SEARCHING FOR ARIZONA'S BURIED TREASURES

A Two Year Odyssey

By
Ron Quinn

Including Bonus Section:
Diary & Notes By Captain Donald W. Page

Illustrations by Ron Quinn
2013

Searching for Arizona's Buried Treasures: A Two Year Odyssey
Including Bonus Section: Diary & Notes By Captain Donald W. Page

Illustrations by Ron Quinn
Editing by Mary Bingham
Production by Robert E. Zucker

Published by BZB Publishing, Inc.,
P.O. Box 91317, Tucson, Arizona 85752

Printed by CreateSpace, an Amazon.com Company.
Available from Amazon.com, CreateSpace.com and other retail outlets.
Printed in the United States of America

First Edition, 2013
ISBN-10: 1939050405
ISBN-13: 978-1-939050-40-3

**Ron Quinn (right), and brother Chuck at our Clifford Well base camp
soon after their arrival in Southern Arizona in 1956.**

*Dedicated to
my brother Charles Quinn,
Walter Fisher and Roy Purdie.*

Author's Note

This manuscript recounts the wild adventures my brother Chuck and I had during our odyssey across the deserts and barren mountains of Southern Arizona.

We camped out for two years while treasure hunting, exploring and living a life few would undertake today. We met some of the most colorful characters imaginable fighting the harsh environment and gaining two lifelong friends, Roy Purdie and Walt Fisher. We heard tales from old Indians and Mexican vaqueros— some bordering on the "Twilight Zone."

Searching for hidden treasures few have ever heard of, we discovered places that have never been visited by others to this day. We never lived the same day twice. Each day was a new, exciting adventure finding strange Indian caves, ancient stone walls and lost Spanish settlements. These two wonderful years would become the most adventurous times of our lives.

Many years later the four of us finally unearthed a medium-size treasure south of Tucson, Arizona, which consisted of 82 pounds of Spanish gold bullion. Other trips were made throughout the years, but none as lengthy as our first two year odyssey.

Some of my articles have appeared in various publications including *Arizona Highways*, *Southern Arizona Trails*, *Fate* magazine and a number of newspapers. The *Tucson Citizen*, a local paper, ran several stories about our adventures.

This book will make interesting reading for the armchair adventurer.

Ron Quinn
August, 2013

About the Author: Ron Quinn

Ron Quinn has been a prolific writer of treasure hunting and paranormal stories over the past fifty years or more. This book is a compilation of treasure hunting stories, some published and some unpublished. It has a special focus on Southern Arizona and his favorite town of Arivaca.

Southern Arizona Trails or *Southern Arizona Trails International,* as it was called for a short time when it included stories in Spanish, is the source for the majority of these stories. *Arizona Trails* was published in Tubac, Arizona from 1986 to 1991 by George McGill. Ron's stories were greatly enjoyed by the local residents and from time to time sparked controversy.

Several of Ron's stories also appeared in national magazines as well, including: *Southern Arizona Trails, Treasure, Treasure Search, Fate* and *Arizona Highways.* Credit is noted where those articles have been published.

In transcribing and editing Ron's stories for this book, especially the stories that appeared in *Southern Arizona Trails,* many typos, transposed sentences and paragraphs plus some unusual punctuation occurred. For the ease of the reader, and hopefully more pleasurable reading, many have been corrected. However, the content of the stories has been left intact. These stories are over 50-years-old, so some changes are to be expected. Tumacácori National Monument has been redesignated as Tumacácori National Historical Park. Other similar changes will be noted from time to time throughout the book.

A few editorial notes have been added for clarification or to bring an article up to date. Spanish accents have been used when appropriate. As an example, Tumacácori is used when referring to the old Spanish mission. However, Tumacacori without the accent is used when referring to the mountain range or mine. Spanish words like *vaquero, carreta,* and *arrastras* are italicized as appropriate.

Ron's great sense of humor is reflected in his stories and especially his cartoons.

Treasure hunting with Ron, his brother Chuck, and their good friends and partners, Roy Purdie and Walt Fisher is a fun read as well as a great book for novice or seasoned treasure hunters.

By the way, Ron assigned pseudonyms to himself, partners and some friends to protect their identity in several of the early articles. Their real names have been included in most cases.

Mary Bingham, Editor
Robert Zucker, Design

Contents

Preface

My brother Chuck and I had always been avid outdoorsmen, interested in what might lie beyond the next mountain range. At that time, the early 1950s, we lived with our parents on Vashon Island, located between Seattle and Tacoma, Washington.

On weekends and summer vacations, both of us could be found with our older friends, Don and Jean Schuette, exploring, camping, gold panning and enjoying the beauty of the towering Cascade Mountains of this picturesque state. The Schuette's were close friends of the family, and these adventurous excursions continued until I entered the Army in 1953.

While stationed in Germany, Chuck would occasionally write. In one letter he mentioned purchasing a book on buried treasures. It was entitled, *Lost Mines and Buried Treasures Along the Old Frontier*, by noted author, John D. Mitchell.

Mitchell was also a writer for *Desert Magazine*. Fascinated by the tales within its pages Chuck proposed, if I was interested, that we should seriously consider taking a trip in search of these legendary treasures supposedly hidden by the Spanish padres that once occupied the Southwest. This ignited my adventurous spirit and plans were made.

Upon my release from the service we both worked and saved for almost a year. Chuck already was employed and had saved a considerable amount.

My mustering out pay, plus savings was used to purchase a 1950 Willys 4 x 4 Jeep Wagon. Other essential equipment needed to maintain such a lengthy adventure, were also obtained during the year. A 9 x 9 foot tent, sleeping bags, cots, stove, etc. The list seemed endless.

Of course our parents opposed the idea of us roaming the desolate regions of Arizona, especially Mom, as she feared for our safety. However, we were a hearty bunch and the stories we read of Arizona's harsh environment didn't frighten us. We were aware of the sudden flash floods, violent thunder storms which ravish the deserts, dancing dust devils, extreme summer heat, and the dangerous deserts that patiently wait for us to enter their kingdom and make a mistake. We both were well versed in the art of survival and these tales didn't alarm us.

At that time I was 23, Chuck 26. Neither of us was married so why not embark on such a journey? Youth is only given to us once. Enough capital was saved to sustain a two year trip. That is, if we didn't experience any major problems with our vehicle.

Jason searched for the *Golden Fleece*. Our odyssey would almost parallel his voyage, minus flying harpies and other strange creatures. He sought a fleece of gold, traveled to hidden lands, encountered mysterious people, fought savage seas and returned with haunting tales of his journey.

Chuck and I would seek Spanish gold, explore hidden places, and climb mysterious mountains seldom visited by modern man. We'd meet fascinating people, fight the desert elements and discover many hidden things. We also would return with stories of our odyssey across the wilds of Arizona.

Many diehard prospectors still search the barren wastes in their quest for these elusive lost mines, hoping to discover the golden wealth that may lie within. Historical evidence proves many of these treasures are factual. But one should not be too gullible when it comes to all these tales, as not all are true. One must know how to separate fact from fiction. Chuck and I soon would enter this exclusive club of "rainbow chasers," as we're often called. We realized our chances of finding anything were quite remote. But like they say, "nothing ventured, nothing gained."

Our final destination would be the desert community of Arivaca in Pima County, AZ. This small village lays some thirty-odd miles north of the Mexican border and near the heart of the mysterious Tumacacori Mountains where the majority of these treasures are supposedly hidden.

The next few years would become the most adventurous in our entire lives, living and traveling the rugged land, searching for treasures and meeting some of the most colorful characters imaginable. We would discover secret places high among the craggy peaks and hear tales which border on the *Twilight Zone* and most of all, discover a freedom few have had the privilege to experience.

We would also find two lifelong friends and partners, Roy Purdie and Walt Fisher, perhaps the greatest treasure of all.

Quinn's account surrounding the concealment of Jesuit treasures

During Arizona's early history, the Spanish built several missions across the Southwest. The majority were located in highly mineralized regions. After gold and silver were discovered, the converted Indians, both Pima and Papago [Tohono O'odham], worked the rich deposits. This continued for several hundred years. These treasures were often stored within the confines of the missions or nearby in bullion form.

During this time several Indian uprisings occurred. The peaceful Indians didn't like working in the dangerous mines where many died in accidents within these unsafe tombs.

The big Pima Rebellion of 1751 temporarily drove the Jesuit order out. This began by burning missions, killing padres and attacking anything Spanish. The padres heard of the impending revolt and decided to hide their wealth, then flee. The hordes of gold and silver were hidden in mines located deep within the surrounding hills and carefully concealed, while others were hastily buried in caves and other locations.

With some of the faithful mission Indians, they traveled westward. Many died or were killed in route, taking their secrets with them. The triumphant Indians had no interest in the "yellow metal" and over the years the mines were slowly forgotten, until legends, rumors and old Spanish documents began surfacing, telling of these lost treasures. The search has continued ever since. Several have been discovered. "One" medium size treasure was found by us during a cool afternoon in 1984.

RON & CHUCK'S ODYSSEY

Chapter 1

THE ODYSSEY BEGINS

Ron and Chuck's Willys Jeep ready for departure from Vashon Island.

Chuck on Fish Creek north of the Superstitions.

On March 20, 1956 we bid farewell to family and friends, and left on the first leg of this extraordinary journey, promising our folks to write several times a month.

Chuck kept the diary and his first entry read:

We are on our way at last. Who knows what adventures we'll encounter before writing on the last page of this book?

Little did we realize what a memorable trip it would be!

After four days and 1,500 miles we arrived in Phoenix, Arizona. We had ordered a metal detector from Gardner Electronics, a small company located there. The management told us it wouldn't be ready for several weeks. We asked them to ship the machine to Arivaca when ready.

We decided to relax a day after the long weary ride to Phoenix. That evening we camped at Fish Creek. The area borders the Superstition Mountains. Home of the "Lost Dutchman Mine." Chuck and I would eventually explore these famous desert mountains, but not until the following year.

After a day's relaxation we headed for Winkleman, a small mining town beside the San Pedro River. Both of us were intrigued by a story entitled, the "Lost Yuma Ledge." This gold deposit is believed to be hidden east of this river, just south of the town. Many have searched, but all have failed. We decided to spend several days exploring the area before continuing on toward Tucson.

After locating Romero Wash we followed it some three miles west. Camp was established several yards south of the sandy arroyo. The region was carpeted with cholla, also known as "jumping cactus," the most dangerous of the cactus group. Their thin sharp needles can easily penetrate a boot.

The area was true desert, made up of fine sand, broken shale and periodic outcroppings of conglomerate. Rattlesnakes were no doubt lurking among rocks scattered across the uneven terrain. The hills supposedly harboring this gold ledge rose abruptly toward the west, all craggy and threatening.

The following is a condensed version of the remarkable tale of found and lost gold.

A frontiersman, known only as Yuma, began trading among the Indians. He was well liked and trusted by most and eventually married an Apache girl.

While living among the Arivaipa Apache, he heard rumors about where the Indians obtained gold for trading. Yuma was eager to learn this secret, and after considerable persuasion, induced the Chief to show him the location.

Accompanied by the chief they traveled by horse across the barren hills. After riding some nine miles they reached a long ridge west of the San Pedro River. Before them in a crater-like depression was an outcropping of rose quartz, rich in coarse gold.

After obtaining several pounds of the rich ore, the Chief carefully covered it with dirt and rock. He told Yuma never to return after this first visit, or he'd be killed.

Arriving in Tucson, Yuma showed the ore to a friend named, Crittenden, whom he had known for years. They decided to return to the Arivaipa country and sample the discovery thoroughly.

After traveling about ten miles north of Fort Grant, which is near the San Pedro River, they camped beside it and waited till morning. After searching the following day, the ledge was found. Not seeing any Apaches, they removed some forty pounds of gold ore. This ore brought to Tucson produced $1,200 in gold.

Knowing the Apaches might be on the lookout, they decided it was too dangerous to return at the present and develop the mine. Yuma returned to trading and Crittenden continued his freighting business.

Months later, Yuma and his wife were killed by renegade Apaches near Growler Pass located in central Arizona. Crittenden tried returning alone and was never seen again. He was apparently killed also.

The Apaches never revealed their secret to another white man, and today it's doubtful any living Indian knows the location. The rich gold ore still lies among the lonely hills guarded by the desert itself.

For three days we searched the hazardous terrain. All that was found were several pieces of rose quartz indicating we were in the correct locale. We made plans to return after the detector arrived and search once more.

The days were exceptionally warm, but the temperature dropped dramatically at night. That evening I stepped from our tent and gazed upon this awesome yet beautiful landscape. The full moon was slowly rising over Sombrero Butte, covering the desert floor in an eerie yellow glow. During the day the deserts appear dangerous and unfriendly to those entering its harsh domain. At night it takes on a quiet peaceful solitude. Occasionally, a lone coyote would make its presences known by its mournful howl. Yes, we had finally arrived in Arizona, and wondered what the next two years would bring.

After breaking camp the following morning we headed for Tucson, some seventy miles away. After checking into a motel for several days, we spent countless hours researching stories at the Arizona Historical Society. Afterward we visited the museum at the University of Arizona. Their mineral display supposedly held a sample of Yuma's gold, but nobody knew of it.

MURPHY WELL ADVENTURES

Chapter 2

CARRETA CANYON TREASURE

**Chuck & I at the doorway of the old line shack
where we spent a stormy night at Murphy Well.**

**Carreta Canyon with the remains of the old mesquite tree
where the *carreta* (cart) broke down.**

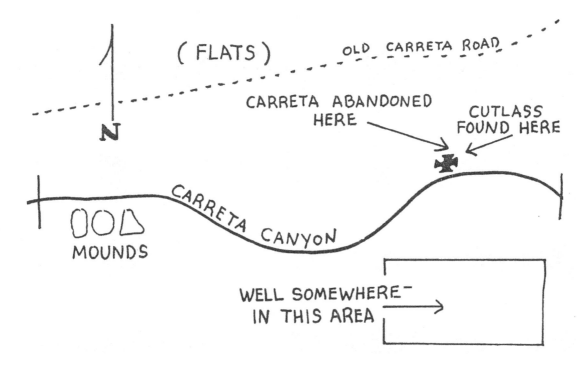

Map of Carreta Canyon.

Dreaming of treasure.

rom Tucson we traveled southward toward Arivaca, some sixty miles away. Off in the distance the towering Tumacacoris rose from the valley floor, like a fortress wall, daring anyone to enter. In the following months, Chuck and I would challenge this sun baked monument of rock and search for the treasures it guards so jealously.

The road leading to Arivaca was a nightmare of holes, bumps and twisting some 22 miles across the desolate terrain. As we sped along kicking up dust and rocks I could see the lofty sentries of the desert scattered across the hills. The giant saguaro, some reaching heights well over twenty-five feet, was here during the Spanish occupation.

Arivaca consisted of approximately 18 adobes. Trucks, jeeps and other vehicles lined the main street. Even a lone white burro was seen wandering about. Two general stores occupied the town, one on either end with the local cantina squarely in the center. The largest store housed the post office and was our first stop. We notified the owner, whose name was Marge Schwanderlik, to hold all mail for us under general delivery.

This dusty oasis had a population of some 75 residents, prospectors, miners, proprietors, cowhands and retirees. Some still searched the barren hills for that elusive "pot of gold."

Several of the Mexican families had husbands who worked for local ranchers or the county maintaining the roads. By the road's, condition they surely weren't doing their job well.

Some of the elderly sat beneath scattered mesquite trees watching "Front Street" go by, undoubtedly quite curious about us. The town had its share of characters we would have the privilege of knowing throughout our stay.

We looked up John D. Mitchell, author of our book, *Lost Mines and Buried Treasures Along the Old Frontier,* who was living here. His adobe was located beside the second store, owned by Hack Townsend. We knocked at his door and were greeted by a rather distinguished looking gentleman of about 75. He wore an old western suit with frayed cuffs, had white hair and mustache, and resembled an old Kentucky Colonel who had fallen on hard times.

After introductions, Chuck said, "We'll be in the area awhile and would like your opinion regarding several stories which appear in your book."

Mitchell bid us welcome and we entered his modest home. One of the main tales which enticed us was, "The Lost Treasure of Carreta Canyon." Upon hearing this, Mitchell said, "Oh, that's almost been found."

Surprised, we asked for details. He wouldn't say much other than it was located at the upper head of Lobo Canyon, which he stated meant "*carreta*" in Spanish. Not knowing the language we assumed this was correct. We had only been in town twenty minutes and the plot was already thickening regarding this mysterious canyon and Mitchell.

Thanking him we left and drove to our first camp at Murphy Well, some 13 miles east of Arivaca. It took us almost an hour to make the journey over the tortuous desert roads.

Camp was set up beside the canyon just below the menacing Tumacacoris that loomed above us. Plans were made to visit the treasure site the following day. If a treasure was being uncovered, surely there would be guards to discourage unwanted guests. I was also curious why there wasn't a new road leading toward Lobo Canyon.

That evening we hiked around the immediate area to look the country over. From the outside these mountains look easy. Inside, it's a maze of gloomy dark canyons and high craggy cliffs. Water is almost none existent within its boundaries and old faint trails seem to lead nowhere. High above several buzzards could be seen gliding on out stretched wings, waiting for something to drop. We hoped they didn't have us on their menu. This indeed was rugged country and we realized why these alleged treasures have never been discovered.

The area near camp looked quite mineralized, as large white quartz veins could be seen cutting across the hills. It was strange though, that no modern mining activity has ever been carried out here. Yet, the mission padres supposedly had some rich silver mines working for over a hundred years.

The following morning we hiked toward Lobo Canyon. After an hour's climb we discovered we had taken the wrong turn, missing Lobo by half a mile. The terrain was extremely rough while climbing the rocky slopes. You'd take one step forward and slide back two, while loosening rocks underfoot. These would bounce then cascade down into the dark canyon far below.

It began getting windy so we returned to camp. Upon arriving we found the wind had blown our tent down. As the gusts became stronger it was decided to move into an old line shack nearby, no doubt used by the local rancher as salt licks were found within its interior along with an old potbelly stove.

The cabin was in the last stages of collapse and the howling wind blew through cracks making weird whistling sounds. Chuck smiled, saying, "Guess the mountains are welcoming us." We erected the tent, nailing its corners to the wooden floor. That evening we heard something walking above on the rafters, then drop to the floor. "What the hell is that," I said. We stepped from the tent with flashlight and gun in hand. In the far corner was the biggest rat I had ever seen. I swear, the damn thing turned and snarled as Chuck put two slugs in it. After disposing of the carcass, no other disturbance was heard. By morning its body had been carried away by some other carnivorous predator.

As we prepared to leave on our second attempt to reach Lobo Canyon, a cowhand rode in. He worked for the Arivaca Ranch and was searching for a sick bull. Spotting our equipment, he smiled saying, "You're prospectors?"

His name was Louis [Luis] Romero, a true Mexican vaquero. He was weather-beaten from years on the range. His face and hands resembled leather left out on the desert for several seasons. He appeared to be in his late 60s and was quite friendly.

During our conversation we happened to mention Mitchell. Louie, as most call him, frowned saying, "You're not involved with him are you? He's nothing but a crook."

Louie went on to tell us about his shady mining deals, from selling worthless claims to "salting" old mine dumps. We told him about meeting Mitchell, and our search for Carreta Canyon.

When Louie heard Mitchell told us *lobo* meant *carreta*, he burst into laughter and said, "That damn liar, *lobo* means wolf."

Mitchell had been looking for this canyon himself and asked Louie often if he knew its location. If anyone came inquiring about Carreta Canyon, Mitchell would try discouraging them with tales of it being found like he did with Chuck and me. He didn't want anybody else searching for it.

During our stay in the area Louie would occasionally stop by looking for fresh water. While visiting, he told us remarkable stories regarding this area. Chuck called him a walking history book, and we learned much from listening to him.

Over the weeks since our arrival, we had been searching for various treasures east of camp, as there were several clues to their whereabouts. We also spent days looking for Carreta Canyon, as the remains of the *carreta* (ox cart) were supposedly still visible beside the canyon.

Louie told us to meet him near Cedar Canyon at 1:00 in the afternoon and he'd show us Carreta Canyon. He had taken a liking to Chuck and me and decided to share this information with us. Louie never trusted Mitchell and refused to tell him anything by saying he "heard the tales of mission treasure but never believed in them."

At 12:30 p.m. we left, traveling overland dodging cactus and menacing rocks. Ten minutes later we spotted Louie atop a hill. He motioned us to follow and started down a long gentle slope toward a large flat bordering a canyon. Unbeknown at the time, Louie would be instrumental in our search for several other treasures.

**Chuck looks over the 3 suspicious mounds pointed out by Louie Romero.
Louie told us the mounds had been there as long as he could remember.**

As we approached the canyon's edge, he pointed toward three suspicious looking mounds, saying they had been there ever since he could remember. A short distance away was the remains of an old mesquite tree. Louie informed us the ox cart once stood beside it. His father had shown him this site as a young lad. He said, very few people know of this place, and only this section is known as Carreta Canyon; also, the large flat had once been farmed by the Indians and a well had been sunk near the canyon's edge. Over the years it slowly filled with gravel during the rainy seasons. No trace remains, but Louie pointed toward the general area.

He continued, saying, the old carreta road used by the mission padres from Tumacácori Mission, passed through here. It then followed the flats, skirting north of Jalisco Ridge, then down into what is now Mexico. Portions of this ancient road can still be seen cut into the soft rock where it crossed several rugged canyons.

As the tale goes, during the rebellion of 1751, the padres loaded the cart with gold, silver and precious altar fixtures. With several oxen pulling, they headed west with a number of loyal mission Indians. As they reached this flat near the well, the axle broke. After concealing their vast treasure they abandoned the ox cart and continued on.

The most popular version of this concealment story claims, the group from Tumacácori met another party traveling east from the mission at Sonoita and were informed the revolt was widespread. Both parties decided to hide the treasures and flee to the safety of the west coast. It's rumored they hid the treasure in a nearby silver mine. I doubt they met another party heading east. If the revolt was spreading they surely wouldn't journey "east" into the conflict but west away from the killings.

When the axle broke they wouldn't take the necessary time to bury the load or carry it into some mine tunnel, perhaps a mile away. Not with the Indians hot in pursuit.

The most logical reasoning would be to dump the treasure down the Carreta Canyon well, until such time as they could retrieve it; which they never did, as King Charles III expelled the Jesuits from the New World in 1767.

We asked Louie, why he showed us this location, when there were others he knew much longer. He said, he knew most of Arivaca but never associated much with them. Most of his time was spent at the ranch, or visiting his wife and family in Tucson on his days off. Louie was kind of a loner. Besides, as he told Mitchell, he never put much stock in all the tales of lost treasures, as did the other cowhands.

Of course we told him we'd share anything we found. He only smiled, as if he knew this was all wishful dreaming.

We sent Gardner in Phoenix several letters inquiring about our metal detector, as it was now over a month. They said it would be shipped soon as there were some difficulties at the plant. Two weeks later it arrived.

Upon receiving the detector we returned to the canyon and began our search. We checked the three mounds but found nothing, then searched in the vicinity of the well. Afterward, we trenched in the area of this well, but found no evidence indicating it was there. If such a well did hold the treasure, and say it was fifteen or so feet deep, the range of our detector wouldn't reach that depth.

It became frustrating but we continued, checking the entire flat. Besides, the summer heat was approaching, cutting our search short as we only worked until noon.

Louie occasionally stopped by during our search. One time he rode up within ten feet of us. We never heard a sound until he called out, "Louie come for his share of the gold." I replied, "Not yet Louie, not yet." Several times while at camp he'd ride in, never making a sound. It was spooky at times. It seemed he just appeared out of nowhere.

We told him we'd continue until the whole region around the flat was searched. Before riding off, Louie told us about some symbols he once found carved onto a rock formation near Dicks Peak. He promised to give us directions next time.

Chuck and I spent another week searching, but found nothing until we checked beside the old mesquite tree. We received a strong signal, so I dug. After two feet my pike struck something metallic. We both gasped at the possibilities. It turned out to be a Spanish cutlass some 27 inches in length. The blade was rusted but in remarkable condition. Some lettering was visible near the base of the blade but this was unreadable. The handle was quite decorative and was made of brass.

Being it was discovered in the area of the *carreta*, it could have been accidently lost during the unloading of any treasure. This was proof something occurred here, and added credibility to the tale.

We were encouraged to continue the hunt, as we believed something lies buried within this area of the canyon. Most likely, if such a treasure exists, it's within the elusive well. Louie was quite surprised upon seeing the cutlass. It also rekindled his interest in these stories of hidden gold.

By now most of Arivaca was curious about us. While leaving the post office, a young slender man approached us by the name of Randall Hill. He was another prospector and through him we met several others.

His camp was beneath two large cottonwoods bordering the Arivaca Creek just west of town. We visited him often discovering he was another honest, hard working individual, trying to pry a living out of old mother earth. This went for many living in and around this town of Arivaca. We eventually came to call it our second home.

In the following weeks we left lots of shoe leather in the Cerro Colorado and Las Guijas Mountains in our search for mineral deposits and several lost mines. Most of these desert ranges are unbelievably rough and few venture into their interiors. But Chuck and I could often be found climbing along their rugged skylines.

THE OLD CARRETA TRAIL

Southern Arizona Trails, Vol. 3, No. 83, May 10, 1988, Page 19

I have heard a large majority of the stories centering around the lost mines and treasures of Southern Arizona but occasionally a new one comes my way. While attending the Tucson Rock Show several months back, I met a fellow from Phoenix. About fifteen minutes into our conversation, the subject turned to lost mines, etc., and I was told the following tale.

The old Carreta Trail ran from Tumacácori Mission, skirted the north end of the mountains, wound through the rugged mesquite-covered foothills south, passed the present town of Arivaca, zigzagged through the northern approaches to the Oro Blanco Mountains, then twisted back and forth across what is now the boundary between the United States and Mexico, eventually arriving at the dry little outpost of Sonoyta, [Sonora].

It was a major road and today hardly any trace of it remains, but just south of the old Paul Bell place, portions of it can still be seen cut into various rock formations that line the banks of several arroyos.

An old prospector by the name of Williams operated a mine in the area of this trail, believed to have once belonged to the padres from Tumacácori.

Williams packed his rich silver ore over this trail to the eastern side of the mountains. It was a region of wild Apache bands returning from raids below the border, and if they caught any white man, it was sudden death if he was lucky.

One day in the late 1830s a small party of travelers, most likely prospectors, were picking their way along the old trail when they came upon a burro grazing some distance from them. They were about to pass it by when one of the party saw that the animal was bearing a pack.

They rode up to investigate and to ask directions of its owner. The burro was indeed bearing a pack-saddle that looked to be quite new. Lashed to each side of the animal were large rawhide sacks.

They looked around but could not locate the owner. They also shouted but received no answer. Thinking that the owner might have strayed off or was injured, they searched the vicinity but found no one.

Afterwards, they investigated the rawhide sacks and found they contained silver ore which they later described to be of "incredible richness." When nightfall approached the small party made camp, determined to wait until morning before taking the burro and it burden.

During the night strange sounds were heard. Thinking it might be Apaches, the men remained quiet.

They were up with the breaking of dawn and made another search of the area, but turned up nothing. It was now concluded that the owner was nowhere in the vicinity. Whatever fate had overtaken him could have occurred miles away.

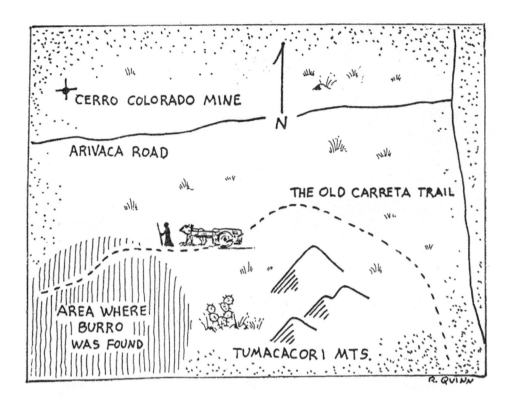

Area where the burro was found.

Placing the burro in their own pack train, the men proceeded on their journey certain that somewhere in the area was a mine of fabulous richness, its owner probably killed by Apaches. Near the end of their own journey, this party were themselves attacked by Indians and two of the men were killed. The third managed to escape into a thicket where he concealed himself under a narrow ledge until the hostiles left.

When he thought it was safe to move, he could find no trace of their animals, including the burro they had found. Scattered on the ground where the attack took place was the silver which the Indians had thrown away.

The lone survivor of the sudden attack made his way safely to a small settlement where he told the story of the ambush and the silver. No immediate search was made for the source of the rich ore, and the sole witness to the account drifted on, never to be heard of again.

I would venture to say that the silver belonged to Williams, and he was killed by the Apaches while transporting it along the old Carreta Trail. Years later, a few diehard prospectors searched for the mine, but never succeeded in find it.

I have my suspicion old Williams found the Cerro Colorado Mine, believed to have been worked by the padres before it was shown to Samuel Heintzelman, who bilked the man that showed it to him out of a $500 payment with 50 cents, "good enough for a Mexican."

Whether there is any truth to the above story is for you to decide. The facts, if any, are extremely vague. The tale, however, is quite interesting and just might be true.

CLIFFORD WELL ADVENTURES

Chapter 3
ROY PURDIE & DON

Roy Purdie, our third treasure hunting partner & friend.

Chuck & I at our base camp at Clifford Well.

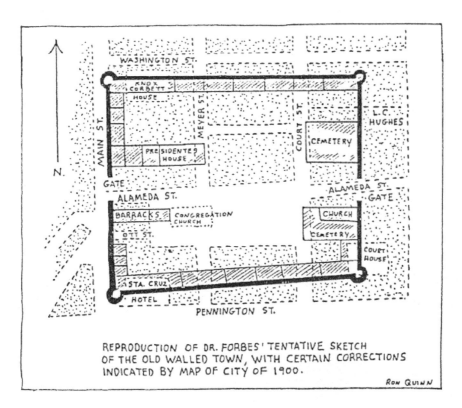

Dr. Robert Humphrey Forbes was the first dean of the College of Agriculture and Dean Emeritus of the University of Arizona. A close friend of historian Frank Lockwood, his books and files are located at the Arizona Historical Society in Tucson.

W hile obtaining gas at Townsend's store, we happened to meet a friend of Hack's by the name of Roy Purdie. Roy was about fifty and worked as a merchant marine, shipping out occasionally from Seattle or San Francisco. After several months at sea, he'd head for Arizona to visit friends and treasure hunt.

We talked for hours and found Roy had a great personality and knew a great deal about the old Spanish treasures. The three of us met several times while in Arivaca and we invited him out to our camp, which at that time was at Clifford Well.

During one of his visits he saw our detector, which few in the area had the privilege of owning. Roy asked if we'd be interested in searching for some coins near Tucson.

Roy knew a Don Page [1] from Berkeley, California. Mr. Page was a noted amateur archaeologist, historian and world traveler. Both were friends, so they formed a partnership, as Don was too old to venture out into the mountains. Don furnished the documents, maps, etc., and Roy the leg work.

Roy called Don, informing him about meeting Chuck and me. Don agreed that three searching was better than one, so a partnership began with a handshake, and lasted forty years.

Roy camped with us and told the following story concerning buried coins, he heard from Don back in 1955. It was also published in *Southern Arizona Trails*.

---

[1] Note: Donald W. Page was an assistant Tucson City Engineer in the late 1920s and early 30s, and the co-author of Tucson—The Old Pueblo with noted historian Frank C. Lockwood.

TUCSON'S HIDDEN RICHES

Southern Arizona Trails, Vol. 3, No. 62, December 15, 1987, Page 27

T he mission of San José del Tucson was located about one and a half miles southwest of downtown Tucson and was the poorest mission in the Pimería Alta chain. Even though this fact was known, rumors continue that a sizable treasure was buried at the site.

I've heard many insist that most of the silver buried there came from a rich mine hidden somewhere within the Tucson Mountains, north of Gates Pass. This region is now within the boundaries of Tucson Mountain Park.

Mining is restricted, but you can still hike around the area. In doing so, you could keep an eye peeled for anything looking suspicious. No *arrastras* have been discovered in the vicinity, so if a mine did exist, the ore was undoubtedly sent by mule to the grounds of this mission. Once there, the rich silver was removed from that which was crushed.

During 1768, Padre Garcés was in charge of the mission of San Xavier del Bac. When Captain Juan Bautista de Anza noticed the increasing violence of the Apaches, he had the garrison at Tubac, some 30 odd miles south, moved to Tucson to protect the settlers. [2]

Later, Padre Garcés had a new mission built nearby and name it San José del Tucson.

I doubt if anything remains of these ruins today, but once Roy and Chuck visited the site in '57, and only saw several piles of crumbling adobe where this large mission stood. Nevertheless, where mission ruins are found, there will also be found tales of treasure, and this old mission was no different.

I once read a copy of a diary written by a padre from either Tumacácori or San Xavier. Within its pages, he mentioned there were 177 working mines in the surrounding area. Most were located in the Santa Rita Mountains east of Tubac.

How large these workings were was not mentioned, but I'd guess most were only shallow diggings that were worked out in several months.

Out of these 177, I'd make an educated guess that perhaps no more than 20 were of any significance. These would fall into the category of the Tumacacori Mine, Guadalupe, San Pedro, La Purísima Concepcíon Mine, etc. These mines supposedly produced large amounts of gold and silver for many years.

Roy, our partner, had a document from historian Don Page. From a specific location near the west wall of *El Pueblo de Tucson*, one could look west and spot the mine opening on the eastern slopes of what now are the Tucson Mountains.

---

[2] Note: The Tubac Presidio garrison was relocated to Tucson by Hugo O'Connor, in 1775. Anza was leading an expedition to California to establish San Francisco at the time.

If my memory is correct, we all were standing somewhere in the area of the old courthouse. Of course we didn't see any mine in the distance, but after 200 years who would? The region was just north of Gates Pass, about a mile or so.

When Don Page visited the site of the old Tucson mission in the 40s, he mentioned there had been extensive digging in and around the ruins by treasure hunters. The only things found were several Spanish coins and a few skeletons.

I also read that sometime in the 1880s, a J. D. Burges [Captain John D. Burgess] once found a bronze box that was described as a "treasure box." It was not disclosed if anything of value was found in it.

Roy also had another document describing an old Spanish reduction works. It was located on the northwest corner, where the bridge now crosses the Santa Cruz River on West Grant Road.

Supposedly a box measuring 18 x 24 inches was buried at the site, containing silver dollars. Over the years the river bank has no doubt eroded back many yards, and into the area where this reduction works once stood.

There is a rumor some Mexican woman was out collecting firewood along the Santa Cruz in this region and spotted part of a box protruding from the high bank. She returned later with her sons and after removing the box, opened the lid and found it contained more than a thousand coins.

The above incident occurred sometime during the 1930s. If the tale is true, nothing is known about what became of this large amount of silver coins.

The three of us spent one afternoon searching the area with our detector. While working a spot near the bank I received a strong reading. By using the outer edge of the search coil, we estimated the size of the object below to be 18 x 24.

After digging perhaps six inches, Chuck's pike broke through some rotted wood. This was the third time in 18 months we thought we had "hit it big," but Lady Luck wouldn't be smiling on us this day.

It turned out to be an iron frame and the same size as the coin box. Attached to it was a thin piece of plywood. We all gazed at each other with looks of disappointment. Roy's expression was like he just bit into a sour lemon.

After stopping off at a restaurant for something to eat, we headed back to Arivaca. If nothing was discovered during a day's search, Chuck would often say, "Well fellows, we got shot down again."

One thing about this treasure hunting game, you usually wind up with your hands full of nothing and a head full of memories, but there would be many tomorrows and many other treasure-leads to follow in the months to come.

THE LITTLE-KNOWN RICH AMOLE MINE

Southern Arizona Trails, Vol. 3, No. 63, December 22, 1987, Page 27

I n a previous article entitled "Tucson's Hidden Riches," I mentioned a mine supposedly still hidden somewhere in or near the Tucson Mountains. In reviewing my research material, I discovered it was named the "Amole"— a Spanish diggings that is little known, and once produced gold and some silver.

The exact date of its discovery is unknown, but it was in full operation during the time San José de Tucson Mission was completed.

In Don Page's documents, he states: "The Spanish workings were very rich in both gold and silver, and was believed to be the richest mine in this part of the county." It was also stated, that coins were minted from the silver removed from the mine.

On page 1 of these documents, Don mentioned that by using a spy-glass the workmen near the mouth of the Amole could be seen. The entrance was located close to a great rock or crag, and the point from which the observation was made was from the west wall or main gate of the walled town (Tucson). This would be in the area where Alameda St. now intersects Main St.

Further on in Page's documents he states that one time a Spanish general whose headquarters were at this mission was returning to the Amole Mine with an escort of 50 men when the column was attacked by Apaches and a number of his men killed. The attack was made somewhere in the foothills of the Tucson Mountains. The ore from the Amole was believed treated at the *arrastras* and furnace about 50 yards north of the northwest corner of San José's defensive wall, as slag has been discovered in this area. At that point there was a 13 x 40-foot adobe building that is said at one time to have been used in connection with the reduction of the ore from this mine.

Concerning the 18 x 24-inch box of coins buried near another old reduction works, mentioned in "Tucson's Hidden Riches," further research by this writer has uncovered another tale which could be a second version of this rather interesting story.

When the Spanish left the country (at the triumph of the War of Independence), they buried a large copper *peron*, a bowl about 12" deep and 24" in diameter, filled with coins under or near the smelter.

Again, from Don's notes dated Feb. 4, 1929, Don and friend Glenton Sykes tried to locate the place from Don Augustín M. Tomé's description but failed. Don and Tomé drove out still later and he showed Page the spot which is on the west bank of the Santa Cruz River, but again nothing was discovered. He was also informed by Tomé that the people of Tucson used to come out to hunt for metates, manos, pots and arrowheads, of which there were many to be found in earlier days. Tomé hunted around until he unearthed a small piece of slag, and told Don that when he was a boy he used to find many large pieces in the vicinity just north of the Tucson Mission.

Also from his notes of May 31, 1929, Charlie Bell, another associate, and Don drove out and found abundant indications of a large Indian village, the pot shards being both of the early and late type of potting. Bell discovered several arrowheads and a large piece of furnace brick, together with a good-sized piece of slag.

In his notes Don does not mention at which location these were found—the area just north of San José de Tucson or the region northwest of Grant Rd. near the Santa Cruz.

On June 5, 1929, Tomé and Don again drove out to the mission location, and he tells Don that about five years ago a girl, the daughter of a family that lived in a "hut" just north of the old road, dug a hole in the ground and unearthed one side of a large copper pot that was covered with a plate.

Prying up the lid a little, she found the bowl filled with money (coins), but when her mother saw this she made her cover it up again, saying that it must be something that Don Felipe, the owner of the land, had hidden. After they moved and quite sometime later, they told this to Don Felipe, who sent Tomé out to look into the matter. But in the meantime the old house had been removed and he was unable to locate the right spot. He believes that it was close to an old *acequia* ditch that runs east. Tomé says that the discovery seems to check with the old tale about the Spanish burying the coins at the reduction works.

Other interesting discoveries mentioned in these documents include the following:

Pre-Columbian artifacts found by Tomé at the old lime kiln on Silverbell Road. The ruins of the Cañada del Oro, known as the Rancho Viejo, and the "Mission of Ciru," as mentioned by Archbishop Jean-Baptiste Salpointe, Don Augustín M. Tomé and Fabian Romero.

A boulder found by Don Page on the western slopes of the Tucson Mountains, bearing what is believed to be an inscription by Fr. Francisco Hermenegildo Garcés. No location is given where this boulder might be found. Perhaps it's in another document I do not have.

The following was taken from Don Page's notes concerning Tomé, a close friend and a very knowledgeable individual when it came to the early history of Tucson.

According to the inscription on Don Augustíne's headstone, he was born about 1857, but when I knew him, my impression was he looked much older. Some of his reminiscences date back to before the American occupation of Tucson, and as they are unquestionably authentic, I am convinced that he must have been born about 1850. His name does not appear in the Arizona Census for 1864, and I am wondering if there are earlier census returns from which his age can be checked.

Don Augustíne's family was living in Tucson as early as 1775, as in that year an uncle of his, also named Augustín Tomé, a soldier in the presidial company, was killed by the Apaches when on his way to the Amole Mine referred to earlier.

Another bit of interesting information I discovered tells about a treasure hidden somewhere in the vicinity of the Tucson mission, but it gives no specific location. It states one should dig at the spot and find a block of wood. Under this will be found the dies used in the casting of the coins and a little deeper under there will be another thick block of wood. Under this will be one or more *perons* (large copper pots or caldrons) filled with silver, and under this again another pot or so filled with minted silver and gold coins.

No doubt many of these treasure locations have homes occupying the site. Perhaps in some backyard a good size treasure is waiting to be discovered. It also would be interesting to find the lost Amole Mine, to see if it's located within the boundaries of Tucson Mountain Park or on state or private lands. Most likely its hidden somewhere on the eastern slopes of these mountains and mining is forbidden there. Not much mining activity has been carried on in this area, but like that old saying, "Gold is where you find it."

Chapter 4

THE LION CANYON TREASURE

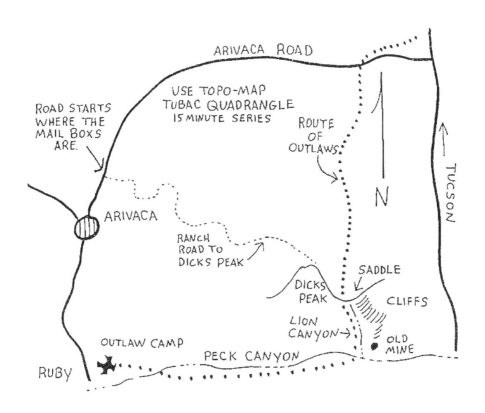

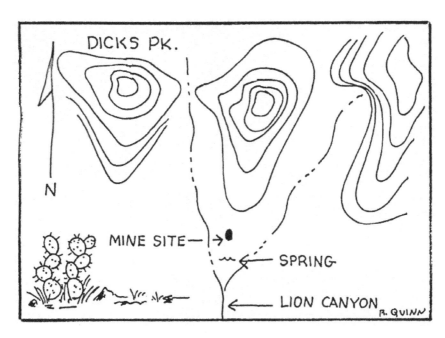

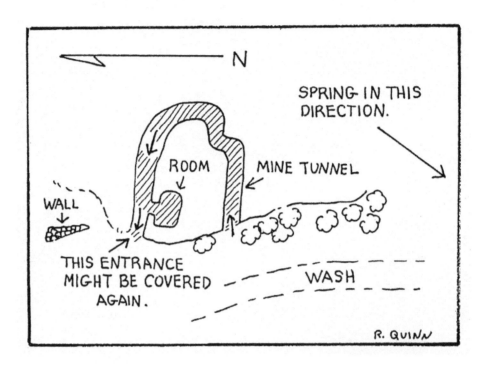

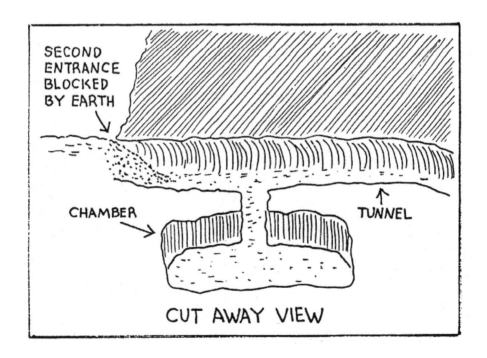

Mine site with shovel marked Cortez on the right behind detector.

Spring located near the mine site.

I t was late June '56 and the summer heat was becoming extremely uncomfortable. We'd depart before sunrise and return by one. This gave us approximately eight hours of searching before the heat drove us back to camp.

Several times we made plans to leave this furnace of an area for the cooler areas of the state, but another treasure tale would prevent us from doing so. If you leave the Tumacacoris, you eventually always return. If you leave you always feel a tugging at your sleeve to return. It's known as "The Curse of the Tumacacoris."

Here is the story as it appeared twice in *Southern Arizona Trails*.

OUTLAW LOOT AT LION CANYON

Southern Arizona Trails, Vol. 2, No. 18, January 1987, page 14
Southern Arizona Trails, Vol. 3, No. 34, June 9, 1987, page 20

While prospecting near Jalisco Ridge, my brother and I and partner, Dave,[3] met a very interesting vaquero by the name of Louis [Luis] Romero. He rode for the Arivaca Ranch, and during a windy March day happened upon our camp and rode in. He had been searching for a sick bull and spotted our tents, and thought he'd ride over and see who we were.

In the weeks that followed he'd usually arrive at camp around 4:00 p.m. looking for some cool water. When Louis had the time, we'd chat about various stories concerning buried "something or others," and after awhile we became friends and would look forward to our talks with him. This man was a walking book of knowledge when it came to this particular area. It was a shame they didn't have portable tape recorders then, (1957) as we missed so much by just taking notes.

We asked about him while in Arivaca one afternoon and received nothing but high praises. He was only a lone vaquero, but his trustfulness and honesty was without blemish. One individual said, "If Louis tells you something, you can bet ya life it's true."

One rather interesting story he told us involved three outlaws that robbed a bank. Afterwards, they rode south and soon found themselves near Dicks Peak. There is a low saddle east of the peak and this makes easy access down Lion Canyon. From here you travel west along Peck Canyon, then [you] have clear sailing to the Mexican border.

Louis believed they hid the money somewhere between the saddle and where they camped that fatal night.

That evening they made the mistake of camping, and not continuing straight for the border. Their campsite was in the vicinity of the mining town of Ruby, Arizona.

Guess they wanted to be near a saloon to buy a bottle or two.

---

[3] Note: Partner, Dave, mentioned in this story is actually Roy Purdie.

The posse that was following saw their campfire and the sheriff had his men dismount and move in quietly. One member of the posse witnessed the hold up and recognized all three. Guess the sheriff wasn't in a good mood after the long ride, so he didn't call out, "hands up" or read them their rights. They opened fire, dropped all three within seconds. One outlaw had extremely long shoulder length hair and was kneeling beside the fire when all hell broke loose. It's said, after all the shooting was over, he still kept the same position for a moment or two, then fell face down into the fire. His hair went up like dry tinder in a ball of flames.

After checking the campsite and not finding the money, they waited till morning then searched further out for any signs of newly disturbed earth where the loot might be hidden, but found nothing.

Being the three were on the run, I doubt if they'd take the time to dig a hole and bury it. When one starts down Lion Canyon after crossing the saddle, there are numerous caves on the left side. They range in size from a barrel to that of a truck. This would make an excellent place to conceal something for a short period of time.

After hearing this tale of ill gotten wealth, we decided to move camp to that area. Two days later we made the hour-long climb to the saddle and stood gazing down Lion Canyon. High cliffs to the left were dotted with caves of various sizes. We began checking these first, then slowly moved further down. I even had the others hold a rope so I could lower myself to search the ones we couldn't reach from below. Dangerous but necessary.

On the second day of this adventure we had searched most of the caves, but no saddlebags of money were found. At one point I found myself on a narrow ledge that seemed to get smaller with each step. As I was about to turn around, Chuck called from below and said they could see the entrance to a cave from their vantage point. They stood watching as I made my way around the ledge and spotted it. The opening was about four feet high and some seven feet deep.

I almost lost my balance when I spotted an old rusted shovel half hidden in the shadows. I felt my heart quicken as I thought what the implications might mean. I called to the others that I found a shovel. They started up and soon were standing beside me. I removed the shovel which looked quite old. The wooden handle was cut short, and ideal for carrying on a horse. The thoughts that were going through our minds at the moment, only a true treasure hunter would know. Chuck worked the floor with the metal detector and slowly moved toward the entrance. All eyes were on the needle and, Dave was saying softly to himself, "Jump damn ya, jump!" There was no "jump" and nothing was found in the area around the cave either. As Chuck would say, "Well, we got shot down again."

It was near noon as we decided to have lunch at the cave as it offered some shade from the bright early May sun. Afterwards, I reached for the shovel to examine it closer and almost lost my lunch. Stamped on the metal and where the handle is attached was the word, Cortez; not Cortes. Looking further down I saw the words Cortez Metal Works. Did the others get a laugh over that! Dave said when I first saw it I had an expression like I had just seen a ghost. I have to admit, it was a surprise.

Two shocks in one day were enough. First, finding the shovel and then seeing that word, "Cortez." Sometimes this treasure hunting is hard on the nervous system. We took pictures of the cave and shovel then moved out.

Further down canyon, we discovered an old mine. The entrance was open but there was a small cave-in further back. The entire area looked as though somebody had just walked away and abandoned the diggings. By the items left behind, we guessed the year to be the '30s. There was rotted clothing, rope, drill steel, miner's spoons, cooking utensils and just about everything it took to put in a tunnel like that. Near the entrance were four bags of cement long since turned hard due to the rain.

We came to the conclusion that [the] shovel must have come from this mine. Why it was left in the cave will never be known as there wasn't a sign of mineralization near it. Nobody would just walk off and leave their entire camp. If the truth was known, I'd guess some old prospector was living back there alone, and perhaps fell from that ledge where the shovel was found. If so, the animals would have taken care of any evidence in short order.

We checked both the dump and mine and couldn't find a trace of mineral. Dave said, to warrant this big of an operation the miner had to be on to something, but what?

Louis also mentioned that back in '38, some stranger would drive his horse and wagon to within a quarter mile of that saddle. He would never talk to anyone, but would wave occasionally when Louis would ride by. This loner would arrive in early October and remain 'til the end of the year, then pick up and depart until the following October.

There was evidence of him being there as holes were dug at various locations. On the eastern slope of Dicks Peak there are large open cuts dug about 12 feet deep and placed about 25 feet apart, right up the side of the slope. He was searching for something that if he discovered anything, Louis never knew. One year the stranger never returned.

This entire area around this peak is one weird place. When you're there awhile, you get an odd feeling and it remains with you until you pack up and leave. We met two other treasure hunters from California out searching for the lost treasure of Carreta Canyon. They also felt the same while in this canyon near Dicks Peak.

Perhaps it's all the strange things that have gone on here all lumped together. The abandoned mine, the stranger, perhaps violence and the strange sounds Louis and other cowboys heard coming from the canyon, while camping near it one night during "round up time." All these things together could be setting off some strange vibes. The closest I can describe the odd feeling is…like you're not wanted there.

The Lost Treasure of Carreta Canyon is quite well known in the area, and groups even today, venture into those lonely hills in search of it, but that's another story.

The tale about this outlaw loot is only known by a few, as all the old timers from the '50s have long since passed away, including our very good friend Louis Romero. He died at 93 in his sister's home in Tucson, Arizona.

He, like us, believe it's still hidden somewhere between the saddle and where the outlaws met their violent end.

One more note: years later it's rumored some hiker discovered several gold coins in this vicinity. Was it part of the loot dropped by the fleeing outlaws? Again, only the mountains know.

ANOTHER MINE MYSTERY

Southern Arizona Trails, Vol. 3, No. 50, September 29, 1987, Page 23 & 21

T hose interested in prospecting and treasure hunting have, at one time or another, heard tales of people stumbling upon abandoned mines while hiking the hills. Old sites where everything owned by the previous owner had been left behind to slowly rot away in the harsh environment of the desert hills.

Such a mine was discovered [by] the three of us while out exploring. The location was just south of Dicks Peak, near Lion Canyon.

At that time, Roy, a partner of ours, came along to help search for a cache of stolen coins, supposedly hidden in this area by several fleeing bandits. They were eventually caught near the mining town of Ruby and died in a hail of lead while resisting arrest.

While checking out the terrain above the canyon floor, we discovered an old rusted shovel in a small cave. The mine was found later about a hundred feet below this point.

By the looks of the encampment and various items scattered around, I'd say it was abandoned sometime in the 1930s.

Four large sacks of cement, long since hardened by moisture, were rotting just inside the mine entrance. On a large flat rock nearby were all the cooking utensils. Several tin plates were rusted through from rain water dripping from a ledge over the years.

A short distance away was a cluster of mesquite trees, and swinging lazily in the afternoon breeze from a branch was an old lard bucket.

We also found some drill steel and a miner's spoon beside an unfinished stone dam. It was built across a small wash and looked perhaps six feet high in the center and some 18 feet in length. Roy disappeared and soon returned pushing an old wheelbarrow.

Afterward we returned to the mine. There we found a small cave-in, with rotted clothing protruding from it.

Our first thoughts were that it might have collapsed on the previous occupant. With the tools available, we dug into the pile of loose rocks, expecting to unearth some human bones, but none were discovered.

Further back, we came across rotted old boots, different size ropes, a hat—half eaten by some rodents—and some other miscellaneous items.

On a shelf cut into the wall stood a corked bottle, half full of some kind of alcoholic beverage which none of us would sample. Nearby was a small tin box marked aspirin, but the contents had long since decomposed to a grayish powder.

A short distance back, the tunnel dropped off some eight feet before continuing. Using a rope, I climbed down while Chuck and Roy remained behind. Thinking back, it seemed I was the one always taking the chances.

We carried a flashlight, as we never knew if we'd find some cave or other deep opening during our daily trips into the remote country.

The tunnel was now about eight feet below the outside surface. As I inched my way along the dark passageway, it slowly made a half circle back toward the entrance.

Off to my left I spotted a hollowed-out chamber with a doorway leading into it. As I approached the end of the tunnel, it angled up and was blocked by dirt.

I could see some daylight coming through near the ceiling, so I called to the others to go outside and see if they could locate the opening. Several minutes later I heard them digging at the loose earth. As the opening became larger, I saw Roy's smiling face peering down and a few moments later they crawled in and joined me below.

We examined the walls, ceiling and floor but couldn't find any trace of mineralization. Afterward we checked the mine dump, but still nothing. Not even a small quartz vein could be found cutting through the rock, which was nothing but barren old andesite.

There wasn't a single clue anywhere indicating what the miner was after. I did hear several accounts of individuals searching for buried treasures they thought were in the area by sinking tunnels through solid rock in hopes of discovering the hidden chamber that held the treasure.

To me, it would be much easier to try to locate the original entrance then go blasting and digging through countless yards of rock.

While the others continued to search the area, I went drifting off to other locations, like I usually do. In a short while I came upon a natural spring hidden in the center of an outcropping of rock. The water was cool and refreshing and was seeping out from beneath two boulders.

I called Chuck and Roy and they also were amazed to see running water in this dry, desolate terrain. We found out several days later that not even our knowledgeable friend Louis Romero, who had been riding this country for 30-odd years, knew if its existence.

These springs are mysterious, as some will dry up after many years while others will appear at new locations. I have no idea if the one we discovered in '57 is still there—we returned to it the following year while passing through and filled our canteens there.

The unanswered question is: Why did the party or group involved in this mine abandon the diggings and leave all their equipment and personal possessions?

If a single individual was responsible for the operation, he either met with foul play, died while away from the mine, or lost interest in the project and left, leaving everything behind.

I find this most unlikely.

I heard a story once about some old prospector who had a silver mine somewhere in this general area. He would bring his rich ore to Nogales, and after selling it, would spend the evening drinking at several bars.

One night was rather cold, so after downing a bottle or two, [he] went to sleep in a nearby alley and froze to death.

The mine we found might have been his diggings, but that event occurred in the late 1890s, not the 30s, as some of the items indicated.

If this was the mine, there's a chance it was later discovered by another prospector who stumbled upon the claim and worked it till the ore ran out. If this was the case, surely we would have found some evidence of silver.

Before leaving the canyon, we filled our canteens at the spring and gathered up most of the drill steel and the six-foot miner's spoon. They came in quite handy as walking sticks during our long struggle up the mountain to the opposite side of the range.

Yes, another unsolved mystery added to all the others that abound in these harsh and lonely hills.

Chapter 5

THE THREE Xs

Louie Romero's rock with the 3 Xs.

After our unsuccessful search for the outlaw loot, Louie Romero told us of the symbols he had seen chiseled on a boulder. They were near Dicks Peak, the same location we had just searched. A couple of days later before daybreak we made the second long climb again, arriving at the saddle just as the sun poked its fiery face over Sardina Peak.

The boulder was found half concealed among the mountain brush. These markings consisted of three Xs and two parallel lines. On top of the large boulder was the faint outline of a snake, its head pointing south.

There are several meanings concerning the Xs. Three supposedly means, "on way to treasure." If Roman numerals are used, three Xs plus two lines could mean the number 32—perhaps 32 Spanish *varas*? That would be approximately one hundred feet. One X represents "one line, land mark, divide or 10."

A snake has several meanings. Head or tail points to next sign or proceed with caution.

Searching further out, we came upon another rock on edge, with a hole in its center. Whether natural or crudely dug, could not be determined. This rock was located some hundred feet northeast of the boulder. Peering through the opening, looking north, an outcropping of rock could be seen about a hundred feet away.

Chuck and Roy came upon a large donut shaped circle of stones near the center of the saddle. All three sites formed a perfect triangle.

Later that afternoon, Louie told us the outcropping seen through the hole, once had symbols carved onto the surface. The Formation was soft lava and over the years erosion had taken its toll, until the signs were completely obliterated.

This was the same region Louie Romero told us the lone stranger would visit each fall. Did he eventually decipher the meaning of these symbols and discovered a treasure? There were numerous open cuts on the eastern slopes of Dicks Peak believed to have been dug by the same individual. At the intersection of Lion Canyon and the nameless canyon we found the abandoned mine.

Was the stranger also searching for something besides mineral? We were certain something was or is still buried at this site. Returning we searched the entire area with our detector for some five days, most of the time remaining overnight. Nothing was found including any new signs. Perhaps the stranger did in fact find something. Quoting Louie, "One year he never returned."

Periodically we'd return to the saddle and search again in the hopes we might have missed something. Nothing was ever discovered. There is a strong possibility if a treasure was buried there it has long since been spirited away.

Chapter 6

CRAZY DAVIS

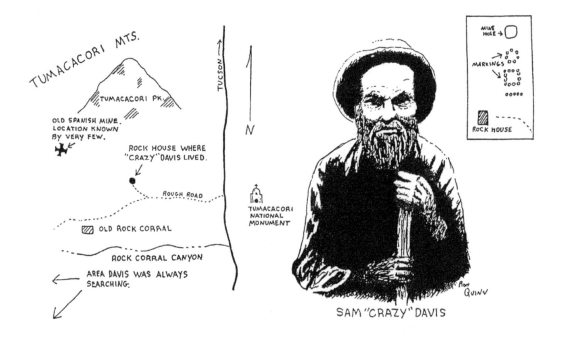

Looking over the ruins of Crazy Davis' rock house during a later visit in the 1980s.

Roy decided to visit Don Page and see about shipping out for awhile. If there weren't any good ships he'd return in a few weeks. If we moved camp, a letter and map would be sent to his post office box in California.

During our travels we met some unusual characters. Most resided on old abandoned mining claims, while others were content to live by themselves in far off locations. They ventured into civilization only when the last can of beans sat on the shelf. From their lips we heard some of the most outrageous tales imaginable.

CRAZY DAVIS

Southern Arizona Trails, Vol. 2, No. 14, October 29, 1986, Page 19

VISITS WITH 'CRAZY DAVIS'

Southern Arizona Trails, Vol. 3, No. 48, September 15, 1987, Page 18

During our odyssey around Arizona my brother, Chuck, and I met some very unusual characters. Most reside in small hamlets scattered across the state, while others are content to live by themselves in "out of the way places." This type only venture into town when the last can of beans is on the shelf. From their lips we have heard some of the most "outrageous" tall tales imaginable.

The character which comes to mind the most was an old recluse called, [Sam] "Crazy Davis." He lived in a rather small rock house built on the ridge above Rock Corral Canyon and just inside the boundary of the Coronado National Forest, west of Tumacácori Mission. There was no water nearby, so this elderly, thin, "desert rat" with the sunken eyes would have to fetch it from the gas station located near the highway and carry it up hill for almost two miles. We met him through another prospector from Arivaca, who has long since returned to Texas.

Each time we found ourselves in this area, we'd bring Davis ten gallons of water, and to him it was like finding gold. One time we happened to pass the junction and spotted him lugging a five gallon can up the road, and most of us know what that weighs. Of course we stopped and gave him a ride. Within a few minutes we deposited him at his meager dwelling. If he had had to walk, it would have taken Davis close to two hours.

While there we gave him about five more gallons which we poured into the large wooden barrel within his house. Just a few yards north of his place there were rocks laid out in various designs, and a couple of feet behind that, a pit about 15-feet deep. The story Davis told was quite "farfetched" but worth relating. It seems these markings indicated there was a large treasure buried below them. (The truth of the matter was, he placed them there himself years before.)

Davis asked us not to walk across the rocks as "they" might hear us. I looked rather shocked and said, "They?" He was digging about ten feet north of the rocks and Chuck asked, "Why there, and not at the marking?" The old gentleman looked at us quite serious and replied, "If I dug straight down the spirits would hear me and move the treasure again." He continued and said, "By digging here I can approach the treasure from beneath so they won't hear me."

This poor lonely soul had lived out here on the desert so long that his mind was completely gone. The sad thing was, he believed wholeheartedly in what he was saying, and the pit looked as though it hadn't been worked in years, as desert vegetation could be seen growing from the bottom.

This strange individual could talk for hours and be very rational when the subject of Tumacácori's lost mines and buried treasures came up. He knew all about these legendary treasures, the padres leaving the area during the revolt of 1751, and knew more names, dates and other facts regarding these stories than most people we met that considered themselves to be an authority on this subject.

To this day, I believe he knew the location to at least one of these mines, but the facts were jumbled together with his fantasies and he couldn't distinguish between the two. He kept insisting that the lost mine was quite near and pointed toward the area southwest from where we all were standing. Geologically speaking, there isn't a trace of workable mineral in this particular area of the mountains. Treasure hunters better than us have searched this area before and after we ever arrived, and nothing has ever been discovered to indicate a rich silver mine is hidden there.

Davis would give exact measurements to several "Spanish mines" around the hills, but before we could obtain any "real" information he would again go drifting off to a "never-never land" and talk about ghosts, spirits and other nonsense. He then would return to some degree of reality and start all over again, about so many *varas* to this point or from his place to the mine. It was difficult to "pin him down" to a definite location. As I mentioned before, it was all jumbled within his head, but I still believe old Davis knew something, but we didn't know how to extract the truth from him without also obtaining his fantasies.

He would also talk about a tunnel which was dug from the mission to a hidden spring near the edge of Rock Corral Canyon. The padres would use it to fetch water when the "hostiles" were in the area, and it was unsafe to venture from behind the protective walls of the mission. Davis insisted he knew its location, but was afraid to enter it again as the spirits would surely get 'em next time. He went on to say a large portion of this tunnel had collapsed when he first discovered it, and that bags of native silver were stacked beside the wall. Remains of his rock house are still visible on the ridge that overlooks the canyon. I heard two stories about what happened to him after we left the region. One is that he died of natural causes several years later. It's said, he was found at the bottom of his pit with a pick in hand. If you believe it, I guess the spirits finally caught up with him, as he made his last attempt to reach the "treasure."

The other, is that the Forest Service evicted him from the property, tore the rock house down and placed him in some institute. Davis did tell us where to find a "real Spanish mine" (without a treasure in it of course), and this we did locate. [Probably the San Pedro Mine.] That was back in '57 and I doubt if many residents in this area know of its location today, unless there are some that spend a great deal of time in these mysterious mountains and discovered it by accident.

This next part is only rumor, but like I mentioned earlier, I'm quite sure Davis knew something concerning one of these mines. It's said some individual was digging around the floor of the old rock house and discovered two large pieces of "native silver." Question: If true, where did Crazy Davis find them?

I still enjoy hiking the hills and reminiscing about the good times we spent in this area. Perhaps most of the stories being told concerning these lost mines and treasures, have been blown clear out of proportion, from the retelling of 'em down through the years, but I have to admit, they do make interesting reading. I believe however, there is some truth behind several of these tales.

During the autumn and fall months you'll find me again out there camping, hiking and of course searching for clues and treasure signs among the many canyons cutting deep into this mountain range, and perhaps recapturing a few moments of those wonderful years we spent "chasing rainbows" in the Tumacacoris.

Chapter 7

WALT FISHER & POP

W hile in town we heard from friends about some fellow camped out our way. He had trouble with his Jeep Wagon and had hiked to Arivaca from Jalisco Canyon, a distance of perhaps ten miles. Randall Hill had taken him into Tucson for a new fuel pump. On their return Randall drove him back to his camp, arriving near dusk. This gentleman's name was Walter Fisher.

**Walt Fisher,
partner number 4.**

Roy & Chuck at the Clifford Well base camp.

After thanking Randall, he began replacing the pump and Randall returned to town. Upon hearing this and realizing Fisher hadn't arrived in town as Randall had expected, Chuck and I drove up Jalisco to investigate. Halfway there we spotted his jeep coming down. Stopping, we asked if everything was okay. Accompanying him was an elderly fellow he introduced as Pop. After some small talk he thanked us for showing concern and drove off.

Almost a week later Roy returned from the coast, and while we were in Arivaca we spotted Walt and Pop. After introducing them to Roy, we asked both to stop by camp sometime. Walt was searching for some Indian cave believed to be in the vicinity of Jalisco Ridge.

Later that day we discovered Walt was an attorney from Chicago and had given up his practice to explore the Southwest. When asked why he did such a foolish thing, Walt said he was disgusted with all the lies, double dealings, etc., associated with the profession.

One time while in an elevator he overheard two lawyers discussing a case. One said to the other, "What do you mean you'd give him a break. You give him a break when he's got his foot on your neck, not when you have yours on his."

Walt continued by saying, the law profession was rotten to the bone, and he wanted nothing more to do with it. Peace of mind and honesty meant more to him than money, a rarity in today's world.

Walt was about 40, wore glasses and shaved his head. Smiling he said he had very little in the first place, so why not shave it all off. He also had five degrees in various subjects and was the most highly intelligent person we had ever known, bordering on genius. People with this level of intellect are often a little odd in their ways, and this appeared at times. Nevertheless, Walt turned out to be an honest and lifelong friend.

"Pop," Walt's friend who passed away soon after this picture was taken.

While camping near Death Valley, Walt happened to meet Pop, who was prospecting. They camped together for several weeks, hiking the low easy valleys as Pop was about 76 and couldn't handle the rougher country.

When Walt decided to move over to Arizona, he asked Pop if he'd be interested in coming along. After dropping off his truck at relatives near San Diego they headed for Tucson.

Several days later they arrived at camp. The four of us spent three days exploring various locations toward the south, including Carreta Canyon. Pop was half deaf and kept saying, "Speak up. I'm missing all the key words." Being too old to climb he remained at camp, reading and doing various chores.

We had interesting evenings sitting around a crackling campfire discussing the alleged tales of lost gold and Arizona's wild history. Throughout the conversations, Pop would occasionally shout, "I'm still missing the key words. Speak up." He was quite comical at times and also told us interesting stories about being a deputy sheriff in North Dakota during the turn of the century.

There was much laughter and joking as the moonlight danced off the surrounding cliffs. To us there was no better life than this. Relaxing among friends under the stars and planning for the next day's adventures.

Walt was interested in searching for another cave, supposedly hidden near Bartolo Mountain southwest of camp. The Apaches allegedly hid their guns there before surrendering to the local cavalry. Later that evening we found Bartolo on our topographic map. We would follow Apache Canyon south as far as possible, then hike the remaining distance. Plans were made to leave early the next morning.

After a quick breakfast of hot cereal and flapjacks, we left in two jeeps. The traveling was rough along the canyon's rocky bed. Finding a flat area beneath some mesquite trees we parked the jeeps and began the long hike. Bartolo could be seen rising defiantly against the early morning sky.

Rumor has it an arsenal of weapons was concealed by the braves, and would be used once again after jumping the reservation. This occurred many times during the Indian Wars, surrender, jump the reservation and go raiding once more. To us it was conceivable that such a story could be true concerning these weapons as others have been discovered throughout Arizona.

We each took a different slope. The way some of the rocky faces on the cliffs had cracked in several locations, it looked as though the stones were placed there by human hands to cover an opening. Careful examination proved otherwise.

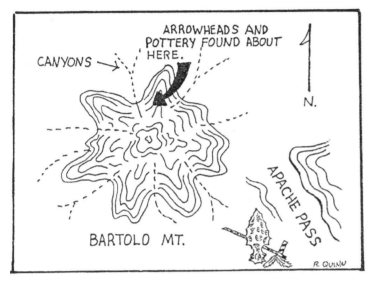

Area where the Apaches are rumored to have hidden a cache of weapons before their surrender c. 1886.

To the east of us was Apache Pass, not to be mistaken for the famous pass of the same name located north of the Chiricahua Mountains of Cochise County.

We met several hours later near a flat and had lunch. None of us found anything of great importance, but we were determined to keep searching for two more days. By 3:00 in the afternoon nothing was discovered, so we returned to camp and Pop.

At 6:30 the next morning, we again were searching on the mountain. This time we investigated the southern slopes. The terrain was rough going, but we slowly pushed on toward the summit. If any cave was in the vicinity harboring weapons of the past, its entrance was concealed well.

That afternoon, while descending the northern slope we happened to find several broken arrowheads. Our first thoughts were, "this sure looks suspicious." At least it proves Indians were here at one time. After searching the area closely, we discovered a few more arrowheads, and a large piece of pottery wedged in a crack in the rocks near an overhang.

It might have been my imagination but that old "gut feeling" came over me that something could be hidden in this general vicinity. Looking about there were several locations where a cave could be. So every foot was covered including any rocks that looked movable, which were moved and searched thoroughly, but no entrance to a cave was discovered.

We decided to explore the western slopes before abandoning the hunt, so an extra day was added, but still nothing. If a cave does exist within the area, its hidden well.

Even today when I'm camping near Bartolo, I still have that old gut feeling there might be a cave hidden within the shadows of this desert mountain. It would be interesting to make the discovery, and prove the tale was true after all.

Two days later Walt and Pop left for parts unknown, but promised to keep in touch. This friendship with Walt, like Roy, continued long after our adventurous trip ended. Both became what is known as, "true friends."

49

Chapter 8

THE GOLDEN FLOOR

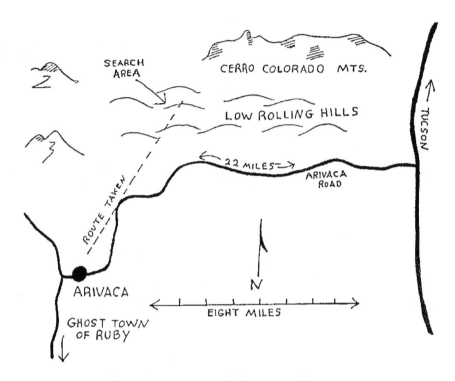

Map of first area searched for the stone floor. They left empty-handed.

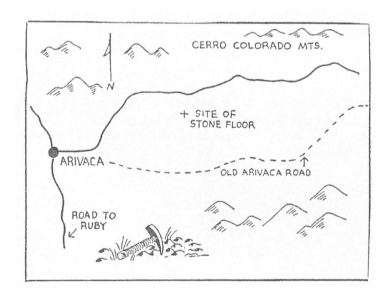

Second area searched for the stone floor.

T his story was told to us by Charlie Bent, a native born resident of Arivaca. He also was somewhat of a character but quite reliable.

Southern Arizona Trails, Vol. 3, No.23, March 24, 1987, Page 2

**A.J. Allen searching the stone floor
with a metal detector.**

Just south of Arivaca, a small village located in Southern Arizona, lays the ghost town of Ruby. All that remains of this once thriving mining town are numerous buildings, some of which were still livable. Desert vegetation grows among old rusted mining equipment scattered around, while doors swing lazily in the breeze.

Back around the turn of the century, it was a booming community that produced gold, silver, lead and some copper. It also employed well over two hundred people.

On their days off, two miners whom I shall call Jack and Bill, as their real names aren't known, would hike the country around Ruby and Arivaca prospecting and hoping for that big strike we all wish for.

During one of their two day trips, they ventured northeast of Arivaca about six to eight miles. The region is mostly low rolling hills, cut by numerous arroyos and small canyons. It's not difficult to navigate with a jeep. Occasionally you'll reach a deep arroyo or two with steep sides and have to find another way across. Also you run into a fire fence or two erected by the ranchers.

That evening as the sun bedded down behind the Baboquivari Range, they searched for a suitable campsite below the hills, as a strong wind was kicking about and making things a little uncomfortable. Finding a small flat area surrounded by gentle rolling hills, they removed their backpacks, made a fire and settled in for the night.

They finished breakfast just as the sun poked its face over the Cerro Colorado Mountains. They would start prospecting and work their way back toward the Arivaca Road, which was some three or four miles to the south. From there they could hitch a ride to Ruby and be able to start work the following morning.

Both had been doing this weekend prospecting off and on over the last six months, but never located anything of great value. They enjoyed it anyhow as it got 'em out of the underground mines and into the fresh air.

As Jack was relieving himself behind some bushes, his eye caught sight of something shining near his feet. He stepped back and discovered they had camped on a stone floor of some old adobe. The walls had been completely eroded down, but portions of the corners were still visible.

He called Bill over and they removed one of the stone slabs. Underneath they discovered two gold bars, estimated weight around 18 pounds each. They then pried the other stones up and found 17 more bars. After the excitement of finding them died down some, each took two bars, placing them in their backpacks. They decided to place the others back under the stone floor, hike to Arivaca, purchase horses and return for the remainder.

With each carrying 36 pounds they managed to reach Arivaca that afternoon, after numerous rest stops. Great excitement was aroused as word drifted about of their find. Of course nothing was said about the other gold bars. When asked where they found them, they would only say they discovered them while doing some digging. After selling the gold the two partners purchased some horses and other equipment.

That evening after some of the excitement had settled down, they rented a room at one of the local boarding houses. Before dawn the two were well on their way out of town, heading toward the area of their find.

You guessed it. They couldn't relocate the area. Back and forth they traveled checking all spots that looked familiar, up one arroyo and down the other. Had they gone too far or not far enough? Should they have taken the arroyo back a ways or that branch off they just past? Perhaps they were closer to town, so that area was checked. Try as they may, the adobe floor couldn't be found.

In a short while they were completely confused and returned to Arivaca. Word of the find got out, but none of the townspeople knew of the area where the discovery was first made.

Whenever the two miners left town, somebody was always following. In a few weeks the two disappeared and were never seen again.

Rumor has it that several years later, a group of Mexicans arrived in Arivaca from San Diego in search of an old adobe in that very same area. They too left empty handed after weeks of searching. If this gold is still hidden beneath that stone floor, it's no doubt covered with dirt and desert growth and completely concealed. One could stand right at the spot and never realize it, unless a piece of adobe was visible.

The cache would be great hunting for those that enjoy using a metal detector, and had the time to cover all the low areas around these rolling hills. To date, I haven't heard of anybody discovering the gold bars. The above story has never been in print, and is one of those little unknown treasures that very few people know of.

Yes, we put in quite a number of weeks ourselves searching but left empty-handed, like most hunters do.

THE GOLDEN FLOOR REVISITED

Southern Arizona Trails, Vol. 3, No. 27, April 21, 1987, page 7, 24

S everal weeks back, you read my account of two miners from Ruby that discovered a cache of gold bars beneath an old stone floor they happened to camp near one evening during the 1930s. Its location was estimated to be about eight miles northeast of Arivaca.

Each carried two bars that weighed around 18 pounds apiece. The other seventeen were left hidden beneath the floor. They hiked to Arivaca, purchased horses to retrieve the others, but were unable to find their way back to the site. Many weeks were spent searching, but try as they may, the stone floor could not be found.

Finally one time they left town but the two never returned. Either they rediscovered the cache and decided to leave the territory or they met with foul play.

A. J. Allen of Arivaca read the article and contacted me. He said he found such a floor many years ago in that vicinity, and could find it again.

In the "Letters to the Editor" column, April 7th issue of *"Arizona Trails,"* he wrote, to come on down and we'll check the site out, and split 50/50 if anything is found.

After traveling about seven miles we left the road and started overland. In a short while we stopped on a slight rise. With detector in hand, along with canteen, camera and pick, we hiked a short distance. It was a windy day, and our hair, "what we both had left of it," was blowing wildly in the breeze.

Earlier, upon arriving in town, A. J. mentioned a few locals had shown interest in the story, and some even said he should go out on his own and search the area. He flatly said, "No."

We left at 10:30, and during our drive we occasionally looked back to see if anyone was following, but this was done mostly as a joke.

Within a short time we arrived at the site. Most of the floor was covered with several inches of earth and some desert vegetation, but the outer corners were quite visible. The foundation measured approximately 7 x 14 feet.

A. J. began the slow process of searching with his Mayan detector, and we listened for any increase in the pitch of the detector tone. This sound did increase a number of times, so I removed several large slabs, but nothing was found below. We discovered later it was the slabs themselves that were giving us the false readings. After A. J. finished, I searched the same area a second time, but again nothing.

Afterwards, we both took pictures of the site, and some accompany this article.

The floor was found south of the present road, but it was still north of the original Arivaca Road that wound its way through the flats during the time Ruby was in operation. None of this road is visible today, but A. J. said it was located a mile or so south of where we stood.

The odds were against us finding anything, but in this treasure hunting game one must follow up any leads, no matter how small they might be.

There's no definite proof the floor we searched was the one the two miners discovered, but it definitely was located in the correct area.

Before leaving town, I saw Randall Hill and he mentioned he had found another floor in that same vicinity while out searching. He didn't disclose its location and I didn't ask.

Also, most of these stories have never been in print before, and they offer a "refreshing breeze" from the others, which have been told and retold around campfires and local bars for the past hundred years or so.

I decided to write this follow-up story after visiting the site. The majority of the stories that appear in "Treasure Trails" are true. Some of these lost treasures might have been discovered many years ago, but the finder decided not to mention this, and kept the discovery a secret. Others are just tales we heard during our years of treasure hunting in the southwest.

Documentation is difficult to find on some, while others have been proven to be factual. The remainder has to be left to the credibility of the story teller.

Chapter 9

THE LOST VILLAGE ADOBE

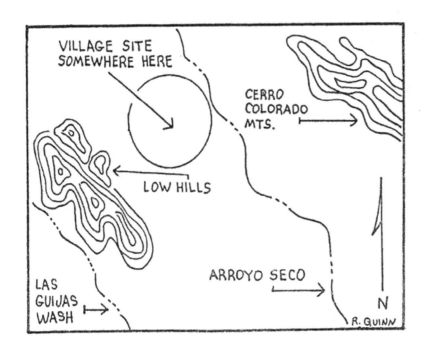

Chuck with Nicho in Arivaca.

Southern Arizona Trails, Vol. 3, No. 54, October 27, 1987, Page 23

Somewhere between the rugged Cerro Colorado Mountains and the northern slopes of the Las Guijas range, one can find the faint remains of an old forgotten adobe village. Nicho, a local character who had lived in Arivaca most of his life, once told our partner Roy that he knew the location of an old Spanish settlement. Nothing remained but the stone outlines where the buildings once stood. Also nearby were the mounds of six or seven graves.

The old gentleman had only one leg and moved about with the aid of a heavy homemade crutch that could also be used as a weapon if the occasion ever arrived. We even saw him pushing a wheelbarrow once. This was accomplished by holding the crutch tightly under his armpit and swinging it forward as he walked.

The old fellow was full of tall tales, but occasionally he would spin a yard that had some truth behind it. A great deal of the time he was intoxicated, so you never knew if the story being related at the moment was true or fabricated. Anyway, he was a nice old guy and we had a lot of laughs when he was around.

Roy told us about the site, so next time we saw Nicho we asked if he would show us the old settlement. He agreed, and a couple of days later we all piled into Roy's open jeep and headed east on the Arivaca Road.

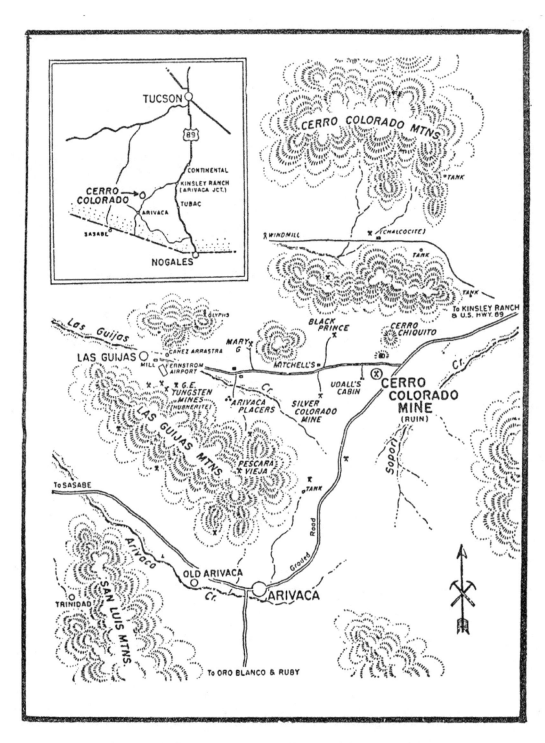

**COPY OF RARE MAP SHOWING ARIVACA
MINING DISTRICT. MAP PROBABLY WAS
MADE IN THE EARLY 1950s.**

After all these years I'm not [exactly sure] but I believe it was in the vicinity of the old Cerro Colorado Mine. We then traveled along several back roads with Nicho in the front seat pointing the way with that deadly crutch. We drove perhaps four or five miles, then started overland with old Nicho again shouting directions. When we picked him up in Arivaca we knew he was mildly intoxicated, and how he managed to locate the site remains an unsolved mystery.

After bouncing along for another mile, he had Roy change directions several times as he became confused as to where the settlement was. We finally got back on the right track and headed northwest, with all of us joking and laughing most of the way. A short while later we approached a deep wash that could have been Arroyo Seco.

We followed it north for perhaps half a mile, then Nicho pulled himself up on his one leg and started looking around as we traveled merrily along. A few seconds later he yelled, "Stop," and pointed toward the other side of the arroyo. He said the village was on the opposite side near a large group of mesquite trees.

Roy (right) and I metal detecting at Nicho's lost adobe village.

Reaching the other side we hiked another few hundred yards and came upon the site. Nicho was correct when he said nothing remained but the stone foundations. By the looks of the place, there were perhaps the remains of six graves on the side of a nearby slope.

While Nicho relaxed in the shade of some trees, we assembled our detector and began our search of the area. Later on Chuck took a picture of Roy and me, with me holding the instrument.

In the picture (above), the Cerro Colorados are directly over my shoulders, and a portion of the stone foundations can be seen just under the search coil.

I noticed we were a mile or so from a small group of hills to the west. I believe these are that low range of mountains called the Las Guijas. There were five dwellings there at one time, on to the east of the Las Guijas range and near the wash of the same name.

We spent most of the afternoon searching and digging, but nothing was discovered. Nicho claimed a friend of his once dug into one of the graves and removed a gold cross and chain from the skeletal remains.

We had been prospecting and treasure hunting for almost two years and never dug into any old graves, and we weren't about to start now, even with Nicho coaching us on from where he sat beneath the trees. However, we did check the gravesites out with the detector, but received no reaction.

The mystery here is: Why were the adobes erected at this location, and why five?

Unless the residents were working a mine somewhere in the general vicinity, they must have lived at the site for quite a spell due to the amount of graves nearby. There has been extensive mining activity in the region, as the northern slopes of the Las Guijas Mountains are pockmarked with dozens of prospect holes. Also, the old Las Guijas Mine is located in the center of all these workings.

On our return trip Nicho pointed toward the dark, forbidding Cerro Colorado Range and mentioned there was a cave hidden somewhere up among the towering cliffs. A large box of gold coins was believed to be buried in the rear.

He went on to say there was an "l" or "M" carved above the entrance where the loot was hidden. This one we never got around to searching for.

If I had to locate this settlement today, I believe I'd have some difficulty, as it sits on a large flat and there aren't any notable landmarks close by. The wash east of the site, I'm almost positive, is Arroyo Seco.

We only visited the site once, and that was with Nicho. As I mentioned earlier, he told many tales, but this one happened to be true. We often thought how many other interesting places he might have known of but had forgotten about over the years.

Another interesting point: This old village was in the general area where those two miners discovered the 19 bars of gold beneath that stone floor. I also wonder if there is a connection. During our search of the village, we didn't uncover any stone floors.

On returning to Arivaca, we thanked Nicho for showing us the old site and gave him $10. He seemed surprised at the gift and thanked us, then headed across the street toward the local cantina.

As the sun started to set behind the San Luis Range, and the long shadows began creeping outward, we headed back to camp near Sardina Peak.

That evening Chuck wrote about the day's activities in our diary. It was another adventure added to all the others we had been on, but surely not the last.

Other adventures awaited us down the road. Nothing of monetary value was discovered at the old forgotten village, but we had found and visited another part of Arizona's interesting history. I doubt if anything has been written about this small settlement, or for that matter, if its location was even known.

If it had a name, only the sleeping residents buried nearby know it.

Chapter 10

THE TURQUOISE NECKLACE

One afternoon while Roy was climbing a dangerous slope, his attention was drawn to an object beneath a rock overhang. Before reaching in to investigate, Roy checked the interior carefully to see if any unfriendly desert animals, such as rattlesnakes, were using it for shelter against the heat of the day.

Not hearing the distinctive sound of this deadly varmint, he reached in cautiously and removed the object. It was a small clay pot with something wrapped in leather within. This turned out to be a turquoise necklace some 16 inches long. The stones were attached to a thin piece of dry rawhide, but crudely made.

Why it was hidden at this remote location is unknown. No turquoise is found in this region, so it must have originated from Northern Arizona.

If you keep a watchful eye out while exploring these rugged canyons, there's an excellent chance something might be found. But caution must be taken before placing your hands into any openings.

One individual discovered a Conquistador helmet and breastplate while hunting near the eastern slopes of the Cerro Colorados.

This terrain isn't all that rough, and many have explored the region since the 1800s in their search for silver. The armor wasn't found earlier as nobody had taken the time to inspect the narrow but deep cracks that run parallel in the sedimentary formations along most of the canyon walls in this district. These openings were frequently used to quickly stash items before moving on, like bandit loot, etc. Why this armor was left behind will never be known.

SAN LUIS WASH ADVENTURE

Chapter 11

TULLY'S GOLD

Location of the Tully place on San Luis Wash.

A s supplies grew low, the three of us drove into town to stock up. Most of our food was canned, as anything fresh doesn't keep. While Roy was filling our water barrel, I happened to glance down Front Street. There, driving into Arivaca in his gray Willys was Walt. Stopping beside us he shook his head in disbelief. Rolling down the window he said, "I came looking for you guys. Didn't expect to find you this fast! Thought you might be out of this area by now."

We noticed old Pop wasn't along. Walt said after searching near Yuma, Pop became ill and he drove him to relatives in San Diego. Walt knew Pop's excursions into the hills were over. He was just too old.

We asked Walt if he'd like to camp with us as there were several sites we planned to investigate. Two hours later we returned to camp, which was now located in the San Luis Mountains. With Walt's tent erected beside the others, the place began to resemble a "tent city." It was nice to have the old gang together again.

They were great friends, fun to be with and honest as the day is long. Roy said he'd be around for several months before shipping out again. Being a merchant seaman, he had this wonder lust, and couldn't remain in one place too long. We all knew there'd be a lot of fun, laughter and adventures during the coming months. While in this area we planned to search for the "Tully Gold," another story told to us by Louie Romero.

HIDDEN GOLD AT TULLY WELL

Southern Arizona Trails, Vol. 3, No. 22, March 17, 1987, page 16

In 1885, Frank Tully [4] owned a large ranch along the San Luis Wash and located near the mountains of the same name. He was a man in his late 60s, who came to the Arizona Territory forty years earlier and carved his domain out of the savage wilderness, while still a young man.

Now old and crippled with arthritis and angry at the world, he spent most of his time sitting in the shade of the cottonwoods and reminiscing on past glories.

He had just sold a large portion of his ranch and cattle for $60,000 and was one tightfisted individual when it came to handing out money. His wife Sue, and two children Dan and Terry, [5] which she had late in life, were in their twenties and still lived at the ranch. They didn't live poorly by any means, but had to account for almost every dollar spent. Old Tully would say, his money came hard and slow through hard work, and it was going to go out the same way.

Of course, he never trusted banks, as they were (quoting him) "...easy pickings for the outlaws, the lazy bastards of the world, that didn't want to work for a living."

Every dollar from the sale was stored in a large steel chest, anchored to the heavy floor beneath his bed. He never feared robbery as he employed four fulltime *vaqueros* and most were better than average when it

---

[4], [5] This is probably Charles "Carlos" H. Tully. His second wife was Isabelle "Belle" and they had two children, Mary and Alice.

came to handling fire arms. Besides, he needed their loyalty and got it, by paying and treating them well. Some say, better than his own family.

When the monthly bills came due, he'd lock himself in his room, remove the exact amount needed from his "treasure chest" then hand it to his oldest boy, Terry. There was no physical abuse toward his family on his part, as he could barely get around himself, but living with him was a daily chore.

His wife and children still loved him, in their own way, but they didn't like his foul mouth or the way he'd put them down during a disagreement. He might have been crippled but there was nothing wrong with his lungs. When something didn't go right according to him, his voice and language could raise the dead.

Early one morning the rest of the family left for Tucson by wagon, as it was almost a day's journey to reach the town. They would attend to their business, remain the night and return the next afternoon. Old Tully saw them off and two *vaqueros* went along as guards, as the Indian problem was still "alive and well" in parts of the territory. There hadn't been any serious trouble in several months, as the U.S. Cavalry would chase 'em back across the border every time they poked their thieving heads across it.

That evening after dark, the two remaining *vaqueros* were in the bunkhouse playing cards. One happened to look out the window and saw somebody carrying a lantern. Walking to the door he called out and asked who it was. The booming voice of Tully came back out of the night. "It's me damn it, go back inside."

A few moments later the Mexican again saw the lantern. It was moving toward San Luis Wash, and a few minutes later he saw it coming back. This went on several more times and the two *vaqueros* thought Old Tully was just restless as he was alone in the house. Picking up their cards they continued the game, and thought no more about it.

When the family returned, they noticed the old man wasn't ranting and raving about how much money they had spent on some worthless junk they never would use like they had in the past.

In the days that followed, he spent more time alone in his room, gazing out the window, which faced San Luis Wash. A few weeks later, old grouchy Frank Tully died in his sleep. After he was laid to rest in the small cemetery north of the ranch house where a few words were spoken over him, the family returned to his room. There they found the key and opened the chest. A look of horror crossed their faces as out of the $60,000 only about $1,500 was left.

They knew the only time he was left alone for any length of time was during their trip to Tucson about four weeks earlier. All three searched the house systematically, looking in every place that could conceal that amount of money, but nothing was found.

With the help of the four Mexicans they kept the search going for several weeks. They looked around the cemetery, corral, barn, and even down the well. The *vaquero* that saw old Tully that night making round trips toward the wash, told the family and the search was centered there. Holes were dug to a depth of three feet; then trenches were dug, some twenty feet in length, and these crisscrossed the entire area beside the wash, and still nothing.

At that time of the year, the arroyos and washes weren't running with water, so they dug beside all the boulders within the wash up to a distance of 600 feet from the house.

The fifty-eight thousand dollars has never been found to this day. Even when the family sold the remainder of the ranch, they still returned each year with the permission of the new owner in search of Tully's gold, and each time they left empty-handed.

Nothing remains of the original ranch house or the other buildings but the well. Today, only holes can be seen where treasure hunters from the area have been digging. On the topo map you will only find the words, "Tully Well" where the large ranch house once stood. Just above are the letters, CEM to indicate where the small cemetery is.

After hearing this intriguing tale, all four of us spent around eight days searching the area. Camp was established beneath the very cottonwoods Frank Tully would sit under and reminisce about the past.

We, like the others before us, searched every square inch of that area, and the only thing found was an old lock and hasp. It was buried about four inches down in the vicinity of the main house. Old Tully was loud, demanding and difficult to live with, but he still loved his family. Why he hid the money from them will never be known. They even looked for a map while going through his personal things, but of course none was discovered.

One explanation could be that he lost his mind and thought his family was planning to steal it. We know he couldn't walk very far or even dig a hole, but somehow he managed to find a hiding place that even God couldn't locate.

From the house to the wash was about a hundred feet. He couldn't carry all the money at once, as his numerous trips that night verifies this. The *vaquero* thought he made perhaps four or five trips. If my memory is correct, Louis said, the round trips took about 15 minutes. How slow he moved, that wouldn't leave him much "burying time."

The big question here is, where could he have hidden that gold in so short of time, where nobody could ever find it? If he just buried the money in some random hole, close by, it would have been found by his family. Louis said, "You couldn't imagine the amount of digging that went on there over the weeks." So here we have another tale of vanishing gold, and I'm certain it's still hidden somewhere along the banks of San Luis Wash. Remember when old Tully became real quiet and would just sit in his room gazing out the window toward the wash? Well, some of the older residents of the area claim, as I do, the S.O.B. was looking right at the spot where he hid his gold—but where?

The following is another piece to add the tale that didn't appear in the above article.

During the mid-1970s while visiting Harvey Riggs in Arivaca, he related this interesting tale to us. Around 1962, a descendant of the Tully family descended on Arivaca. She was a stoutly gal of about 50 that looked as though she could handle any situation that came her way. Her quest was the missing gold.

She'd camp at the site in a small trailer towed by her old Buick. After searching several weeks or so, she would depart, only to return each spring. This continued for a number of years. The last attempt to unlock the puzzle was 1965. After only two days at the location, she was seen racing through town, towing the trailer, kicking up gravel, and disappearing in a cloud of dust, never to return. She really put the "pedal to the metal."

Being she was a descendant there's a strong possibility she uncovered a clue leading to the gold's hiding place. That $58,000 in coin on today's market would bring a tidy sum. If indeed she did solve the mystery, it would be interesting to know just where that money was buried.

SOPORI WASH
ADVENTURE

Chapter 12

TALE OF THE PHANTOM GEAR

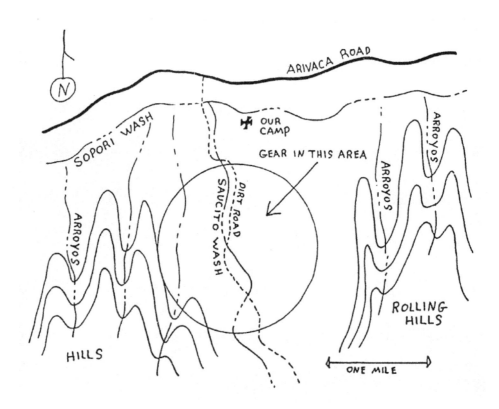

Area of the tow truck treasure hunter's huge gear.

Southern Arizona Trails International, Vol. 3, No. 31, May 19, 1987, Page 24

fter our disappointing search for the "Tully Gold," we moved camp just south of the Arivaca Road, near Sopori Wash.

This odd story has nothing to do with lost mines or mission treasure but it's rather unique, and I have never heard another tale like it before.

My three partners had taken off for Tucson, for supplies and to take care of some personal matters. I hadn't gone as the day before all of us were in Nogales, Mexico, and I had a mild case of "Montezuma's Revenge."

Our main camp was south of the Arivaca Road and located beneath some large cottonwoods that grew near the banks of Sopori Wash. It was a very picturesque and serene location, and almost resembled a scene one would find on a picture postcard. It was a beautiful late spring day and a hot breeze would occasionally kick up, signaling the approach of summer.

I could have enjoyed these surrounding much more, if I didn't have that painful rumbling in my stomach. It comes from drinking water or eating something fresh below the border. I never learn. To keep my mind off it, I began doing some odd jobs around camp that we had been putting off.

A few hours later I heard the distinctive sound of a truck moving about on the opposite side of a hill across the wash. I figured it might be some rancher out checking his livestock, as cattle feed in this area.

A short while later I spotted the truck coming across the wash in my direction. To my surprise it was a tow truck.

Pulling up, the rough looking driver introduced himself. His name was Ken and he asked how long I have been camping here. I said about a month as my partners and I have been exploring the rough canyons toward the east. On the seat beside him he had an old wrinkled topo map of this area. Picking it up he asked how far it was to Saucito Canyon from our camp. I told him about half a mile to the west and indicated on his map where our camp was.

He then asked if we had ever seen a giant "brass" gear buried halfway in a sandy arroyo in this general area. By the portion above ground, he figured it should be seven to eight feet across and four inches thick. I smiled and said, "Where did you ever hear a yarn like that?" Ken climbed from the truck and we both sat in the shade of the cottonwoods. After lighting his pipe, Ken related the following tale.

A few weeks earlier, two fellows that work for him, asked to borrow one of Ken's trucks over the weekend, as neither had a truck and a car wouldn't do. Both liked to rock hunt and some neighbor mentioned they should try the area near Sopori Wash as thunder eggs and some pieces of large black obsidian have been found in the arroyos, especially near Saucito Wash.

Ken let 'em have a truck and both left Saturday morning. The neighbor also told them to hang a left after crossing the third cattle guard on the Arivaca road and follow this faint path a mile or so, and they would be in the right area.

While working the numerous arroyos in search for these bits of treasure, they happened to find this huge brass gear buried halfway in the wash. One remained behind while the other returned with the tow truck. Backing to the edge they attached the cable to the "thing" and tried pulling it free, but the gear wouldn't move.

They then dug around it, trying to loosen it some, and gave it another tug. This time they bent and damaged the town arm. Leaving their prize discovery still in the arroyo, they returned to Tucson and told Ken what happened, and they would pay for the damage to the truck. Ken was very interested in seeing this large gear they couldn't move, so they drew a rough map showing the area.

I told Ken we have never seen anything like that, and I doubt if the thing really existed. If something like that was laying around, the *vaqueros* that rode for the local ranchers would have discovered it ages ago as little escapes their keen eyes.

Ken had the crazy notion that perhaps the Spanish padres used it in their mining operations. No way, I said, and besides, there wasn't any use for such an oddity that size. I asked him why the others hadn't come along, if they knew where the thing was. He replied they had to work Friday and through the weekend.

I told him to forget the whole thing as somebody was pulling his leg, but he still insisted he was going to search. Twenty minutes or so later, he drove off toward the hills behind camp. The last I saw of Ken, he was climbing up the rise, bouncing along with his head out the window looking around. Not having four-wheel drive he was doing pretty good with that tow truck.

For almost half an hour I could still hear him shifting gears and driving about, stopping momentarily then moving on again. The sound became fainter as he moved further away.

When the gang returned from Tucson, I told them the whole tale. None said a word; they just shook their heads and walked away.

This is all in jest, but after returning to this area we heard there was a rash of UFO reports several weeks earlier. If anyone is flying about in these things and build their craft as good as we build cars, there is a possibility one of them "threw a gear" while flying over.

That evening I wrote in our diary a brief description of this strange tale. Even then I called it, "The Tale of the Phantom Gear." That was sixteen years ago.

ROCK CORRAL
ADVENTURES

Chapter 13

A CHALICE FULL OF GOLD

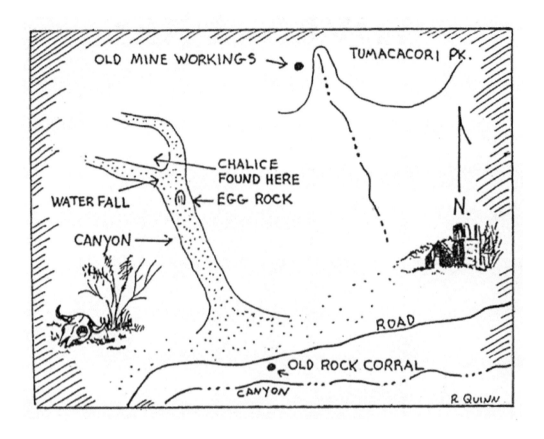

A CHALICE FULL OF GOLD

Southern Arizona Trails, Vol. 3, No. 64, December 29, 1987, Page 23

Several months back I heard a rather intriguing tale from a woman living on Bopp Road, east of the Tucson Mountains. A few weeks earlier she was out with her son and daughter-in-law, doing some gold panning somewhere on the eastern slopes of the Santa Rita Mountains. While there she happened to meet a gentleman the family had known for quite some time.

He also engaged in this pastime, and knew several individuals interested in prospecting and treasure hunting. A close and reliable friend of his passed on a story that centered around that popular area, where most treasure seekers eventually end up at sooner or later, Rock Corral Canyon.

I believe this one locale has been visited by more hopeful treasure hunters than any other site within the Tumacacori Range.

Area where the golden chalice was found.

There are numerous exploratory diggings lying in the shadows of these mountain peaks that have been dug by both weekend and professional treasure seekers.

Many were dug around the '40s and '50s by enthusiastic individuals, believing they knew the locations of several buried treasures or lost mines. These were supposedly hidden by the padres from Tumacácori Mission, during the great Indian rebellion of 1751. Most if not all, left the hills with nothing more than broken dreams and hopes.

New dirt roads have been pushed into various locations in and around this well-known canyon. Almost every year somebody new ventures out among these rugged hills in search of these legendary treasures.

During September of '87, a lone explorer entered into this region and started climbing and searching the rocky slopes in the vicinity of this canyon. If he was looking for something in particular, it's not known. Soon he found himself near some interesting high cliffs and began searching them.

These mountains are mostly composed of andesite, a rather fragile lava rock. And the cliffs have countless cracks, narrow openings and small caves. These range from fist size to one large enough to walk in.

He spotted a small opening that looked as though someone had wedged several rocks in. Reaching up he pried them loose then stepped back in dismay. His eyes fell upon a gold chalice hidden near the rear. It stood perhaps six inches tall.

After the shock of finding such an item, he reached in and removed the goblet carefully. In doing so, he noticed it was extremely heavy for its size. As he brought it down to eye level, he discovered why. Its interior was full of gold coins. If they were Spanish or American mintage, it's not known.

THE WATERFALL

The finder related this story to a trustworthy companion then later displayed the gold chalice and coins. This tale was then passed on to Betty by her acquaintance, who in turn informed me.

Who hid the golden cup within the small enclosure will never be known. But I would venture to guess it was a local Jesuit from Tumacácori.

He might have considered the chalice his own and didn't want it buried along with the other treasures that were concealed during the Indian uprising.

It's also possible a neophyte (a Christianized Indian) who for some reason wanted to keep the cup from falling into hostile hands and becoming lost, hid the goblet in the hole.

But this doesn't explain the coins. If their origin and dates were known, it could perhaps date the concealment of the chalice.

I was told that the party who made this outstanding discovery would be returning for another search. If he did, I have heard nothing, as this woman hasn't seen her friend since first hearing of this remarkable find.

I'm not completely convinced at this time if the story is entirely true, so I'll refrain from any comments until I am reasonably sure about the authenticity of this tale. That is if I can obtain more information concerning this alleged find.

MYSTERIOUS ROCK CORRAL CANYON

Southern Arizona Trails, Vol. 3, No. 85, May 24, 1988, Page 19

S ince writing about the alleged golden chalice, supposedly found in the vicinity of Rock Corral Canyon last September, I have discovered the golden treasure was located in the area of a small waterfall.

The fall is nestled among the sun-baked boulders near the intersection of two narrow canyons (see map).

This rugged piece of country has been well explored by treasure hunters for countless years.

Even today, individuals seeking sudden wealth travel to this remote spot, alone or in groups, in their attempt to unravel the mysteries of hidden treasures which are believed still buried somewhere among the craggy rocks.

This desolate region has been searched more often than any other within the Tumacacori Range.

Why this chalice, if it was indeed found, was never discovered until recently will forever remain a mystery, as this area has been raked and re-raked by experienced treasure hunters and it was never found until now.

I visited this area during March of '88 and it has changed very little since I first trekked up the canyon's rocky bed in July of '56.

Vegetation has increased along its banks and some rock movement is clearly visible, but basically this lonely stretch of canyon still looks the same.

I hadn't ventured back to this locale for many years and I felt somewhat strange as I hiked along. It brought back many pleasant memories of the "good old days."

By using my imagination I could almost hear my brother and partner Roy calling to one another across the canyon as we had done some 30-odd years before.

The gigantic egg-shaped boulder still stood stately on the canyon floor, the large limbs of the nearby tree still embracing it. Many times we had sat beneath its welcome shade.

During this visit, Dean Yedica, a friend and fellow treasure hunter, accompanied me, along with his two friends Dallas and Bernice Strans of Florence, Ariz.

We searched in the vicinity of the falls, which was still trickling some water from the previous rains.

Nothing was found but the old diggings we had discovered 32 years earlier. One outcropping of rock toward the west resembled a pointing arrowhead, but further investigation by Bernice proved it to be nothing more than a natural formation.

Several sections of the canyon had trenches cut into its sides and were heavily overgrown with brush.

Back in '56 we found some faint markings and symbols carved into the rocks above one of these open cuts, but they had completely eroded from view and could not be located.

The upper head of Rock Corral Canyon is in an area where many believe several lost mines might be hidden. However, none to my knowledge have been discovered. There is evidence of extensive digging by those who believe the buried wealth of the padres was hidden somewhere close by.

The small mine entrances once sealed by the Jesuits would be quite difficult to find today. Especially after 200 years of erosion and desert growth. One could stand right on the exact spot and never realize a tunnel was concealed nearby.

Just north of the old rock corral, at the upper head of that long canyon, located on the southwestern slopes of Tumacacori Peak, one can see the remains of an old Spanish workings. Throughout the years several parties have sunk a tunnel just beneath it, in hopes of finding some hidden chamber full of treasure or a rich silver vein, but all failed.

There are about five square miles around this peak that hold tales of buried gold and lost mines. The only thing known to have been recently discovered there was the gold chalice and the coins it held.

If anything else has been found, the discoverer most likely kept the find a secret. The only witness to the discovery would be the silent canyons and lofty peaks that surround this mysterious region.

Chapter 14

TREASURE OF TUMACACORI PEAK

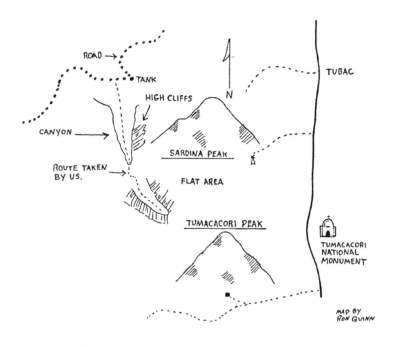

Bats leaving the cave.

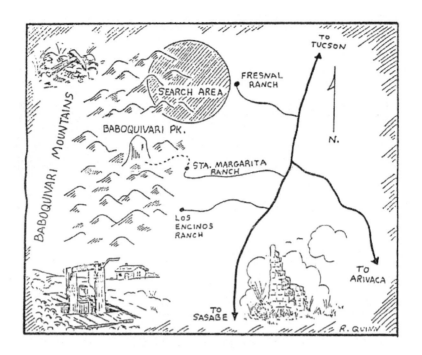

Egg-shaped rock.

TREASURE AT TUMACACORI PEAK

Parts One & Two
Southern Arizona Trails International, Vol. 3, No. 35, June 16, 1987, Page 20
Southern Arizona Trails International, Vol. 3, No. 36, June 23, 1987, Page 20

Part 1

Just west of San Cayetano de Tumacácori Mission, stands the majestic Tumacacori Mountains. Jutting out from this barbaric range is a rugged pile of rock, called Tumacacori Peak. Buried within its shadow, lies a fabulously rich Spanish treasure, so the story goes.

The treasure, which lies buried within sight of these mysterious mountains, was hidden by the Jesuit priests when the Pima tribes revolted against the Spanish oppression in 1751, and this started a bloody uprising. Many missions were destroyed and countless padres killed. The priests at Tumacácori decided to hide their gold and flee to the coast and the ships that would carry them to safety.

Our own connection with the story dates back to the spring of '57 when my brother Chuck and I were prospecting in the area. During this time, we met an old Mexican *vaquero*, who had been riding the country for over thirty years. One afternoon he rode into a camp we had established just north of an old rock corral the Spanish had built, and is still visible to this day. After greetings, Louis [Romero] sat against a tree and lit a cigarette, the smoke circled lazily over his head then drifted off as we talked. Of course our conversation turned to lost mines and treasure, and Louis sat gazing toward Tumacacori Peak. Pointing toward the lofty monument, he said, "Boys, there is a big treasure hidden over there."

He told about the uprising and how the padres hid their gold and silver before fleeing for their lives. Louis also told us that back around the turn of the century, a Papago Indian would pay for his supplies at the general store at Tubac, with gold nuggets. With aroused interest, the storekeeper asked where he obtained such fine nuggets. The Indian pointed toward the western mountains and indicated he found them there, then picked up his supplies and left.

The old Indian returned several times in the months that followed, and he and the storekeeper became good friends. In a short while, the storekeeper again asked about the gold nuggets which the Papago never seemed to run out of.

After some coaching, the Indian told his friend that while hiking the mountains, he had discovered a small cave. The entrance was covered with a large flat rock. In one corner stood sacks of gold nuggets along with church ornaments made of silver. The old Indian knew he could barter the small nuggets without arousing much suspicion, but was afraid to touch the gold bars.

The storekeeper knew some people in the mining business outside the state that would help dispose of the bullion. Upon hearing this, the Papago gave it some thought then agreed to lead him to the treasure.

The next day, they left town on horseback in the general direction of the Tumacacoris. After traveling some five miles, they started up Rock Corral Canyon and made camp alongside its bank. When the first rays of dawn appeared, they started to climb the steep rocky slopes north of the canyon. The terrain was rough and they were forced to lead their mounts most of the way. In a short time, they arrived at the gaping mouth of a long rocky canyon, and here they hobbled their horses. Taking canteen in hand they entered, and soon passed a large rock resembling an egg on end. (This rock can still be seen today.)

No doubt the storekeeper's heart pounded with excitement as they inched their way along the canyon's rocky bed. Soon the Indian turned and began climbing from the sun-baked floor. No doubt an animal was resting above, and hearing their approach was startled and ran. In doing so, it dislodged some rocks, which cascaded down and into the Indian's path. Stopping, the old Indian looked up...turned toward his companion, who was hot on his heels, and said, "Bad omen, we go back. Spirits no want me to show you cave. We go back." With these words, he started down the slope. The storekeeper tried in vain to change his mind, but to no avail. The old Papago disappeared shortly after returning to Tubac.

In the years that followed, cowboys riding in the general vicinity of these desolate mountains came upon the storekeeper searching the barren hills for the golden hoard. He looked till the day he died, without ever finding it.

We had spent quite some time exploring this hazardous country, until the blistering heat drove us out. The area is unbelievably rough and loose rocks underfoot make it dangerous to climb the steep mountainsides. One slip and you go head first into a dark rocky canyon.

The summers are even worse, when the rains come. Dark storm clouds settle across ridges, and thunder rumbles from high mountain walls. Rain comes down in torrents, loosening rock and sending them crashing into the valley floor below.

We were caught out during one of these violent displays of Mother Nature, but found shelter near an overhang. It was a nightmare of light and sound, as lightening struck about us. Rain came down like the heavens were opening, accompanied by a gale-like wind. When the storm moved on we stepped from under the overhang and there was a new freshness in the air, and the temperature had dropped some twenty degrees. To the south, we could see the tail end of the storm. It was moving across the Atascosa Mountains like some hideous monster, growling and splitting sparks as it made its way southward.

It's easy to get to, the mountain that is [Tumacacori Peak]. Just drive some thirty odd miles south of Tucson, and there she is. From the outside she looks easy. Inside, it's a maze of dark and lonely canyons, dangerous slopes, heat, snakes and faint trails that go nowhere. But if you think you'd like to pick up a million dollars or so, and figure a mountain is just a mountain, this is where to search.

It's a sinister land, especially during the summer months. Water is scarce and the temperature will reach well above 120° in the narrow almost forgotten canyons. The hot wind that whistles among the boulders seems to come from the furnaces of hell itself. Buzzards glide on outstretched wings against a cloudless sky, just waiting for something to drop. Snakes, lizards and other creepy things of the desert dart from rock to rock, in search of shade. It seems the very mountains are trying to keep intruders out. Just west of Tumacacori Peak are lofty cliffs, like a fortress wall, forbidding anyone to enter.

As Chuck and I descended to our jeep below, I caught a glimpse of Tumacacori Peak in the distance, and wondered if we, or anyone else would ever uncover its secret and find the treasure it guards so well. This country has changed very little since the sandal footed padres first stepped into the valley.

So, if you plan on entering this sun drenched pile of mangled rock called the Tumacacoris, in search of this elusive treasure, be aware of all I have said. This is a land covered with the dry blood of Spanish padres, Indians, miners and those who thought they could pry its golden secret from the dry earth.

Part Two

Fall of 1958 found us again back in the Tumacacori Mountains, and just looking at them makes my legs hurt. These rocky hills play havoc with your feet, as the area is mostly composed of andesite, a volcanic rock. The entire surface is covered with small to fist-size rocks and it makes walking difficult, as these little monsters hide and wait in thick grass and on slopes, just waiting for you to make a mistake so they can twist your ankle. This is just one of the weapons these devilish mountains will use against you.

After a couple of months of prospecting on the western edge of this rugged range, my brother, Chuck, and I again found ourselves back in the area of Tumacacori Peak and Rock Corral Canyon on the eastern slopes of these unfriendly mountains.

Early one chilly morning as we were preparing to leave camp, I heard the sound of a jeep approaching. A few moments later it rounded some mesquite trees and popped into view. It was, John, another treasure hunter we had met while in Arivaca, earlier last year. He recognized us and came to a stop. What kept that vehicle of his running is still a mystery to us.

After the handshaking was over, John told us he was going to search once more for that elusive treasure near Tumacacori Peak. He told us he had met this old *vaquero*, while visiting Louis, a cowboy that worked for the Arivaca Ranch that we all knew and liked. They started talking and of course their conversation drifted toward treasure hunting. The *vaquero* said that one day while riding the country near Tumacacori Peak, during the middle 1930s he spotted another rider below that flat ridge he was on. The rider was moving up the same canyon which the storekeeper and the Papago had taken years before. (The old *vaquero* knew of this story.)

When the stranger approached the large "egg-shaped" boulder in the center of the canyon, he dismounted and tied his horse to a nearby tree. Removing the saddlebags the stranger continued up the canyon on foot and out of view. By now curiosity had settled in, and being in no hurry, decided to wait till this stranger returned. (If only this *vaquero* would have rode north a short distance, he could have seen where this stranger was going and discover the treasure site.)

Twenty minutes later the stranger came into view. He placed the saddlebags, which looked quite heavy across the back of his horse, then mounted. The vaquero followed, but kept to the high ridge and out of sight. After placing his mount in a horse trailer, he drove back out and turned north toward Tucson.

A few months after the close of World War II, this same vaquero was visiting relatives in Tucson and heard the following story.

It seems his nephew lived near an elderly gentleman by the name of Walt, and over the past few years became friends. Walt was losing his eyesight and could hardly see so Manuel, the nephew, would do various jobs for him that he couldn't accomplish himself.

One day Walt called Manuel over and asked if he would drive him down toward Nogales. If he did, he would make Manuel a rich man. Walt said all he needed was one more load, and what was left Manuel could have, but not to mention this to his family. With curiosity aroused, Manuel agreed, and said he could borrow his family's truck over the weekend. Walt mentioned he once had a truck of his own, but sold it after his eyesight began to fail.

The following Saturday both left town and headed south. Walt instructed Manuel to inform him when they approached the old Tumacacori Mission, which today is a National Monument. A short while later the mission came into view and Manuel told him they were near it. Walt instructed him to slow down and look for a dirt road off to the right that went up over a small hill. Spotting it they turned west and followed the road almost a mile and a half into the Tumacacori Mountains. At one time this road terminated at the top of a hill near an old rock-house, but somebody, probably the Forest Service pushed the road in another couple of miles, and right past the old rock corral where the canyon got its name. This cut their walking distance almost half a mile.

Stopping they climbed from the truck. Walt had two strong canvas bags with him and each had a canteen. Taking Walt by the hand, they entered the mouth of this rough narrow canyon. They had to walk slowly as Walt could hardly see the ground and was stumbling most of the time. In a short while they reached the egg-shaped boulder and Walt told Manuel to move closer to the right slope. With outstretched hand he started feeling the rocks as the moved slowly along. He also told Manuel to look for an outcropping of rock about three feet above the canyon floor that protruded from the steep bank.

After searching back and forth for almost an hour and not finding what Walt was looking for, Walt became frustrated and kept shouting, "It's here, damn it…I know it's here." Manuel finally asked what they were searching for, and Walt shouted, "Gold, boy, a whole cave of it!"

Both were getting weary from the search and returned to the large boulder. Walt kept saying, "All I need is one more load and I can't find the damn flat rock." He had left a flat rock about 2 x 3 feet over the small entrance, and couldn't understand why he was unable to locate it, with Manuel's help.

Manuel was curious to know where this gold had come from, and Walt said, he discovered it while out hunting many years before. He went on to say he'd come back once or twice a year to remove a small portion. (Why he didn't remove all of it over a short period and conceal it, say in his home or closer to Tucson, is anyone's guess.) He mentioned there were gold and silver bars, plus sacks full of gold nuggets. The church ornaments were never mentioned that the Papago had seen.

I guess these yearly trips were what the old timer was living on, as he did have a large home and some 200 acres near Tucson. Walt said there was enough left to make several people rich for life. He also hadn't made a trip to his cache since his eyesight began to fail. (Again, if he knew his sight was on the way out, he should have brought back all his truck could carry to be on the safe side. This is the only part of this story I cannot understand.)

When Manuel began doing him various favors and wouldn't take any money for his trouble, Walt started to trust the lad, and decided to take him into his confidence. Besides, Walt was low on cash and had to make another trip to his "vault." After searching in vain once more, both returned to Tucson very downhearted and disappointed.

This canyon is very deep and narrow, and flash floods that rumble down it during the rainy season, could easily change things around. These rushing waters could easily have removed the flat stone, exposing the small entrance. Dirt and rock from above could fall and cover the hole in a short time, concealing it under another storm.

You might ask, "Then what happened all those years Walt was returning and removing some of this treasure?" The area certainly has big flash floods each season, and if he had seen some difficulty in keeping the entrance covered, Walt surely would have found a better way of concealing it or even moving this cache to another area. Like most stories, there are numerous questions that go unanswered.

John had searched for this treasure twice before, without success but after hearing this most interesting story, the old "gold bug" gave him another bite and he just had to make another attempt at it. John asked us to join him in the search, if we didn't have other plans. I doubt if he really thought we could locate it, and I'm quite certain he wanted us along for company. Nothing big was going on so we both decided to tag along for awhile.

After three days of climbing, slipping and falling and moving every flat rock we came upon and not locating a thing, John gave up and returned to Arivaca, and Chuck and I continued our prospecting.

I'm quite sure the stranger the old *vaquero* saw and Walt are one and the same. Walt died several years later and Manuel returned many times with friends to search that sun baked canyon for this elusive treasure. On the LEFT side of the canyon are a few large open cuts, supposedly dug by Manuel and his party.

I believe the only way this cache will be discovered is like it had in the past—by accident. Due to the ruggedness of the terrain very few people venture into this area, and if the racing waters happened to uncover the entrance and nobody was around to see it, the entrance would again be covered by nature after another few flash floods. The steep road leading down to the old rock corral is completely washed out.

The next way sounds somewhat radical, but you could use a large bulldozer and shear away the right bank a portion at a time. I'm quite certain if you did, the Forest Service would be paying you a visit soon. They frown on ventures like this, and to obtain a permit for such an endeavor is almost impossible. You would have to cut away almost an eighth of a mile to be sure you didn't miss the cave. The Forest Service throws a fit if they discover a new hole left by some weekend prospector, so your chances are about nil in obtaining a permit.

Well, that's about all I know of this cache. Nothing has been added to make this story sound more interesting. I'm sure a large portion of this treasure still remains hidden somewhere up that narrow sun-baked canyon.

Another thought is, there is a strong possibility this hiding place could have caved in and there isn't any entrance left. If so, the bulldozer would be the only way.

As I have stated before, these mountains are quite dangerous and they wait patiently there, century after century for somebody to venture in and make a mistake, and to be added to their list of casualties. These mountains are very jealous of their treasures and guard their secrets well.

100 YARDS UP THE RIDGE

Southern Arizona Trails, Vol. 3, No. 78, April 5, 1988, Page 19, 22

O ver the years I've heard stories that perhaps could be true, while others stretch the imagination some. Most concern lost mines, bandit loot and those well-known mission treasures. One particular tale has absolutely no documentation, but I still find the treasure yarn most intriguing. A similar story occurred in Southern Nevada, so there's a strong possibility both tales are one and the same.

The question is: Which one is true?

The version I'm familiar with happened over in the Baboquivari Mountains, northwest of Arivaca. Sometime during the 1880s a considerable amount of placer mining was going on in the vicinity around Arivaca, especially north of town.

At the small general store, the miners would barter their newly found gold for necessities of life. One regular customer, an old Papago Indian also brought in his share of gold, but unlike the others, he didn't work a claim.

His supply of glittering nuggets never amounted to much, so he drew little attention. Most thought the quiet old Indian was just "wildcatting" around the countryside, finding "color" in both the surrounding hills and along Arivaca Creek.

When the placer fields finally gave out, most drifted off to other locations, all except the old Papago. He continued to bring in good-sized nuggets. One was reported to be the size of a man's thumb-tip. Again, he didn't have any claims, but there he would be every month or so with his little leather pouch overflowing with gold.

Eventually he was followed by several suspicious miners wherever he went, but there were only three points in his wanders, the store, his brush hut below the Baboquivari Range and Tucson.

The Indian finally revealed his secret many years later to the storekeeper. A number of years earlier, while hiking through these rugged mountains on the eastern slopes, he sat down to rest near a long rocky ridge jutting out in a northerly direction from the central peak.

As it became darker, he spotted a large number of vampire bats emerging from a hole beside an outcropping of rocks some one hundred yards away. He investigated and found the opening to be an entrance to some abandoned mine tunnel. Climbing down the narrow opening, he discovered a large cache within the interior.

Rotted buckskin bags of gold nuggets were resting beside the wall, their glittering contents scattered on the floor, in another corner stood a pile of gold bars and ancient mining tools. Cut into one wall was a small opening containing a shrine. The old Indian became frightened at the surroundings and quickly turned and hastened away, but not before taking several bags of gold. Later that evening he buried them under the floor of his hut.

The merchant, overjoyed by this information and the promise of the Papago to guide him there, spend the night preparing for the trek into the towering Baboquivaris.

Next morning he was greeted by the Indian, who had second thoughts about telling this to a white man. He had climbed to the location and waited till all the bats had returned to the hole, then closed the narrow entrance with rocks. Before leaving, he also told the merchant, "No more bats. The all will die in hole, and no white man will ever find the mine." Several weeks later the Indian left the area and was never seen again.

The similarity between this account and the article I wrote in the June 16, 1987 issue of the *Trails* parallel one another quite closely. I believe a majority of these stories that sound similar are an off-shoot of the original tale.

A number of mines have been discovered in this mountain range, and undoubtedly this region has been visited by our old friends, the Jesuits. I also believe their sandaled feet have covered every mineralized area in Southern Arizona. Evidence of their passing can be found around the Arivaca mining district.

An old Yaqui Indian who lived in the vicinity remembered hearing rumors of a rich mine once worked by the Spanish in the foothills of the Baboquivaris. Supposedly some old graves and rock house ruins are located east of this range, indicating the region once supported a fairly large population. Most likely the inhabitants worked several mines in the surrounding area.

While relating the story concerning the vampire bats at a party several years ago, I met a gentleman from the University of Arizona. Upon completion of the tale, he insisted there never were any vampire bats in Southern Arizona. "Some large populations inhabit caves in Mexico but not here," he said. Perhaps the old Papago saw another variety and thought they were the vampire species.
I believe this story might only be a tall tale and I wouldn't consider undertaking a serious search for the mine site.

After hearing hundreds of stories about lost mines, etc., it seems to me that most are discovered either by (1) a Mexican woodchopper, (2) an Indian hunting or aimlessly hiking about the hills, (3) a cowboy caught out in some raging thunderstorm, finds shelter in a nearby cave and discovers it full of treasure, (4) a prospector becomes lost and stumbles across a hidden canyon nobody can ever relocate and discovers an open mine, rich with gold and several human skeletons laying beside the entrance.

I have jokingly said to my partners, "We should lose ourselves in some unfamiliar mountains then wait for a fierce storm to hit. As the thunder rumbles down from the peaks and the wind howls around us, we'll wander aimlessly about in search of shelter. If we happen to come across any caves or hidden mine tunnels, we're sure to discover a treasure of two."

It seems to work out like this in most stories I've heard. While hiking these hills, I have seen clues indicating the Spaniards indeed worked mines in the region.

When the padres retreated from the territory in 1751, they didn't burden themselves with heavy bars of gold. These treasures were buried at various locations among the hills. The question that haunts most of us is where? I doubt there are 2,050 mule loads of silver and 905 loads of gold hidden anywhere within the dark confines of the Guadalupe Mine, as some writers claim. If and when any Spanish workings are uncovered, I'm certain gold will be found, but not in these vast quantities.

Many old abandoned Spanish mines have been discovered over the years in Mexico. If they mined gold and silver below the border, then why not here in Southern Arizona, in our own backyard?

Chapter 15

CAMP LOCO

Ruins of Camp Loco

About half of the walls of Mrs. Laura Pierson Shepley [Shipley] Clark's old cabin were still standing. A large tree now grows from the center of the cabin floor.

CAMP LOCO SITE DRAWS AVID TREASURE HUNTERS

Southern Arizona Trails, Vol. 3, No. 108, November 1, 1988, Pages 18-19

Some five miles west of Calabasas and a few miles north of Peck Canyon is a rugged area called Camp Lobo. Supposedly a vast treasure is hidden somewhere among its towering cliffs. Since the 1800s this region has been dug into, blasted and other areas ripped apart by those insisting a fabulous mine and treasure are hidden among the high rocky cliffs that dominate the upper head of the canyon.

The first to seriously search for the treasure was a Laura Pierson Shepley [Shipley]. She came from the upper Midwest, was intelligent, well educated also claimed to be a lawyer, and had money.

Most of the information regarding this woman and the unusual events that occurred at her camp was furnished by Ron W. Anderson of Tubac.

She employed about a dozen Mexican men. After having a small rock cabin built beside a large boulder, the men began digging numerous tunnels and shafts at random locations throughout the area. She was hoping one of her diggings might intersect the hidden mine tunnel, which she was convinced was somewhere in the vicinity.

The majority of this work was carried on beneath the cliffs west of the cabin. No doubt she was searching for the legendary "Lost Guadalupe Mine" and the huge treasure concealed within. It was supposedly hidden by the padres from Tumacácori Mission during the Indian rebellion of 1751.

This digging continued for several years until she eventually ran out of funds, but this did not dampen her quest for the treasure she believed was there.

Shepley also had a bunch of kids with her at Camp Loco—two boys and two girls. It's said both girls became pregnant and left the campsite.

While checking court records at Nogales, Mr. Anderson discovered that in 1936, the Shepley woman had become Laura Pierson Shepley Clark after marrying a man named Bob Clark. It's also not known if the four children were his or hers.

It's believed she chose this site from information received from a Mexican family living in the Yuma-Winterhaven area, as she made frequent trips there.

One time Mrs. Shepley Clark left the camp on a trip, leaving her two boys in the care of one old man. The old fellow died a few days later, leaving the boys alone.

They remained until the corpse began to smell, then left. They hiked out on foot and arrived where Rancho Santa Cruz now stands. Sheriff J. J. Lowe was notified and arrived at the ranch soon afterward. There he obtained horses to remove the body.

Ron Anderson believed that by 1935 the Shepley woman was broke, because court records show that on May 22, 1936, she was the defendant in a lawsuit. She had obtained investment money from several Nogales businessmen.

The plaintiff was a Marvin V. Saylor. A trial day was set, but Mrs. Shepley never appeared. Sheriff Lowe was sent out to bring her in.

Her cabin consisted of one rock wall built oval shaped, or in a half circle out from the huge boulder. This large rock itself was the back wall of the cabin.

She had set up a World War I machine gun on a tripod just outside the door. The sheriff called for her to come out, but the crusty old gal refused.

Sheriff Lowe then climbed atop the cabin roof and jumped down, landing between the open door and the menacing machine gun. He called again for her to come, but she again refused, saying she had no clothes on and that he would have to take her in naked. The sheriff shouted back that he would, if indeed that was her wish.

Moments later she emerged clothed, and was taken to Nogales.

It's believed she was sent to prison at Florence [6] and served two years. Upon her release, she again made a beeline back to Camp Loco. For some strange reason she got the idea the treasure was beneath the dirt floor of her cabin.

With the help of two men, a pit was dug. To cross from one area to the other, a wide plank was placed across the ever deepening pit.

One day a helper of hers arrived at a ranch and informed the owner Mrs. Shepley had broken her right arm after falling from the plank. Soon after this incident she departed from Camp Loco and never returned.

In the mid-1890s a Mexican family from the Tumacacori-Tubac area searched for the treasure in the canyon about three-quarters of a mile north of the present Camp Loco site. These seekers sank a deep shaft, but it caved in one day, entombing two of the men. The search was abandoned soon afterward and it's not known if the bodies were ever recovered.

The remaining party moved away to Yuma. Several times over the years, they returned to search again. There is a strong possibility these were the same Mexicans visited by Mrs. Shepley over the years.

It's believed several of the descendants have returned over the years to search the site once again. Their last trip occurred seven or eight years ago [1980-81].

A group of Blacks searched for the treasure in a canyon just south of Tinaja Canyon shortly after World War I. This is how Nigger Canyon (now called Negro or Black Canyon) got its name.

Mr. Anderson was also informed of another group of blacks, perhaps the same ones, who searched for treasure near the old rock corral, located in the vicinity of the canyon bearing the same name. This is how all those shafts and pits came to be around the rock corral.

Bill Conley, another treasure hunter, and I made a trip to the Camp Loco site last spring. It was a difficult trip, even using a 4 x 4. Parts of the dirt road were washed away, while other portions had rocks blocking our way. These had to be removed before continuing on.

---

[6] Newspapers of the day indicated she went into a mental hospital.

It took us two hours of tough driving to reach the site. Then we had another half mile or so of hiking before finally arriving at the old camp.

Deep tunnels and pits were scattered everywhere, and several were quite deep. While resting near the cliffs, we surveyed the entire area below us. It was astonishing to see the enormous amount of digging and backbreaking work that went into this project. And most, if not all was single-jacking through solid rock.

About half the walls of the old cabin were still standing. A large tree now grows from the center of the cabin floor. What looked like the caved-in remains of the pit dug within the structure still was visible beside the huge bolder that made up the east wall.

From the looks of the junk scattered around, many others have ventured here to search over the years. One hollowed out area at the base of the cliffs had old camping equipment laying about—a table, a broken cot and a rotted sleeping bag and other various items.

After taking pictures, we returned to the truck and began the long, tedious drive out. If a lost mine full of gold and silver does exist in this rugged country, I'm sure it will only be rediscovered by using modern-day technology.

Then again, there is the possibility that nothing lays buried except a few broken skeletons and the dreams of those who dug there.

Chapter 16

OUR FIRST DISCOVERY

Part of an old windlass platform that remained at the site where we filed our first claim.

Open cut on our mining claim.

During our prospecting one afternoon we happened upon an old mine site atop a hill. It was quite secluded and could only be seen when almost upon it. These diggings looked old as if they had been there since the turn of the century. A large open pit was dug; then a shaft was sunk another ten feet below the pit. Across the top was built a platform where once a windlass stood.

Examining the tailings we discovered many small nuggets of pure lead with traces of native silver. If this property was known surely somebody's claim papers would be on it, but none were found.

This discovery looked promising, so we moved camp to the location while Roy was off visiting friends near Tubac. We told Randall Hill to give him directions to our new campsite when he returned.

The next few days were spent running out our claim lines and filing our claim papers in Nogales, Arizona, making the property legally ours.

Barrowing a windlass from Charlie Bent, we began the slow process of cleaning out the old pit. New timbers were placed across the top, as the others were old and dried out from years in the sun. Upon completion we dug further, exposing a dark gray vein of mineral. This ran across the center of the decomposed andesite formation.

Several days later we heard a jeep approaching. Turning to Chuck I said, "Ten to one it's Roy." A moment later his jeep came up the canyon, accompanied by a gust of wind. This always occurred when he arrived in camp. After awhile we began calling him, "Windwagon Roy," after the fictional character, Windwagon Smith.

Roy looked the claim over, saying it had possibilities. While in Tucson we had the ore assayed and reported it contained lead, silver, copper and some gold. This would run about $110 per ton, if the vein would increase in size it could very well become a paying operation. After digging further, the vein would pinch and swell then vanish.

One afternoon, Tata drove clear out from Arivaca to inform us some unscrupulous characters were going to jump our claim as they discovered we had laid out our claim lines wrong. This in fact would make the claim invalid.

Here we had this old man with one leg drive 16 miles over rocky terrain to let us know. Chuck and I thanked him, but ole Tata still acted cranky saying, "We should have known better." It must have been a rough trip for him.

After fixing the lines, we decided to abandon the property until a later date. We didn't have the necessary capital to warrant such an expensive operation, but the claim was still in our names. If the vein widened to several feet we would have commercial ore. This would entail sinking a deep shaft some hundred feet or more, in hopes it would increase in size, and there wasn't any guarantee of this happening, also, timbering would have to be done all the way.

We decided to move camp over toward Sardina Peak, and continued our "rainbow chasing."

SARDINA PEAK ADVENTURES

Chapter 17

"THE BUCKLE AT CAVE IN ROCK"

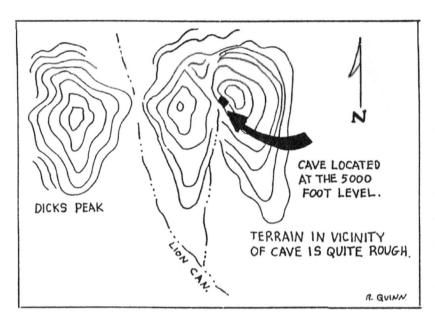

Map of "Cave in Rock" and sketch of the buckle I found.

Southern Arizona Trails, Vol. 3, No. 51, October 6, 1987, Page 23

Located in the center of the Tumacacori Mountains, high up on the steep side of a nameless peak is a large cave which I named "Cave in Rock" back in '56. Its gaping entrance is approximately 20 feet high by 40 feet wide and is some 30-odd feet in depth. It's been visited over the centuries by various individuals, as different dates and initials have been cut into its dark walls.

One rock near the entrance has a date of either 1600 or 1700 carved into its surface. The exact year escapes me, as I haven't been back to the location since 1967.

I do not remember if this particular cave was mentioned in the Arivaca area during this time, so perhaps it's not well-known to the populace of this region. My brother, Chuck, and I discovered it while exploring the rugged country east of Dick's Peak.

It looked like a perfect place to hide something, like bandit loot, etc. So of course, we decided to make a return visit and check the area out with our metal detector.

As Chuck began searching around the entrance first, I inspected the cliffs beside the cave, as numerous wide and deep cracks ran vertically down the side.

"Cave in Rock," name given to a big cave near Dicks Peak by Chuck & I.

Like most treasure hunters, my heart beats with anticipation at the prospects of finding something of value. One large crack was quite deep and as I crawled about in the narrow opening, I was hoping to round a corner and perhaps spot some old Wells Fargo box half-buried in the loose earth that had fallen from above over the years.

As I looked up, I spotted a large round boulder teetering between the two narrow walls. It no doubt had been there for countless years. But to me, it looked as though it could come crashing down at any moment if it had a mind to, so I moved on.

Of course, no money bags stuffed with double eagles were found, so I returned to the cave.

As we ate and discussed this interesting area, I started scratching with the heel of my boot at the layer of dirt that covered the floor. In a few moments I uncovered a small buckle. It wasn't rusted, due to the dryness of the cave and resembled a clasp from a rifle sling. I gave the buckle to a friend who collects such things while I was in Washington State.

To me it looked as though it came off a cavalry sling, having a horse and rider on top. Careful inspection revealed no other markings. After examining the buckle several more times, we thought it also could have come from suspenders issued by the cavalry.

We were curious to know why it was left here, so we searched the interior of the cave and dug at random locations where the detector couldn't reach, but nothing else was found.

Later that afternoon, we hiked back down to our jeep on the slopes of Dicks Peak.

We made another climb to the cave a year later as Roy, another treasure hunter we met while in Arivaca, wanted to see it.

I've heard many say that this country has been searched and researched hundreds of times, and there is little left to be discovered. But almost every time I venture out among these mountains and others, I always come across something new.

It might be some faint markings on a rock face, an odd-looking buckle, a hidden tunnel leading to a chamber inside Cerro Pelón, or some broken arrow heads. There is also the old Spanish cutlass we discovered while searching for the treasure of Carreta Canyon.

Returning to Cerro Pelón for a moment: It's a small hill about a mile or so west of Tubac. It's an interesting place to visit, as Indians once lived there. A crack runs up from the chamber to the outside, making a natural chimney in the rock.

This well-hidden entrance was discovered accidentally while the three of us were searching near its base during the fall of '57. I believe the passageway is still concealed behind the shrubs that border the southern slopes of this strange hill.

I doubt if anyone will come across a "lost mission" with a fabulous treasure buried beneath its foundation or find some ancient Spanish mine heaped high with gold and silver bullion. But there are other interesting things still to be discovered deep within these Tumacacori Mountains — I haven't found them all and never will.

The secret is to keep an eye out for anything that looks out of place while climbing around. If there are any lost mines, and I believe several do exist, their entrance is no doubt well concealed after 200 years, with very few clues, if any, on the surface.

While treasure hunting with the gang here in Southern Arizona—they would always do an excellent job of searching—it was always me who would be found crawling about and exploring the most unlikely places, or hanging dangerously by rope to reach some suspicious-looking hole or ledge.

Mainly I search for those little secretive places where somebody might have hidden a treasure or two.

Chapter 18

GHOST HORSES

Southern Arizona Trails, Vol. 3, No. 27, April 21, 1987, Page 7, 24

Another odd occurrence took place while Louis Romero and seven other temporary ranch hands were preparing for "roundup time." Their base of operations was set up near one of the larger corrals, located on the northern slopes of Dicks Peak. Several trucks had been moved in and parked nearby, and camp was arranged beneath a large clump of mesquite trees.

The first two days went rather smoothly, as cattle were rounded up, brought in and branded, while others were placed in the corral for shipment.

We [Chuck and Ron] were camped on the ranch during one of these roundups, and it was quite interesting to watch.

On the third night, after their meal, the cowboys sat around smoking and carried on small talk among them. Louis said that most evenings you could hear the sounds of the night, and hear the rustle of leaves above caused by the gentle breeze, but this night was unusually quiet. The night was as still as the dead, and the livestock acted nervous.

Around eight-thirty the group prepared to bed down for the night, as they'd be up before the crack of dawn. All of a sudden, from far off they heard the rumble of approaching horses. Louis said, it grew louder and one could hear the clattering of hoofs among the rocks scattered over the slopes of Dicks Peak. This also was accompanied by the whinnying of dozens of horses.

As the sound grew louder, the cowboys looked at one another with startled expressions; then suddenly dove for cover behind anything available. They expected to see an enormous herd of horses come galloping through camp, but as the sound grew nearer, it cut off abruptly on the opposite side of the wash.

Afterwards, they searched the area with lights but couldn't find any signs of horses or tracks. The next morning they searched again in the light of day, but nothing was found.

Louis mentioned that many years before the ranch had a horse named Dick. Several times a month the animal would jump the corral, and later would be found grazing on the slope of a mountain southeast of the ranch. This is how the mountain became to be known as Dicks Peak.

Many strange occurrences have happened in these mountains, and none have ever been explained to this day. One can either laugh these stories off as fiction, or like us, listen to them with an open mind, then draw your own conclusions.

Chapter 19

THE APPARITION IN CARMEN

Southern Arizona Trails, Vol. 3, No. 82, May 3, 1988, Page 22

This mysterious tale was related to us back in '57.

During this period we had been spending a considerable amount of time searching the mountains and foothills several miles west of Carmen, a small roadside community located between Tubac and Tumacacori.

Our partner Roy knew several people in the immediate vicinity. While visiting one of his friends, after purchasing supplies at Tubac, he told us the following story.

THIS IS WHAT THE APPARITION COULD HAVE RESEMBLED FROM THE DESCRIPTION GIVEN

A Mexican family residing in Carmen, whose name I have long since forgotten, had put their 6-year-old daughter to bed around seven one night. Her parents then settled down for the evening, listening to the radio and finishing some last-minute chores.

It was exceptionally quiet that night, and not even their neighbor's dog was barking as it usually would, and there also was a heavy stillness in the air.

Several hours later, their daughter let out a scream, breaking the silence.

Both hurried into her room, expecting to find she had fallen from the bed or had a disturbing dream. Little Maria, as we'll call her, was kneeling in the center of the bed, crying and trembling, and pointing toward the single window in the room.

After she was quieted down some,

her mother asked what was wrong.

Maria said she had awakened and saw a yellow glow coming through the window. Turning, she spotted a ghostly apparition looking directly at her. Different colored small balls of flickering lights drifted lazily around its head. When she cried out, it slowly faded from view.

Both parents agreed she must have been dreaming. Afterward, her father took a light and searched around the house to assure little Maria that nothing was out there. He found nothing unusual as the beam cut through the surrounding darkness, revealing only the scattered mesquite trees and nearby cactus. He did, however, feel uneasiness in the night air.

Returning inside, he found Maria still insisting she had seen the strange flowing yellow specter. It was past 10 o'clock before the frightened girl again drifted off to sleep.

The parents retired to their bedroom and were asleep by 11. A short while later the mother awoke with a feeling of impending danger. She thought this was brought about by Maria's frightening experience earlier.

Glancing toward her daughter's partly opened door, she froze in fear. From within the room she saw a light yellow glow. With trembling hands she shook her husband until he awoke.

They crept silently toward the door and gazed in disbelief. Floating gently outside the window peering in was the apparition described by little Maria. The mother grabbed the small crucifix hanging around her neck, crossed herself while still transfixed by the mysterious sight before her.

The ghostly specter was looking down at the sleeping girl with both its arms outstretched at its sides.

Tiny balls of colored lights were seen dancing slowly around its upper body. From what they could see of its features, it was difficult to determine if the glowing phantom was male or female.

It must have sensed their presence, as its large white eyes, with small black pupils slowly looked up at them. Gathering all his courage, the father ran for the door and darted around the house. As he came around the corner, the apparition was slowly drifting over the land toward the west. As it reached a high point, the glowing figure vanished. The strange hovering night visitor was never seen again.

A great amount of speculation can be injected into this odd encounter.

Was it truly a ghost? If so, what about the dancing lights? In the numerous stories I've read about such sightings, never did I hear about balls of hovering colored lights accompanying the spirits. Could there also be some religious overtones here?

Finally, there is always the possibility the strange thing could have been some type of "E.T." It might have landed over the nearby ridge and decided to see what us earth folks really look like close up. Perhaps the reason it returned twice. The lights could have been some kind of energy field surrounding it, but this is only speculation offered by several individuals I know.

If just little Maria had seen the figure, I'd say it was her imagination or a bad dream. Two people, I'd be somewhat skeptical but I would listen to the story with an open mind. When all three spotted the thing, then it's time for some deep serious thinking.

During the last few years I've come to believe that almost anything is possible. That famous quote comes to mind: "There are more things in heaven and earth than are dreamt of in your philosophy."

Chapter 20

THE GUN

While exploring in the vicinity of Sardina Peak, I happened to slip, sliding down a small incline. As I came to an abrupt and jolting stop, I noticed an object protruding from the earth beside several rocks. To my surprise, it was an old revolver like those used during the Civil War. It was cap and ball, and the cylinder still held four cartridges. Its wood handle had long since rotted away, and its workings were rusted together.

Spotting the others, I called telling them of my discovery. Checking the area carefully we found a small cave some twenty feet from the hand gun. In its rear were portions of what resembled an old saddle bag. Later Chuck found another piece of leather with a buckle attached. Undoubtedly it was a belt buckle.

It would be interesting to know what occurred at this location. Perhaps some bandits had a disagreement over the split of a robbery. One could have killed the other, leaving his partner's blood spilling out onto the unfriendly earth, along with his revolver.

It's just speculation, but something deadly happened, as nobody would deliberately leave their weapon behind. During our travels we came upon several sites like this where there is a story but no answers. If these lonely mountains could talk, the stories they could tell.

Chapter 21

THE TREASURE THAT "WAS" AT LOBO PEAK

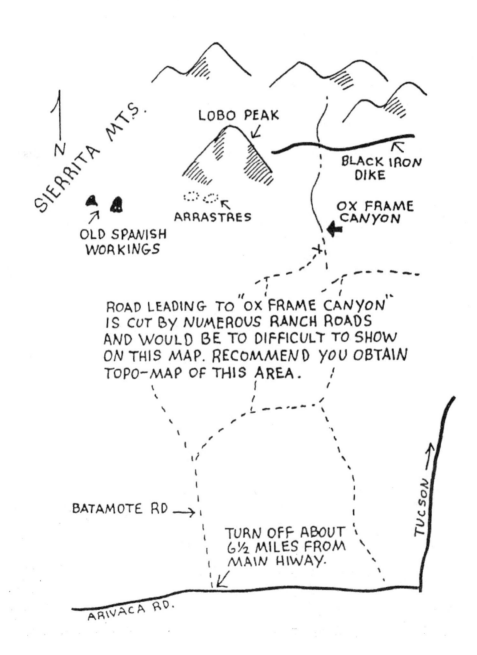

Southern Arizona Trails, Vol. 2, No. 20, March 3, 1987, Pages 18-19

W hen you get yourself involved with partners when it comes to treasure hunting, make certain you know 'em quite well. My three partners I have known for over thirty years and we trust one another with our lives. It's a relationship honed to the finest edge and exists to this very day. I have known some partnerships that became so bitter, they made "Who's Afraid of Virginia Woolf!" look like "The Waltons." A true partnership takes more than several weeks or a month to cultivate as the following story will indicate.

Sometime during 1980, a young man in his early thirties by the name of John, met a Larry about the same age at a local health studio (both names are fictitious). When they discovered they shared the same interests like camping, hunting, hiking and most other outdoor activities, they soon became "friends."

Several weeks later, Larry stopped by for a visit on a Tuesday evening and noticed a book in John's apartment on treasure hunting. Larry also was interested in the subject, but was apprehensive about mentioning it as some friends in the past had laughed at him for believing in such nonsense.

John had a detector and all the equipment it took to go either treasure hunting or prospecting over the weekends. Most of his searching was carried out just south of Tucson, in the vicinity of the Tumacacori Mountains, where the treasures from this mission are alleged to be hidden.

After making himself comfortable, he told John a story that his grandfather had vouched was true. It involved four outlaws and the gold they hid at their secret hideout located somewhere in Southern Arizona on the side of a single small mountain, dark in color, that overlooked a large valley. They dug an open cut some fifteen feet into the bank, then placed timbers they borrowed from a nearby abandoned mine across the top. This was then covered with dirt, rock and some desert vegetation. The opening at the front gave them ample view of the valley below, and they could spot anybody approaching from miles away.

These outlaws were a breed apart from others roaming the territory, as they trusted one another. Each would bury his share of gold in the rear of this manmade cave, without fear of it being touched by the others. They continued their life of crime, and it was later discovered these four never killed anyone during their robberies. It was also rumored, they would give a handful of gold pieces to some families "down on their luck" they occasionally would come upon during their trips across Arizona. Sometimes they'd be gone several months but eventually would always return to the secret hideout which nobody ever discovered during their absence.

As the tale goes, three died during a shootout with officers of the law and the fourth was wounded; then later sent to Yuma Prison, "hellhole of the Southwest." While there the outlaw met a very young inmate that was married, but would be getting out shortly. His crime was being "dirt poor" and trying to provide for his family in an illegal manner.

The aging outlaw felt sorry for him, so told the youngster where to find his old campsite and the gold that was still buried there. He knew he'd never leave prison alive, as he had difficulty breathing and his coughing was becoming worse. (He probably had tuberculosis.) He told the lad there was perhaps fifteen to twenty thousand dollars there, and he should use it to buy himself a ranch for the wife and family, and make a fresh start in life and stay on the right side of the law. A few months later the youngster was released and rode off, never to be seen again by the kindhearted outlaw.

For some reason, Larry believed the gold was still buried out there and hadn't been removed by the young inmate. The mannerism in which Larry told his story was almost like that young inmate could have been a distant relative, and he knew definitely the cache was never recovered. His grandfather just knew too many facts regarding this tale, just to have heard it from another party. Could the grandfather have been the inmate's son?

Larry said he'd been out searching for it, but really had no idea where to start, only that the site was located south of Tucson. He went on to say, even if the location was accidentally discovered by some rancher or "weekend prospector," he had doubts they'd take the time to dig aimlessly about in hopes of finding something of value. To anyone seeing the site, it might just appear as another old prospect hole which are so numerous around the southwest.

Larry began to describe the area again, but this time mentioned one of the "guide posts" to the campsite. Upon hearing its description, John knew exactly where it was located, and "volunteered" this information to Larry without thinking the situation over for a moment. Just east of the hill was a deep canyon with a large "black iron dike" cutting across its bed. This dike can be traced for miles and runs, east and west.

Again without thinking, John reached for his portfolio of topo-maps, found the correct one and laid it out. He had been prospecting there and had seen this dike, which was located in "Ox Frame Canyon," at the extreme southern tip of the Sierrita Mountains.

That single dark colored hill was no doubt Lobo Peak. From there one can see in all directions, except north, and this small hill stands out from all the rest. Both agreed they would make a trip out there the following Saturday and search for the campsite. If any gold was discovered it would be a fifty-fifty split. Larry said, he'd drive over at 5 a.m. and meet him outside the apartment.

Come Saturday morning, 5 a.m. came and went and no Larry, so John gave him a call and no answer. By six he drives to his place and finds out he moved late Friday evening from a neighbor. It took awhile but the realization finally settled in.

Early Sunday, John drove out to Ox Frame Canyon, which is about a three hour trip. He parked where the road terminates then hiked toward Lobo Peak. After climbing some three hundred feet, he discovered the old site. It had caved in long ago, and did resemble nothing more than some prospector's old exploratory hole. Rotted timbers were protruding through the vegetation, but the rear showed fresh evidence of having been dug into quite recently. A large pit was dug the width of the hole and pieces of old dry leather were found and parts of a broken jar.

It seems his "friend and partner" had pulled the old fast one and came out early, found the site and no doubt discovered the gold, then skipped with the entire cache. If that young inmate was a relative, perhaps Larry thought it all legally belonged to him, and he wasn't about to share it with anyone.

When buried, the coins' face value was around twenty thousand. At the price these gold coins would bring on today's market, it had to be worth well over $200,000.

John had no idea Larry would pull something like this, so he returned to Tucson and tried putting the whole incident out of his mind. He did however tell friends that if he ever ran into Larry, blood would flow. It's rumored that several year later, John found out Larry was living somewhere in Las Vegas. He tracked him down but what happened afterwards is unknown.

The area just west of Lobo Peak has a most interesting history. On the flats below, one can find the remains of two "unfinished" *arrastras*. Further away are several old diggings, long since abandoned. We heard from a local rancher that some miners discovered the workings in the late 1800s. After investigating the site it was determined to be early Spanish. The tunnels were enlarged and the miners spent half a winter trying to discover what the Spaniards were after, as they wouldn't have started building two *arrastras* unless rich ore was uncovered. Others worked the site in the 30s and did extensive exploratory work, but they also couldn't find the ore.

While these same miners were moving earth below the tunnels, seven human skeletons were discovered buried in a kneeling position, minus skulls.

What apparently happened, these Spanish miners were jumped by Apaches, which had a burning hatred for all Spaniards, and buried them up to their necks. Afterwards, they either killed them out-right, or tortured the men, then left the Spaniards to die slowly in the harsh desert with just their heads above ground.

No doubt Ox Frame Canyon received its present name from somebody discovering an old Spanish ox frame in the vicinity of these early Spanish workings. The mystery here is why were the *arrastras* under construction when no visible ore has ever been discovered in the area? Another mystery added to the pages of all the rest.

As I mentioned earlier, "know your partners well," as when that glittering gold appears, that inner monster from the "id" known as "greed" will raise its head to the surface and turn partner against partner.

Chapter 22

HOME FOR THE HOLIDAYS

B y now December was approaching, so we decided to drive home for the holidays. We bid farewell to friends in Arivaca saying we'd return in the New Year. Roy wanted to visit relatives in San Bernardino, so plans were made to meet in Arivaca in mid-January.

During our journey northward we noticed our oil pressure dropping. Checking, we discovered a serious leak at the main bearing. It took a quart of oil every 50 miles, and this increased throughout the day. Then a knocking sound could be heard.

About 50 miles from Boulder City, Nevada, the engine really started knocking. We slowed down to a crawl and limped into town about 90 minutes later.

Stopping at the first garage we saw, Mack, the owner listened and said, "Motor's shot." He ordered a rebuilt one from L.A. after he knew we could pay for it. We phoned home informing Mom of our trouble, and we'd be late. Three days later it was installed and ready to roll. Then, in 1956, the total cost was $360 for motor and labor— unheard of today!

By the fourth day we again were on our way. Mack said to keep our speed about fifty for the first 500 miles, to break in the new motor. This wouldn't be difficult, as we were traveling at that speed most of the time due to all the gear we were carrying. We rolled into our driveway three days later. Our folks were happy we arrived home safe. Mom worried the entire time we had been gone—natural for any mother. However, we did write as promised.

While home, our close friends, the Schuette's visited several times to hear of our adventures and view all the pictures taken. It was also nice sleeping once again on a soft bed.

After two weeks of visiting, we said goodbye once more and left on the second leg of our odyssey. Mom gave us a kiss, and Dad shook hands saying to continue writing. Chuck's first entry on our new diary read:

January 8th. This morning we left Vashon on the second leg of our trip. We made good time and arrived in Medford, Oregon at 9:00 p.m. So far the new motor is running fine.

Four days later we rolled into Arivaca, setting up camp near the old Silver Shield Mine in the Cerro Colorado Mountains. The gang was happy to see us, and informed us nothing new occurred during our absence. Mitchell was still trying to unload a worthless claim, and high grade was going to be shipped any day—same old Arivaca.

Eight days later Roy came "blowing into camp," and our search for Spanish treasure began once more. When Roy learned of our motor trouble, he reached into his pocket, handing us $300. We refused the offer, but Roy kept pushing it back. "We're friends and partners aren't we?" Roy was that kind of a friend—"all for one and one for all." Unbeknown at the time Roy would be getting that money back, plus 300 times more.

Chapter 23

THE GREAT WALL

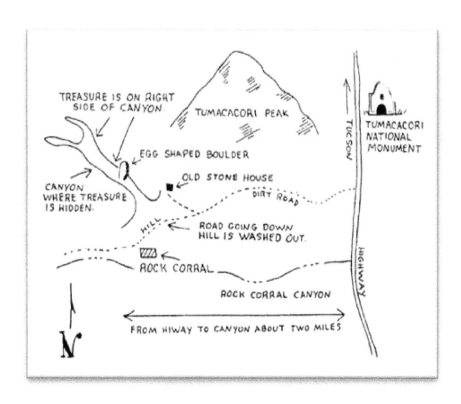

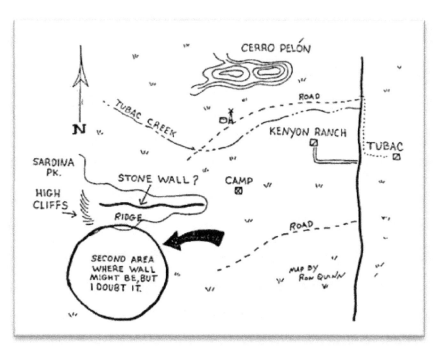

Ron standing next to the Rock Wall in 1957.

And standing near the same spot in 1985.

**Arrows point to the two end of the rock wall located on a ridge
near the edge of the mysterious plateau.**

Bill Conley Jr. at the Great Wall.

hat we discovered during early 1957 still remains shadowed in mystery. It was an odd shaped stone wall we came upon by accident high atop the Tumacacoris. It was not a Hohokam Indian Wall, which are quite numerous in Southern Arizona.

We happened upon the structure while searching for a hidden cave once used by the notorious Apaches during the 1880s. The cave is alleged to contain rifles, handguns, ammo and saddles, decorated with silver. A very impressive find if located. The cave is supposedly located near high cliffs, of which there are many, on the eastern side of these mountains.

This region is extremely hazardous, especially during the summers. Temperatures can reach 110° or more, as we discovered during our first summer on the desert. Hot winds whistle among the boulders and seem to come from the furnaces of hell itself. Luckily we'd be searching during winter months.

This story was told by Roy's friend, Breezy, owner of the old Tubac Inn. After hearing this story we decided to move camp and begin searching for the elusive cave. After seeing the rugged area, one can understand why it's never been found.

After weeks of climbing ridges, cliffs and deep rocky canyons infested with snakes, we found no trace of the treasure cave. However, several caves were discovered which turned out to be "javalina dens," home to the wild boars of the desert that can be quite ill tempered at times.

Of course, our hunt for the cave was unsuccessful, if in fact it ever existed. We enjoyed this hunt and there was always the chance we'd stumble upon something else while exploring. We found a "big one" the following day.

While hiking through this sun baked country, Chuck and Roy happened upon a large overhanging rock and called me over. The ground beneath was littered with bits of flint and many broken arrowheads. This definitely had been where Indians once made these fine pieces of workmanship. Gathering some of the best we moved on, and into a mystery that plagues us to this day.

Later while climbing a high lonely ridge near Sardina Peak, a lofty mountain which dominates the northern boundaries of these unfriendly hills, we came upon a wall—a very mysterious stone wall. The structure where it begins was only a foot in height. But, the wall slowly increases in size as it winds across the summit for almost a third of a mile. It ends near several boulders, where it measures nearly five feet high.

Gazing at this monumental piece of engineering, one could see no purpose for its existence. Midway along its twisting route there's an odd half moon circle, formed by the wall. It would be many years before we discovered its alleged meaning.

I'm not trying to be overly dramatic, but while in the presence of this wall, you have a strange feeling you're not welcome. This could have been brought about by the eeriness of the location. The wall is built well, and many months of labor must have gone into its completion, perhaps centuries ago. After exploring and trying to determine why the thing was ever built, we had lunch beside some boulders. Later we took pictures and returned to camp.

One day Louie Romero rode in. We asked what he knew of the wall.

Looking at us with a wide grin, he said, "What have you been drinking? There is no wall up there." This was strange as he was raised here and knew the land like the back of his hand. However, he might have missed it, as he only rides the low rolling hills most of the time, not the rugged ridges where cattle seldom venture.

Luckily we had been to Tucson and had the film developed. After viewing the pictures, Louie said, "I have never seen this wall or heard of it." This only deepened the mystery.

During 1985 I met, Bill Conley, another treasure hunter. Over the months we became close friends and made frequent trips into the surrounding mountains. During one I happened to mention the wall. Bill was curious to visit the site, so plans were made.

A few days later, after an hour's climb and crawling through catsclaw which tears at you without mercy, we arrived at the wall. After seeing the unique structure once again it brought back pleasant memories of the adventurous times we spent among these harsh hills.

Bill was fascinated by the wall, and he also couldn't imagine why it was built. He brought his camcorder and taped some 15 minutes of the monument showing various portions of the strange oddity. Bill also couldn't understand why it slowly increased in size. Using ones imagination, the wall almost resembles a giant snake stretched out across the summit with the small section being its tail, and the largest its head.

When first discovered in '57, I had Chuck take a picture of me beside the wall. I asked Bill to duplicate the picture and pointed toward the ledge where Chuck had taken it. A few hours later we descended to Bill's 4 x 4 and returned home.

Unbeknown to us at the time, another mystery was to unfold concerning this discovery. When I compared both pictures, the '57 photo and our recent one, I couldn't believe my eyes. I called Bill, saying I'd be right over as there was something he must see.

He also saw the difference. A large portion of the wall had been "moved." A section had mysteriously been straightened out. Almost 20 feet was moved further north. In our recent picture this is quite obvious. The wall is also much wider. A boulder, near me and above, was against the wall. Now you could walk between both. I hadn't noticed these changes until viewing the photos, as memories do fade over the years, but pictures don't lie.

It was difficult to fathom who or what would undertake such an enormous task, moving tons of stones out in the middle of nowhere, just to straighten a section out. Also, when did this transformation occur? Other portions could have been moved, but not having pictures to compare, this would be almost impossible to determine. What we had was a second mystery. But soon, another would follow.

Months later I happened to meet a gentleman from Sedona, Arizona, by the name of Anderson. He also was interested in Southwestern legends. So, I mentioned our wall with the half moon circle. He looked at me in amazement and said quite loudly, "Do you realize what you have found?" His explanation would only deepen this mystery.

I was informed we had discovered the legendary "Healing Wall," once used by the ancient Indians. The half moon circle was the altar and many miracles were performed there. In all our travels we had never heard of this legend, and we heard them all. Not even from old Indians we had known had we heard this story, perhaps they knew but kept it a secret.

On a topo map of the region, I pointed out the wall's location, but due to Anderson's age, I doubt he ever attempted the long grueling climb to the site.

The *Tucson Citizen*, a local newspaper, found the story interesting enough to publish an article about the wall. During the interview I never mentioned its location. I didn't want any weird cults invading the site, thinking the ancient wall was somehow magical. Several of my friends believe it is. As far as I was concerned, no graffiti or unruly crowds were going to slowly destroy this site, as so many in the past have been. Quoting a paragraph from the article:

"University of Arizona researchers, who have not visited the site, say it is unlikely to have any connection with prehistoric Hohokam Trincheras walls and terraces that dot hillsides in Southern Arizona and northern Sonora."

The vicinity where this mysterious structure is located is quite remote. Not many venture into this desert domain. The area is also known for its legends of treasures and other strange mysteries. We investigated many during our years roaming the southern portion of Arizona.

If you ever decide to explore this hazardous country, be aware of all I have said. These haunting hills are unforgiving, and have changed very little since the sandal-footed padres first stepped into the valley. As for the wall, it still stands there, high above the valley floor on that windswept ridge. Its secrets, if any, are guarded by the lofty peaks that look down in silence. Who rebuilt it and for what purpose remains a mystery. Anderson might have been correct when he said ancient shamans once practiced magic there. If this is right, it could explain the feeling of being unwelcome. Perhaps we were standing on sacred ground.

If I visit the site again and discover the wall back in its original position, my belief in the paranormal will greatly increase. People living within the shadows of these ghostly mountains have no idea of the secrets they hold. The wall is just one of many.

THE STONE WALL

Southern Arizona Trails, Vol. 2, No. 15, November 11, 1986, page 7
and

THE MYSTERIOUS STONE WALL

Southern Arizona Trails, Vol. November 3, 1987, page 23

We heard another interesting tale concerning a "stone wall" located somewhere on the ridges which fan out on the eastern slopes of the Tumacacori Mountains. After discovering the chamber within Cerro Pelón, we moved camp further south and began our search for this elusive wall.

During our stay in Arivaca, we heard a story that I would place in the "rumor column," as there isn't any documentation verifying its authenticity.

When the Indian Wars were going hot and heavy, hostiles would jump the reservation, kill and burn, then hide their weapons before again surrendering to the cavalry.

These arms consisted of rifles, handguns, ammunition and other items stolen during their raids.

All this was concealed in a small cave located above a stone wall that was built along the spiny back of a ridge on the east side of these mountains.

After spending several months on the reservation, the hostiles soon got itchy feet and would leave during the night. They headed right for their hidden arsenal and would start raiding again, but not before concealing the entrance with rocks and brush.

Our partner, Roy, knew the proprietor of the Tubac Inn and from him heard another tale about some Mexican gentlemen who discovered a cache of rifles in the area, which is directly west of Tubac. The story goes they were on foot and during their long hike out, discarded many of the old rifles because they were trying to carry too many.

Their discovery was made near the flats below the mountains and not in the vicinity of the stone wall. If this tale is true, I doubt if it was the cache hidden by the Indians. I was told there were several Mexican saddles decorated in silver that were among the weapons. If this was the case, I'm quite certain these men would have taken them and left the rifles behind.

After two days of climbing and searching, we finally came upon the wall, and here we have another mystery. Who built it and why?

I have seen walls similar to this built on the flats and gentle rolling hills, but never along the top of a rocky ridge for no apparent reason.

It starts right at the edge of the ridge and snakes its way back toward the mountains for almost ¾ of a mile before terminating below some high cliffs near Sardina Peak.

In all our years of exploring the mountains and deserts of Arizona, this is the only place I cannot pinpoint on a map, but I know the general area.

The only excuse I have is that we found it 29 [now 53] years ago and the exact spot is a little vague. It's either located just south of the road that lead to Cerro Pelón or the next ranch road about a mile further south.

My guess is it was the Cerro Pelón road and the ridge is just southwest of it. Checking my topo map, Tubac quadrangle 15-minute series, I believe the wall is located in Township 15, which is just northeast of Sardina Peak. There is an elevation number (4102) on the small peak, and I'm reasonably sure the stone wall begins at this point.

I'm also certain that during our track toward the ridge, one could see a portion of the wall by using binoculars.

The wall is from three to four feet in height, and several feet wide and changes in size as you follow it along. It terminates between two large outcroppings of rock and is quite large at this point.

We had lunch in the shade of some boulders, and none of us could determine why such an enormous task was undertaken.

We came up with several reasons why it would be built on the flats, but not on a ridge where even cattle would find it difficult to find footing.

There were many large cracks in the high cliffs above where rifles, etc., could be concealed, but nothing was found. We checked the face of the cliffs very carefully for anything that looked out of place and not natural but again found nothing that resembled a hidden entrance.

After many hours of climbing and exploring, we abandoned the search and returned to camp below, just as the sun began to set behind the western escarpment and the long shadows of the peaks began to creep outward across the land.

Chapter 24

MYSTERY OF THE SHRINE

Southern Arizona Trails, Vol. 2, No. 21, March 10, 1987, Page 16

During 1964, so the story goes, a man named Fernando and his 14-year-old son Ramón went dove hunting over the weekend. Their camp was located near Diablito Mountain, which is at the extreme north end of the Tumacacori Mountains.

To enter this particular area one must take the old dirt road which parallels Puerto Canyon for several miles before terminating at the base of the mountain.

Ramón didn't like hunting but enjoyed camping under the stars in the clean desert air. When his father was off hunting, Ramón would like to hike and explore the surrounding country. He had spent a great deal of time in the outdoors with his father and wasn't a stranger to the desert. His father had told him not to venture far and to always keep camp in view.

On Sunday, the boy hiked a few miles southwest of camp and lost sight of it, but this didn't worry him any, as Puerto Canyon was just off to his left and camp was located a few hundred yards north of this canyon. After hiking awhile, he spotted some rabbits and began to chase them for fun. One cotton tail darted behind some thick brush with Ramón in hot pursuit. As he stood up, the youngster saw a small holy shrine about two feet in height made of stone and mortar and in its center stood a statue of the Virgin Mary. Being Catholic, the boy crossed himself then knelt for a few moments.

Spotting another rabbit he gave chase and fell down a rocky slope, skinning his arms. Ramón had been around many abandoned mines while out in the hills with his father and recognized he was lying beside a small mine dump. Not seeing any entrance to the mine, the boy explored awhile then started back to camp.

Arriving at camp he found his father already there. Seeing Ramón's skinned arms, he asked what happened. The boy told of finding the shrine and falling down a mine dump, cutting his arms. He then pointed toward the area where the shrine was. Noticing how far away it was from camp, his father became angry and told Ramón he had gone too far and could have gotten lost in that maze of canyons. His father was interested in seeing this discovery his son had made, but it was late afternoon and time to break camp.

I have heard stories that when the padres were mining this area they would build and place these small shrines near their mines, like the one discovered by Ramón. The Indian laborers (neophytes) would pray before these shrines upon entering these narrow dangerous mine tunnels, and again when they emerged, after putting in many long hard hours in these "death traps." (If I had worked in one, I'd pray also.) I never found any documentation verifying these shrines were used, so it would have to be classified as a rumor. But there is a strong possibility its true.

My brother and I discovered a portion of something resembling these shrines while exploring Peck Canyon which is located further south. There is rumor of two lost silver mines in that particular area. Where Ramón discovered his is in the region of The Lost San Pedro Mine. This mine is vaguely mentioned in some documents so I'd place it in the "rumor column" also.

The following weekend they returned with two relatives, names unknown. Ramón headed south a ways as the others followed. Upon reaching a large canyon, which had to be Puerto, the small party hiked up the canyon a good distance then northwest toward the southern end of Diablito Mountain. Ramón walked briskly along like he knew exactly where he was going, and the others had confidence they would soon see the shrine. Stopping near some low cliffs, Ramón pointed toward some thick brush, indicating this was where he chased the rabbit. Of course, no shrine was found.

The boy insisted he hadn't gone over two miles from camp, and this was the spot. Try as they may, nothing was found.

The only area near Diablito showing any mineralization is located on the western side. Where Ramón stated he found the mine dump is nothing but old andesite and rhyolite, and there isn't even a mine hole within miles. But like the saying goes, "Gold (or silver) is where you find it."

Now here we have a young honest and somewhat rational boy of 14, who has been in the desert before, hiking along and enjoying the outdoors. He finds a stone shrine, similar to those supposedly used by the padres and he cannot retrace his steps after being gone from the area one week.

I've heard countless stories of ordinary people like Ramón out hiking and finding some pretty rocks. They take one home and later discover its half gold. The party that made the find says, "There's lots of it lying around where I found this one." The family returns to the same campsite and the search is on. You guessed it again, it cannot be found and they claim the area was just a short distance from camp.

I'm far from being superstitious but at times I think there's a curse on some of these discoveries. They seem to vanish after showing themselves to a few, or perhaps these people are stepping in and out of the "Twilight Zone."

Fernando and his group spent the entire weekend searching for something that Ramón just happened upon, but couldn't find his way back to the following weekend. They even searched an extra mile and sill no shrine or mine dump.

I have been at this treasure hunting game since 1956 and still find many of these stories bewildering. The shrine is either there or it isn't. If it does exist at this moment and is sitting out there somewhere in the Arizona sun and cannot be found, then it's one of those strange mysteries that will never be answered.

My brother and I spent quite a few weeks searching for this elusive shrine. We checked every square yard Ramón could have covered, still nothing. A close friend with a plane flew over that area and took 36 pictures from an altitude of 2,000 feet above the mountain. Afterwards we laid all the photos out in order and checked each with a magnifying glass to see if the old mine dump could be seen. Not a thing was found.

All that Diablito Mountain has to offer is sun, scorched rock, dark lonely canyons, snakes and another mystery to be added to all the rest.

Chapter 25

LOUIE'S GOLD

Our friend Luis "Louie" Romero.

While visiting camp one afternoon, Louis told us how he'd "almost" found a box of gold.

The story was quite well-known around the cozy community of Arivaca during the 40s and 50s. Today [c. 1986], only six remain of the original population when Chuck and I arrived in 1956. So, it's doubtful Arivaca's new residents are aware of this tale today.

Sometime during the late 1880s four outlaws stole a shipment of gold and fled toward Arivaca. A posse was formed, but was late in giving chase. Arriving on the outskirts of town, the outlaws reached a long ridge. Knowing the heavy load was slowing them down it was hurriedly decided to bury the strong box. The youngest bandit was sent back to keep an eye peeled for the approaching posse. He stationed himself among some rocks atop another hill some 500 yards distant. He fell asleep while the others searched for a suitable hiding place to conceal their ill-gotten loot.

The young bandit awoke to the sound of gunfire from the other ridge. Not spotting the lone lookout, the posse rode past and encircled the other ridge where the gang was located. During the gun battle the fleeing outlaws were all killed as their young companion watched while hiding. Not realizing the robbers had buried the gold on the ridge, the posse assumed it was hidden somewhere else along their route southward, as the strong box wasn't found among their bodies.

The remaining outlaw was eventually caught. During his trial, he mentioned nothing about the concealment of the gold. He stated he wasn't present during the hiding of the loot. Guess the young lad was hoping to retrieve it after his release from prison, but this was not to be. He died behind bars.

Stories and rumors surfaced years later that perhaps the gold shipment was buried on the high windy ridge just northwest of Arivaca. Throughout the years, locals and others who believed the story, periodically dug at random locations in hopes of uncovering the cache by chance, but none ever succeeded.

During the 1940s, our friend Louie Romero became interested in the story. On off days at the ranch, he could be found digging along the ridge. One day he was searching just after sunset and spotted three men standing beside two large rocks, looking directly at him. As he approached the threesome, the figures slowly faded from view. He departed the area somewhat shaken.

He never spoke of this incident to others, but returned the following evening. This time he noticed nobody had ever dug between the two rocks where the apparitions were seen. As he proceeded to dig at the spot, a cold wind came up, as the sun was already bedded down behind the hills. Light was fading fast, so Louie abandoned the site until another time.

Several days later he discovered somebody had dug deeper at his location, uncovering the strong box. The impression of the box was still visible at the bottom of the hole. Louie said it was a good hiding place, and couldn't understand why nobody had searched there before. Several old excavation pits were within two feet of the location. It was never discovered who finally unearthed the cache of gold. But from that day forward, Louie said, "I no fool around with stories of treasures again." He also regretted not continuing to dig on that cold windy night.

Travelers crossing this rugged terrain often reported seeing ghostly figures moving about on the high ridge. Prospectors and other locals have also witnessed strange activities and lights along the crest of the hill. Even after death, and the reported removal of the treasure, these spirits continue to haunt this region.

Another local we knew personally who actually had seen a ghost near the ridge was rancher Fred Noon. One time Fred took us to a well hidden cave west of the Ruby Road. It was at one time occupied by ancient Indians. Apparently the ceiling had collapsed, perhaps during an earthquake, crushing all the inhabitants inside. Numerous human bones could be seen among the fallen debris. It looked quite dangerous to explore, as some boulders were teetering above us.

While still a young lad, Fred crawled between the boulders and spotted several more skeletons. He never ventured back into the cavern as many sections of loose rocks began to shift. This is another interesting location known only to a few today.

Chapter 26

SILVER BULLION AT SARDINA PEAK

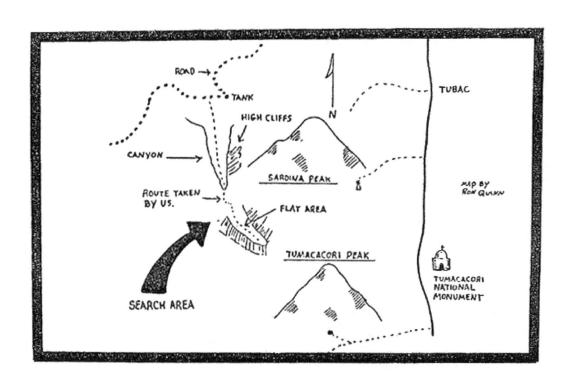

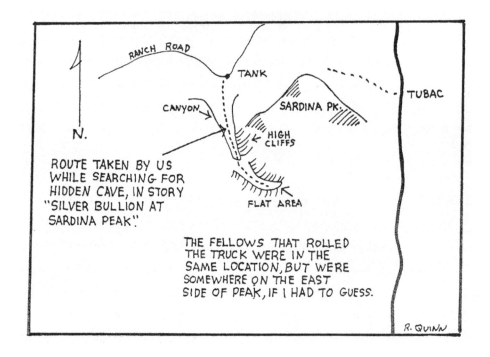

SILVER BULLION AT SARDINA PEAK

Southern Arizona Trail, Vol. 2, No. 13, October 10, 1986, Page 3

S ardina Peak is located at the extreme northern boundaries of the Tumacacori Mountains, and stands out vividly against the blue Arizona sky. Supposedly, a treasure is hidden somewhere on the southwest slopes of this stately peak.

I first heard this rather interesting tale in 1974 from an acquaintance I happened to meet at a social gathering here in Tucson, Arizona. As usual when I'm at a party, the conversation drifted toward lost mines and buried treasures. Dave was quite surprised to discover that my brother, Chuck, and I have been involved in this treasure business since 1956, when we first arrived in Southern Arizona. I told him when the old "gold bug" bit us it did a thorough job.

Dave didn't know all the facts regarding this unique story, but related it the best he could. It seems two men, names unknown, arrived in this area near Sardina Peak around the turn of the century. Somehow they discovered a sizable treasure consisting of silver bullion. Its total weight is rumored at about five hundred pounds. At today's price of silver it would amount to a pretty nice discovery.

Afterward they found a cave on the slopes of the peak which was high enough that they could see the entire western landscape without any obstruction interfering with their view. For some reason, unknown to Dave, they decided to store the silver in the cave for safe keeping. The area was extremely rough and they had to lead the pack animals from the discovery site to this cave, and entered a canyon with high lofty cliffs to reach the area.

Just as the "November" sun began to bed down behind the western ridges, they completed their third and final trip, and camp was set up near the saddle at the head of the canyon.

Locating Sardina Peak on the Tubac Quadrangle 15-minute series topo map, in section 21, look at section 20 and you'll see two deep canyons that flow north. The one furthest from the peak toward the west fits the description of the canyon used.

The following morning, both returned and carefully concealed the entrance with rocks from the surrounding areas. When finished it was completely hidden from view, and one could pass the spot and never notice a cave was there.

One of the clues that could indeed lead a serious treasure hunter to its discovery is, when the sun rose in "November," the area near the cave caught the morning light first, when viewed from the west side of these mountains. My partners and I camped several miles west of Sardina during November of 1984. When the sun rose there was an area that did catch the light first, leaving the remainder of the western slopes in shadow. A few days later we investigated this particular spot and it resembled the region where this treasure supposedly was hidden.

There is a natural pass leading into the area from the canyon used, and I believe this is the "gateway" to where the bullion was concealed. When you cross the saddle keep to the left and climb to a large area that is somewhat flat and has a drop off to the right. If you continue following this, it will slowly rise very steeply and angle toward the left, where it terminates at the face of some rock cliffs.

We searched the entire area for several days and couldn't locate anything that looked "out of place" in the contour of these high sedimentary walls. If this is the area, there's a chance that erosion, along with dirt and rocks falling from above over the years could have given the entrance a natural appearance. The gentlemen that concealed this cave knew what they were doing and did their homework well.

If the two had returned later and removed the treasure, I doubt if they'd take the necessary time to again conceal the entrance. We searched the region completely and there aren't any other caves about. Dave said, "One of the partners died in a boating accident in San Francisco Bay several months later, and the other was never heard of again."

Of course, this tale has many "holes" in it, but this doesn't suggest the story is untrue. As Dave stated, facts have been lost or forgotten in the retelling of it until only fragments remain but the location is definitely correct.

About six years ago I met a gentleman that was very interested in this area. He asked numerous questions about road conditions and wanted to know if water could be obtained from the tanks or windmills in the area. Outside these questions, he was quite secretive. He did, however, ask if the vicinity near this peak was "cave" country.

The big "hole" in this story is, after discovering the silver (if they really did), why rebury it and not take it with them, or at least a portion of the cache? Perhaps they were lucky amateurs when it came to treasure hunting, and after making the discovery, they didn't know how to go about disposing of the silver, legally or illegally. They might have decided to bury it again until these questions could be answered. If so, why conceal it so far from the original site, unless others were involved and knew the location and these two wanted to change it. That accident in the bay of one partner might not have been "one."

It's not difficult to reach this area if you have a 4 x 4 or are well versed in handling a regular truck. The dirt road is quite close to the mouth of the canyon and the lofty cliffs can easily be seen.

During autumn and fall seasons, it would indeed make an ideal weekend camping trip. From the road, it only takes an hour or so to make the climb to the rocky area in which this cache is alleged to be hidden. Even if you don't discover this elusive treasure, the rugged beauty of this country is worth seeing. It's located in the Coronado National forest, and hasn't been invaded yet by paved roads, crowds, screaming kids or picnic tables.

We spent two years ('56-'57) prospecting and treasure hunting in this harsh, yet beautiful desert country. During this time we heard countless stories of lost mines, buried treasures and hidden bandit loot. Yes, it would be great to discover one of these legendary treasures, but if you're just out camping on the western slopes of these rough "sun baked" hills, there is another treasure we found. It's the complete solitude of this country, hearing the early morning sounds of nature, feeling a cool breeze across your face and witnessing a spectacular "Tumacacori dawn."

AN INTERESTING TALE (?)

Southern Arizona Trails International, Vol. 3, No. 41, July 28, 1987, Page 16

S everal years ago while working out at a local health club, I happened to meet a fellow who was quite interested in prospecting. During our workouts, we'd discuss the subject, and also stories of lost mines and treasure.

A friend of a friend of his heard that somebody had bought an old rocking chair at some garage sale. While reupholstering its arms, he discovered an old map hidden inside. It was old and brittle, so after unfolding it he taped the smaller pieces together. It was written in English and told of a treasure hidden halfway up Sardina Peak. It didn't mention this well-known peak by name but had an excellent drawing of it as seen from the east side.

With one close friend accompanying him, they drove to the area. After driving as close as possible in the truck, they hiked the remaining distance. Reaching some high cliffs, they began searching for the marking indicated on the map, showing the treasure's hiding place.

In doing so, they discovered a way to drive a 4 x 4 to within several hundred feet of the area where the marking was alleged to be.

After a few minutes of looking they found the marking on the face of some large boulders on the steep slope. They returned the following day with a rented 4 x 4 and slowly inched their way up the rocky slope. A number of spots were extremely dangerous, but they managed to work around them without rolling the vehicle.

They reached a somewhat flat area and decided not to push their luck any further. The small flat was only a few hundred feet from where the marking was.

Both began digging and soon reached a natural small cave. After clearing the entrance out, they found a small narrow passageway. With flashlight in hand, both crawled several yards then stood up.

All around them were bars of gold and silver. In one corner were rotting sacks of raw gold. Near the entrance, but to the right where they entered, was a statue of a saint. Attached to the hand of its upright arm was a knife.

This might have been placed there to scare off anybody who accidentally discovered the treasure trove and might be superstitious of religious figures, especially ones holding a knife.

They removed a large portion of the treasure, placing it in the truck. After covering the entrance until they could return for the remainder, they started slowly down the steep slope.

Being somewhat top heavy, they hit a large rock and began to tip over. Both jumped free and watched the vehicle roll over a few times before it reached a ledge and fell into a narrow canyon. Being only somewhat bruised, the two retrieved the gold that was scattered about and hid it behind some large boulders, then covered it with other rocks.

They abandoned the truck and hiked to the highway where they thumbed a ride to town.

Both disappeared shortly afterward and were never seen again. The main treasure chamber and the gold that was removed are supposedly still hidden somewhere on the slopes of that peak.

I have hiked and climbed most of the country around Sardina Peak and all its nearby canyons, but have never come across the wreckage of a truck or heard of anyone finding one.

If you read my story, "Silver Bullion at Sardina Peak," in the October 10, 1986 issue of *Arizona Trails*, you will notice the similarity between both stories; same location, two men mysteriously disappearing after concealing some of the cache, etc.

These two accounts "might" have some truth behind them, and could very well be the same story. There is also the possibility it might be a complete hoax. Or it was conceived in the mind of some lonely old prospector living alone in the hills of Arizona. I have come across numerous tales of treasure that are complete fabrications that have cost the seeker time and money in searching for treasures that never existed. One that comes to mind was my article, "The Hoax at Cerro Ruido." (See chapter 45)

Neither of these two tales has any documentation or solid evidence to back them up, but I wouldn't rule them out.

Proving their existence would be quite difficult, unless somebody actually uncovered the treasure.

Most stories and legends that have been passed down through the centuries have some basis of fact behind them, no matter how incredible they might sound to us today. Stories change as they are passed along. Facts are forgotten and fiction substituted, until the tale is completely unrecognizable. The same can be said for stories about lost treasures, but as they often say, "Where there's smoke there's fire."

SIERRITA MOUNTAINS & APACHE WELL ADVENTURES

Chapter 27

LOST SILVER OR OX FRAME CANYON

Southern Arizona Trails, Vol. 2, No. 17, December 8, 1986, Page 10

T his treasure hunting and prospecting can become very frustrating at times, as you will discover after reading this tale of a lost silver deposit.

During the closing months of 1957, Chuck and I moved our base camp to the southern slopes of the Sierrita Mountains. On one of the trips to Tubac to visit a friend we met another gentleman that lived in the immediate area. His name was Frank [Fern Hamill], and he was a pilot that would make frequent flights down into Mexico in his C-47. I'm almost certain these were illegal trips, but that wasn't any concern of ours.

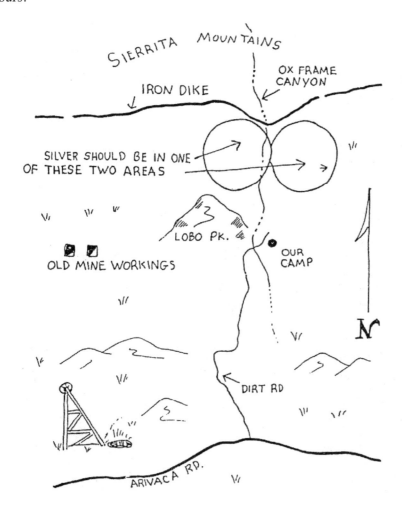

Frank overheard us talking about the location of our camp and the new metal detector we had just purchased. He came over and introduced himself and after the handshaking was over, told us we should search for a vein of hidden silver located in that part of the mountains we were camped near. He said he had once looked for it with the son of the man that made the original discovery.

Frank went on to say that sometime in the late 1930s, a Mexican cowboy that rode for the ranch, who's cattle grazed in the area of these mountains, found himself on the slopes near "Ox Frame Canyon." It was near noon, so he decided to have lunch and relax before moving on and finishing his chores.

About twenty minutes later he remounted and began to ride off, but noticed his horse was limping. Dismounting he inspected the animal's hoof and found a dark stone wedged between the shoe and the hoof. He removed it with the tip of his knife, and in doing so, scratched the surface of the stone and saw the color silver.

He was somewhat of a prospector himself and this lead to a strain in his marriage, as he would occasionally quit working and go "wildcatting" around the hills searching for that elusive "pot of gold at the end of the rainbow," leaving his wife and kids behind to be looked after by his relatives.

After removing more of the dark oxidation that covered the stone, he discovered he held in his hand a pure nugget of silver. He searched the region and found a small vein about two inches wide partially hidden in the grass. Using his knife, he broke off several pieces, placing these in his jacket. He knew the area quite well and noticed the vein was "just south" of a large black iron dike that cut across the country and is very prominent where it crosses Ox Frame Canyon, which was located a hundred yards or so below from where he was standing.

On his return to the ranch he mentioned nothing of his discovery. Two weeks later he got three days off, and returned to his home on the outskirts of Tucson. That evening he displayed the silver to his wife, and informed her he was going to stake the property out and work it. His wife had heard all this before and said, if he wanted to go off digging in the hills again, that she would leave him and return to New Mexico with the children. They would sell what there was and live with her brother and his wife.

He insisted this time it was different as he already had made the discovery. His wife wouldn't change her mind and said, this time it's your family or the hills and to make a choice. She insisted they all return to New Mexico, as when they lived there, he worked and didn't go chasing some dream out across the hills.

After several more minutes of "verbal jousting" he agreed with her and said he loved his family and didn't want to lose 'em, but he had to work until a replacement could be found for his job. A few days later the cowboy rode out to his discovery. He spent most of the morning digging and removed almost twenty pounds of silver, and this he hid behind some boulders in the canyon below.

During the next five days, he managed to dig out another hundred pounds. On the last day he filled in the hole which was about three feet deep with dirt and rocks until it was completely concealed. Packing the silver on his extra horse he left the area.

Two days later he and the family began their journey back to New Mexico. The silver gave them something to live on until he could find gainful employment. His wife wasn't impressed with the silver, as it was this that took him away from her for long periods of time during his trips into the hills. In her way of thinking, it was "ill gotten wealth," as she had seen other families destroyed over "quick riches" and it wasn't going to happen to her.

During their journey, he suggested about returning several times a year to work the diggings as it was a waste to leave all that silver there when they could put it to good use. Every time he brought the matter up, she would give him the same ultimatum.

When their oldest boy turned 16, he told the lad about the silver deposit and how to find it. A year later when they fell on hard times, the cowboy left his wife a note saying he was returning to the discovery and would be back in three weeks. He was never seen or heard of again.

Frank had met his son years before, and from him heard this story. Both ventured into the Sierritas and discovered the iron dike, and they searched during the cool months for almost three years and never discovered the silver.

He told us we should try a hand at finding it, as nobody had ever looked for the deposit with a metal detector. He thought the hidden vein, even though it was three feet below the surface could be found with one. I asked Frank if this was correct, how come he never used one during their search? His answer was, he had commitments and couldn't take the necessary time off to search for it. Chuck asked about the son, and Frank said he lost track of him about two years ago.

Several days later we decided to search for this elusive silver vein. The dike was quite easy to find as it runs for over a mile across the hills. We spent some time checking the iron dike over, as Chuck wanted some samples to test for other minerals. At one time somebody had sunk a five foot hole right in the center of it, and the walls had a greenish deposit on them, indicating copper or nickel.

The cowboy mentioned the vein was "just" south of the dike, but how far would that be? Was he ten, twenty or a hundred feet from it? Another thing, he never indicated which side of the canyon he was on.

During December we spent five long cold days searching both sides, and from the dike, we checked over a 150 feet southward and never discovered a thing which looked suspicious. If the cowboy had dug about three feet, and the vein remained the same size with depth, I doubt if our detector would have penetrated through that much over-burden to give us a signal. To this day, I believe we walked right over the deposit and never knew it.

There was a lot of land movement in this canyon at one time, and there's evidence indicating there is mineralization far below, as when Chuck ran his tests he discovered Chromium was in the iron dike, and our assay report was 25%.

The last time we were there, in '63, most of the property had been staked out by a copper company. Where Ox Frame empties onto the flats there has been some extensive mining operations carried on just west of it, first by the Spaniards, as there are some remains of arrastras in the area. During the '30s and '40s, others have worked the property but all left empty handed. This story is mentioned in my article, "The Treasure that "WAS" at Lobo Peak."

If the cowboy hadn't discovered this vein of native silver, I'm certain the vein would have been eventually found by some old "weather- beaten prospector" hiking the hills.

What became of the Mexican cowboy will remain a mystery, as he never returned to the diggings or his family. Guess he was right when he said, "It was completely concealed." He sure did a good job, as it's never been rediscovered.

Chapter 28

TUMACACACORI'S GHOSTLY SPECTERS

Chuck took this picture of me standing next to an ancient grave piled with rocks tossed by passersby.

(Parts One & Two)
Southern Arizona Trails International, Vol. 3, No. 38, June 7, 1987, Page 18
Southern Arizona Trails International, Vol. 3, No. 39, June 14, 1987, Page 18

Part One

THE TUMACACORI MOUNTAINS

This rugged desert mountain range is located some thirty-odd miles south of Tucson, Arizona. There are an abundance of stories about buried treasures and lost mines hidden within these mysterious sun baked hills, but there are also many tales of ghostly encounters, from unexplained lights, bizarre sounds and apparitions of Spanish soldiers and Jesuit priests.

Just south of Sardina Mountain, a lofty peak that dominates the northern boundaries of these unfriendly hills, one can find a large pile of stones near the summit of a hill, marking an ancient grave. The story surrounding this burial site is almost unknown today to the few residents that now reside in the area. We heard it was customary among the early Spanish settlers to cast a stone onto a burial site that wasn't located in a graveyard as you would pass. This site was near a well-traveled path, and over the years the pile grew to a substantial size.

My brother Chuck and I were doing some prospecting and treasure hunting in 1957 on the eastern slopes of these mountains at the time. One afternoon while visiting friends in Tubac, then a small community located just off the old Tucson-Nogales Highway, we met an elderly Mexican gentleman by the name of Frank Salcido. He spotted our new metal detector in our jeep and told us about a rugged area just west of Tubac, near the foothills of the towering Tumacacoris, where a treasure might be buried.

Cold Blood

About ten years earlier, Frank was working in this remote area, mending fences with several other ranch hands. They camped there one night so as to get an early start on their chores the following morning. The sun had just settled behind the western ridges as they finished their evening meal. A few moments later, they heard the sound of a horse approaching at full gallop and looked up. What they saw made their blood turn cold.

Coming down a hillside north of camp was a horse and rider, but the person sitting atop the mount was minus half his face. The rider was dressed in military clothing, the type worn during the Spanish occupation of this territory. The ghostly apparition came within twenty yards of them, then disappeared behind some large boulders. They heard the horse come to a halt and a few moments later, heard a sound like somebody was pouring a large amount of coins onto the ground. Frank and another member of the work party crept cautiously around the boulders, but the specter had vanished. Frank also mentioned while the horse was approaching them, its hoofs were not touching the earth, and looked as though it was galloping about a foot above the ground. According to him, not much sleep was had that night.

The following evening they all returned to the site where the strange apparition had appeared the night before. They hid below the edge of a nearby dry wash and waited. Sure enough, at approximately the same time, just as the sun began to fade, the ghostly rider appeared again. Down the slope it came and disappeared once again behind the boulders. A few seconds later they heard the sound of falling coins.

Frank asked us if we'd like to visit the area, being we had a detector, and search near the boulders as the sound of coins might be indicating a treasure was buried below. Of course we agreed, and said we would pick him up the following afternoon around five o'clock.

After bouncing overland in our jeep for perhaps twenty minutes, scaring rabbits and other desert dwellers, we arrived at the site. Chuck and I both searched the area around the boulders then checked further out but nothing was discovered. We talked it over and decided to remain the night and see if this specter would make an appearance for us. It was late spring and the nights were quite comfortable, and we did have some camping gear with us, along with food and water. One "never" ventures into the desert without carrying these provisions. The desert can be an awesome place, and it waits patiently for somebody to enter its domain, make a mistake, and be added to its list of casualties.

As it became darker, Frank began to joke and act nonchalant about the whole thing, but we could see he was beginning to act a little nervous. I had my doubts we'd see anything, but I was still somewhat apprehensive. The time the apparition should appear, came and went, but still no rider. Frank had seen it during early fall, and this was late spring, so perhaps it didn't make an appearance this time of the year. To this day I often wonder how I would have reacted if that horseman would have come riding into view.

Skirmish with Hostiles

The next morning Frank showed us the grave mentioned earlier. He said there had been a small battle fought there with the Indians, and a soldier was buried beneath the stones. This grave was about four hundred feet north of the site where the apparition appeared. Frank insisted the specter was that of the fallen soldier, killed during the skirmish with the hostiles. He said all this took place sometime during the 1820s. It was also rumored that the soldiers were carrying gold and a military payroll consisting of "coins" to the presidio, located at Tubac. Chuck took a picture of me standing beside the large pile of stones, before we hiked back to our jeep parked below. Later we also took a picture of the hillside the apparition appeared on.

Native Silver

A rumor sprung into existence years earlier, that some prospector or miner once rode past the grave, and cast a large piece of native silver onto it. This was evident, as a large amount of stones have been removed from the center. No doubt by a party searching for this rich piece of silver ore. This can be seen in the photo taken.

Whether the ghostly specter ever appeared again, we'll never know. Perhaps we were there at the wrong time, as Frank saw it during early fall. If this mysterious apparition does ride the lonely hills during the fading hours of the day, it might be around the anniversary of the soldier's death. Frank wasn't sure of the date they first spotted the specter, but he was almost sure it was during early October. If one could camp at the site during this time, there's a good chance the rider might be seen. The way Frank related the story, one could tell he was very sincere, and believed what he had witnessed. Of course, others were present during these two brief encounters, so they must have seen something.

Note: Another version of this story appeared as "Tumacacori's Ghost Rider" in *Southern Arizona Trails*, Vol. 3, No. 142, June 27, 1989, Pages 22, 26.

Part Two

nother short but rather interesting tale was told to us by Bill Brouse. He was the proprietor of the local tavern in Arivaca. We had just moved our camp to Apache Well, and decided to drive into town for some needed supplies.

I remember it was a hot dry spring day as we drove along the dusty road that leads to this rather picturesque community. About half an hour later, we rounded the bend and parked in front of the local general store. After purchasing what we needed and fueling the old jeep up, we headed across the street to the local cantina and a cool beer before returning to camp.

Bill smiled as we entered and asked how things were going. Chuck informed him we had moved camp to Apache Well, and hoped to remain there until the summer heat drove us out. As he placed our beers on the counter, Bill looked rather startled and answered, "Padre! What padre?"

This is the strange story Bill unfolded.

It seems about a hundred and fifty years ago, perhaps even more, a Jesuit priest, whose name has been lost in the dusty pages of time, had a small mission about 12 x 20 feet, some six miles east of *El Pueblo de Arivaca*, which at that time was a small Mexican village. The inhabitants who resided there and in the surrounding hills gave their most treasured possessions, such as silver and gold crosses, family jewelry, etc., to the padre for safe keeping as they feared robbery. This custom went on for many years and the items grew to a sizable amount. The priest hid these valuables within "sight" of his mission, which today is completely obliterated. The only time these treasures were brought forth was during weddings, a fiesta or other family holiday.

One morning an Indian woodchopper came to the mission for water and found the padre dead of an apparent heart attack I would guess. After the old priest was laid to rest, the villagers suddenly remembered that no one knew where he had hidden their valuables. The search was on. They started near the mission and spread out in every direction, but try as they may the hiding place was never discovered. (We found the location where the old mission stood in November of '57, and searched the entire area with two detectors but nothing was found.)

As the years rolled by, many cowboys, miners and weekend prospectors that ventured into this area have reported seeing a strange dark robed figure walking the desolate country and deep canyons that are numerous in the region. Some claim to have followed the specter, only to see it vanish. Rumor has it that it's the ghost of the Jesuit padre walking the remote country in search of someone he can trust, in hopes of telling them the treasure's location so it can be returned to the rightful families. Bill laughed and said, "Guess there aren't any trustworthy folks left, as the padre is still out there looking for one."

Most of the people that have seen this shadowy figure had never heard the tale until returning to Arivaca. It's reported that some hunter from Tucson that had never been to this particular area before, saw the specter and later asked some residents in town if there was some type of "retreat" or monastery in that area. When asked why, he said while hiking near Apache Well, he spotted a figure in what looked like a monk's robe, walking across a wide dry-wash. When he heard the story, it's said he almost turned ghost white and crossed himself.

So, if you're ever traveling the many back roads east of Arivaca, or are out hunting or camping near the hills south of Apache Well, keep an eye out for this elusive shadowy figure. Most apparitions appear during the dead of night, when the moon hangs low in the sky, but this specter of the past seems to enjoy the light of day, when the sun shines brightly, birds sing and a breeze ruffles the leaves of a nearby mesquite tree.

Many have asked if we ever saw this figure while camping near Apache Well. We were only at the location for three weeks before the heat drove us out, and we returned to the cooler country of Northern Arizona. Just one time while hiking east of camp I saw something move off to my right and turned, for a brief second, I thought I spotted a long robe ruffling then disappear behind a steep rocky bank, but it could have been anything.

After hearing this interesting tale, I believe ones imagination comes into play while in this remote region, and one sees what they want to see. I have spoken to several people that swear they saw this figure, and it wasn't their imagination or some shadow caused by a tree branch. This is the second tale of a ghostly apparition we've heard about while camping in these mysterious mountains. Some other stories were quite funny, and then there are the tales that keep you awake nights. These are the ones concerning lost mines, buried bandit loot and caves full of Spanish treasure.

Chapter 29

DOORWAY TO THE GODS...

Top of the plateau in the area of the mysterious arch.

The mysterious plateau.

Canyon leading to the mysterious plateau.

Southern Arizona Trails, Vol. 2, No. 19, February 1987, Page 14

During our two year odyssey of prospecting and treasure hunting in Arizona, my partners and I heard countless tales of every description. Most were stories of lost mines, buried treasures and some so mysterious, they bordered on the unbelievable.

Many of these tales were related to us ten, fifteen and thirty years ago, by old prospectors residing in out of the way hamlets scattered across this picturesque state.

Out of all these stories, my favorite deals with a natural stone archway hidden deep within the Tumacacori Mountains, and located some thirty-odd miles south of Tucson.

These harsh desert hills are well known within the circle of serious treasure hunters, as several Spanish missions were built in the shadows of these unfriendly mountains. Rumor has it, the padres worked numerous silver mines in these hills for well over a hundred years. Most of this treasure was hastily concealed when they fled for their lives during the Indian uprising of 1751.

The story however does not concern these legendary lost mines, but this strange archway we discovered by accident, before hearing the tale surrounding it. The tale was told to us by an Indian we happened to befriend on a stretch of highway between Tucson and the Mexican border.

We first met John on the old Nogales Highway while returning from Mexico. His old truck had blown a tire, and not having a spare, he stood beside the road trying to hitch a ride to the nearest service station.

We had been prospecting in the area for almost a year, and knew how it felt to be stranded in such a condition. Stopping, we picked him and his flat tire up, and several miles down the road arrived at a gas station. After having the old tire fixed, we returned John to his truck. He couldn't stop thanking us enough as not many white men had shown him such kindness. Afterwards, we returned to our base camp located near the southern boundaries of the Cerro Colorado Mountains, some fifteen miles away.

Two months later, we again were back in the Tumacacoris. One of my partners, Ted [Roy Purdie], had some very authentic documentation about a Spanish treasure supposedly buried in these hills.

Late one afternoon a rider came into camp, and it was John. He recognized us and dismounted. After the customary handshaking was over, we found out he was working for one of the nearby ranches. While returning to the corral he spotted our camp from a distance and rode over as the ranchers always liked to know who is camping on their spread.

He had been riding this country for almost twenty years and knew the terrain quite well. Being treasure hunters, we asked John about several landmarks in the area. Of course he knew their location and volunteered the information. He also had heard the various tales of hidden gold, but never searched for any himself.

He told us however, about this mysterious stone arch and where it was located. I informed him we had come across such a formation about six months earlier while exploring the area he mentioned.

John asked us if we had walked through it. We answered, no, and said we spotted the arch from above and hadn't paid much attention to it. And so unfolds the strangest tale we ever heard.

It seems some Indians were hunting in the nearby mountains around the 1850s, and while returning to camp happened upon the stone archway. Being in a good mood as the hunt was successful, they began chasing each other through the opening in a playful manner.

A short while later, another hunter jumped through but never emerged from the opposite side. Fearing they had entered sacred ground and had angered their Gods, the remaining Indians fled in terror. Arriving back at the village they told the medicine man the story of how their young companion had vanished before their eyes.

As the story spread, others ventured to the high mountain to gaze upon the archway. One Indian did toss several rocks through and these appeared on the other side, until the last was thrown and suddenly vanished. The others backed off in fear and spread the tale about this "Doorway to the Gods," as it came to be known.

Others, curious about the tale would travel miles to look at the mysterious archway, hoping they wouldn't invoke the anger of the Mountain God. Another time, an older Indian approached the opening with a live rabbit he had captured and tossed the animal through several times, but it never vanished. John's father once threw a live lizard in and it disappeared immediately.

John himself has been to the site on numerous occasions and the only time he witnessed anything strange was during the fall of 1949.

A big storm had blown into Arizona and the sky was completely covered with dark clouds in all directions. As he rode past the archway he noticed the sky seen through the entrance was "blue," but there wasn't any break in the clouds above.

Dismounting, he walked cautiously toward the arch and peered through at a safe distance. The mountains on the other side hadn't changed and looked the same, but the sky didn't have a single cloud showing, and sunlight was shining brightly. Fear gripped him and John slowly backed away. Reaching his horse, he mounted and rode off.

I asked him, if the story is true, why haven't any scientists from the University of Arizona located in Tucson, investigated the strange phenomenon? He said his people have known about the archway for almost a hundred years, but the tale has never been told to a white man before.

We asked him why he related the story to us. Smiling, John replied that we had shown him kindness when he was stranded on the highway, and thought he would repay the favor by telling us this rather interesting story.

My partners and I returned to the site of the archway several times, but during these visits nothing out of the ordinary occurred.

It's located in a remote region in the Tumacacori (To-ma-cock-o-ree) Mountains near two high peaks. There are some strange rock formations in the general vicinity, but I'm certain these have nothing to do with the natural stone doorway. On one side of a steep hill is an enormous deposit of geodes or "thunder eggs" and other semi-precious stones. We removed most from the surface, but beneath the ground must be a large amount of these oddities of nature.

Once I approached the opening and slowly passed a long stick through, but nothing occurred. Next I placed my outstretched arm in but again nothing. Ted and my brother stood off to one side shouting I was flirting with danger if the story was true. To this day I regret not letting out a "yell" as I put my arm in, just to see the expressions of their faces. I have to admit though it would have been a dirty trick to play.

This archway could be some "freak" of nature or a rip in the fabric of time, and pulsating very slowly. Perhaps this doorway remains open for short periods, and then closes for minutes, days or weeks.

I often wonder what became of the young Indian supposedly swallowed up by the arch many years ago. If it's some type of a miniature "Bermuda Triangle," did he venture back or forward in time, or into another dimension?

When John saw the blue sky he did mention the surrounding country remained the same, so perhaps he was gazing only a couple of years back or forward in time. If this doorway was visible from the opposite side why didn't the Indian try to re-enter and come back through? It might be he "never" realized a change had taken place, and to him, his friends had vanished. If this is the case, he might have thought they were playing a trick on him and went off searching for his companions. This is only speculation on my part.

Maybe others, such as miners, cowboys, prospectors, etc., have come upon this formation during their travels, but like us, never approached it. As stated earlier, it's located in a very remote area and I doubt if many have seen it. Not hearing the tale about the arch, most would have only given it a quick glance before moving on.

I haven't been back to the site since 1977 and, John no doubt has long since passed away. Perhaps during Indian ceremonies, this strange story is told around open camp fires. There is also the possibility the location as been long forgotten, and the modern Indians of today looks upon the story as just another "tall tale" told by the old ones.

It might be just a legend, but the archway is there. I for one wouldn't challenge it by bravely walking into the "Gorgon's Den." On the other hand, the power that once surrounded this arch could have faded away years ago. I, or anyone else, would be foolish to risk being swept away into some unknown domain to prove the story of the "Doorway to the Gods," told to us thirty years ago by our friend John, is true.

Note: Another version of this story appeared in Ron's article "The Mysterious Plateau" in Fate – Magazine, Vol. 59, No. 3, Issue 671, March 2006, Pages 18-25.

Chapter 30

THE HIDDEN MAIL BAGS

Southern Arizona Trails, Vol. 3, No. 47, Page 15

nother short, but rather interesting tale we heard while in Arizona deals with an Army mail pouch containing around 130 unopened letters. These are nestled away in a natural tunnel beneath the towering Baboquivari Mountains, along with a box of sabers.

They were being delivered to a company of cavalrymen bivouacked near the foot of these mountains, but they never were delivered.

The value of the stamps alone would set most treasure hunter's hearts beating fast. Their condition would be very good, as the caves in this region are remarkably dry.

During hunting season of 1967, a retired gentleman whose name is not known, was hunting among the hills and rocks near these mountains, which are located some 40 miles southwest of Tucson.

He left his truck parked along the Sasabe Road (State Highway 286) which winds its way through the Altar Valley toward Mexico. He left on foot before dawn and headed west across the flats. After an hour or so, he arrived at a natural watering hole. There are others in the area, but they were made by machines for watering the cattle—they are called tanks on topo maps.

Climbing to a high rise, he settled himself near some boulders and waited. As dawn broke and the desert began to awake, he spotted rabbits, birds and other animals near the water.

Within a short time a large buck appeared and started toward the tank. Taking aim, the hunter fired and the deer buckled and fell, then regained its feet and ran off as another bullet kicked up dust behind him. The shot must have gazed the deer, as some blood and hair were found where it had fallen.

The hunter tracked the animal for about half an hour and spotted it again near a large clump of rocks. The deer was limping and walked behind the rocks and out of view. The hunter took aim and waited for the animal to emerge from the opposite side. When it didn't, he moved forward, hoping to find the wounded deer on the ground.

Instead, he spotted a natural tunnel running through the boulders and out the opposite end. The tunnel was about five feet high and some 20 feet long. The deer had escaped the dinner plate by going through the tunnel. The hunter entered, and halfway into the tunnel spotted a couple of old boxes on one side. Opening a box, he found cavalry sabers in one and their handles and guards in the other.

On a small shelf of rock above was a leather bag. Upon opening the bag, the hunter discovered it contained letters addressed to various troopers out of Fort Lowell, which was located east of Tucson.

There were perhaps a hundred or more envelopes in the pouch He removed two and put them in his jacket.

By now the deer had long since disappeared, so the hunter took a last look around and returned to his truck. He missed it and came out on the Sasabe Road some two miles north of it.

After hitching a ride south with another hunter, he found the truck and returned to town.

That evening he visited his son, showing him the letters, and both agreed there could very well be some value to them.

The following morning, both returned to where the hunter thought he had parked the truck. They spotted a water tank after hiking for a while, but he wasn't sure it was the same one. There was a rise east of it so his son suggested they search for the spent cartridge, but couldn't find it.

The two hiked southwest for a while and came across other tanks, but they didn't look familiar. From there they headed north but still couldn't locate the clump of rocks hiding the tunnel.

In the following weeks they resumed the search, but again couldn't locate the tunnel.

Here the hunter made the big mistake of not carrying out all the letters. If it were a 50-pound bar of gold, I could understand why, but a pound or less in letters… There is no excuse he could offer to warrant his decision in removing only two. In other words, he goofed.

I called several stamp dealers and asked what stamps were in use from 1882 through 1889.

Most are worth something, but the real value would be in the covers, or the unopened letters.

There were several stamps or cancelations used during that period that would be worth a great deal if some were discovered on these letters.

The dealer mentioned the complete value wouldn't put two or three people through college, but a few rare stamps could boost the value quite high.

The next is only speculation but could have happened.

I believe two or more troopers were transporting the mail and sabers to the company bivouacked near the mountains. If these troopers had seen some "hostiles" in the area they might have had the time to hide the shipment in the tunnel they might have known. They could have hidden the letters to reduce their weight and have ridden off, but never made it back.

Why I come to this conclusion is that back in the '20s some ranchers discovered some human and horse bones in that very area. There wasn't much left but they did find some cavalry buttons among the bones from an army tunic worn during that period.

It would be quite a thrill to read some of those letters that were sent to husbands and sons out west protecting the frontier.

Then, on the other hand, perhaps it would be infringing on the personal lives of those brave men who have long since passed away.

That decision will be left to the person who finds this tunnel, and I believe it will be discovered one of these days, if it hasn't already.

Chapter 31

THE PHANTOM MISSION

Southern Arizona Trails, Vol. 3, No. 44, August 18, 1987, Page 17

In 1958 I returned to sunny Arizona while my brother, Chuck, remained in Washington state for a while. During my ventures into the mountains and surrounding areas, my path crossed those of several people searching for the damndest things. From some, I heard stories one would only expect to find in those tabloids sold at supermarkets. The stories are presented here for enjoyment only, and I make no claims for their authenticity whatsoever.

The Phantom Mission

It was a cool windy March day, and I was arranging camp at an old site near Ox Frame Canyon in the Sierrita Mountains, where Chuck and I once camped a year earlier.

Glancing up, I spotted two hikers who looked in their late twenties coming toward me. Both carried packs and walked like they didn't have much experience maneuvering around rough terrain. As they drew near, both looked as though they should be sitting behind a desk in some office and not out roaming the wilds of Arizona.

After the introductions were over, they asked if I had ever seen the ruins of an old Spanish mission in these parts. It was supposed to be located "in a canyon" near the southern boundaries of the Sierritas. I smiled and asked where they obtained their information concerning the mission.

One who I'll call Bob, as their real names escape me after nearly thirty years, pulled a cheap-looking men's adventure magazine from this belt and opened it to a story on treasure hunting.

The article claimed there once was another "Tumacácori Mission" located somewhere in this remote region. The story had a very impressive looking map. A drawing of the mission also accompanied the three-page story.

This far-fetched tale went on to mention the old abandoned mission, supposedly built in this location, had a large treasure hidden beneath its foundation.

My two guests were from Phoenix, and after reading the fascinating story, decided to search for this mysterious lost mission. The article stated the ruins were once seen by a hunter in 1949. When he returned with friends who wanted to visit the site, he couldn't locate the ruins.

I informed Bob and his friend that if the truth was known, the entire story was made up by staff writers. They might have read several books on lost Spanish treasures of Arizona and decided to write their version of a buried treasure.

At one time there were about five of these magazines on the market, but they have long since disappeared, thank God.

137

Most of the so-called "true stories" appearing in them are completely false. Some had names like, *True Adventure, "Saga"* and other adventurous titles.

I went on to say this country had been raked and re-raked by miners, prospectors and cowboys. If any mission was here it would have been discovered ages ago, especially if it was located in a canyon or on the flats.

As I spoke, I could sense they would rather believe the printed word than somebody who had spent years exploring the surrounding country and other parts of Arizona, and had heard countless stories about lost mines, treasures and everything else imaginable, from hollow mountains containing Aztec temples, to giant bronze gears half-buried in desert sands.

The old gold bug had bitten 'em good and was chewing away. I could tell they weren't about to give up their search. If nothing else, they would get some needed exercise while out looking.

I asked where their truck was, and Bob's companion said they didn't have one, but had left their station wagon on the old road about three miles back when it became too rough to travel on.

Both complained about their feet sweating and aching, so I suggested they should dry them off and change socks before continuing. Of course, neither had an extra pair so they hung them on a limb to dry in the breeze. I let 'em used my foot powder before again putting on their socks. They were nice friendly guys though, but ill-prepared for a trip into the hills.

Try as I may, I couldn't convince them the story was somebody's "brain child." They also might have thought I was searching for the same mission and was trying to discourage 'em.

The last I saw of the two, they were hiking toward Lobo Peak with magazine in hand. However, they did have a topo map of the region and a compass, so I'm sure they didn't get lost.

Two days later I drove on out, but didn't see their vehicle along the way. We never met again, and the only reference I ever found mentioning a "second" Tumacacori Mission was in a book on treasures of the Southwest. I knew the author, so that alone convinced me the entire story was a fabrication.

Chapter 32

TUBAC MYSTERY TUNNEL

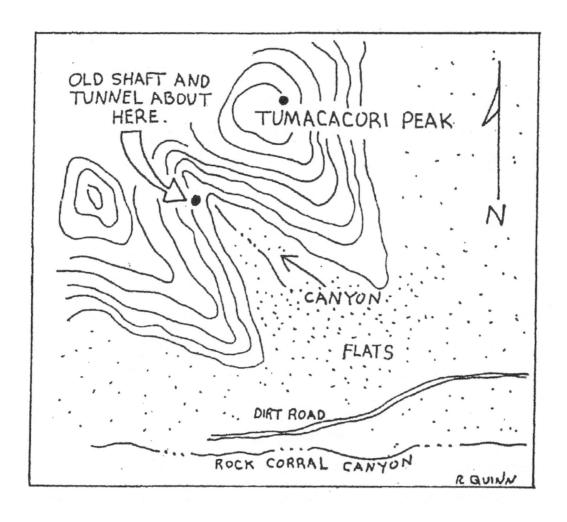

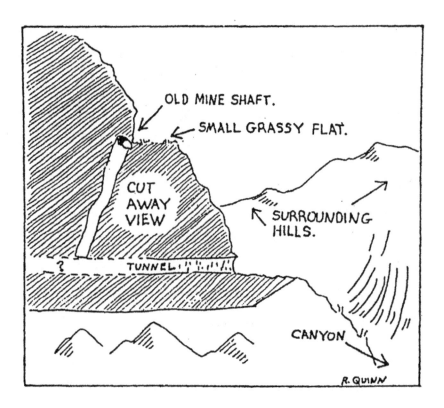

Treasure Magazine, Vol. 21, No. 8, August-September 1990, Pages 30-31

S omebody must have known something back in 1957, to have single-jacked a long tunnel beneath an old Spanish mine shaft in hopes of intersecting it somewhere along the tunnel's route. These Spanish diggings are so well hidden they don't even appear on modern topo maps of the area as a prospect hole, like countless other mines do.

The region I'm referring to is Tumacacori Peak, located on the Tubac Quadrangle 15-minute series map. This well concealed ancient shaft is about two and a half miles due west of Tumacácori National Monument in Southern Arizona.

From the small grassy flat located near the mine's opening, which is high above the canyon floor, one can see far and wide down Santa Cruz Valley.

While out exploring this picturesque and mysterious mountain range, which holds more tales of lost mines and treasures than any other in Southern Arizona, my brother Chuck and I found ourselves near the old rock house once occupied by "Crazy Davis," a colorful character that only had one oar in the water, if you know what I mean. The country north of this location looked rather interesting, so after parking the jeep we began hiking in that direction. It was mid-March and the cool gusty winds were whipping around us as we headed out across the flats toward Tumacacori Peak.

As we approached the upper head of a long rocky canyon, I heard voices coming from above and the distinct sound of somebody single-jacking. Looking up we spotted a long knotted rope hanging from a ledge. Chuck called but received no response.

With our curiosity aroused, we both climbed the rope. After pulling ourselves up about thirty feet or so, we came upon a flat area where several Mexican gentlemen were busy sinking a tunnel. It looked as though they were already in about 12 feet. They didn't act too surprised to see us, nor did they appear angry that some intruders had stumbled onto their operation. We introduced ourselves, and afterwards, they answered our questions freely and were quite friendly.

They told us there was an old Spanish mine shaft above that was partly filled with water. Some doctor from Tucson had discovered it and hired them to put the tunnel in. They were hoping to drain off the water once they reached the old shaft.

I asked if we could see the old mine and they said it was okay by them. After climbing perhaps fifty feet up the steep slope, we came upon the shaft. It was half hidden among the grass and a few trees that grew nearby. Some of the small trees had been cut from near the narrow opening. If they were still there, one would never realize a tunnel was located behind them. It sat on a small rocky shelf that overlooked the valley far below, and was well hidden.

It definitely resembled old Spanish workings, and wound its way downward. The shaft was small, crudely dug and appeared quite deep. The tunnel angled some and the remaining portion was lost in the darkness. We dropped a few stones and heard them hit the water about 20 feet below.

Afterwards, we examined the nearby rock, but couldn't find any trace of mineralization that would have warranted the sinking of such a shaft. The mine dump had undoubtedly been thrown over the edge into the canyon below. This area also was investigated thoroughly, but again, no sign of mineral was found. We remained at the location for perhaps twenty minutes, then bid the three miners goodbye and headed out across the hills.

The last time I visited the site was back in 1972. The tunnel extended quite a ways into the hillside, and then turned slightly to the right about 15 feet in. I was alone at the time, so didn't venture into the tunnel very far. When out in the hills it doesn't pay to enter some of these old abandoned mines, especially if you are alone, as most are very dangerous.

Nothing had changed at the old Spanish diggings above, but while there, I did cast several stones down the dark twisting shaft, but never heard any hit bottom. Last time we were there it was half full of water, so I would have to guess that the miners did break through into the ancient workings.

Later I returned to the tunnel below. Scattered about were bits and pieces of drill steel and other rusted items. By the conditions of the site it looked as though nobody had been there in quite some time.

If any treasure was discovered by the group, the story never became known. A lot of hard labor had gone into this operation, so either they were searching for a particular treasure known to be in the general vicinity, or just "wildcatting around" after finding the old mine, and decided to sink a tunnel toward the water filled shaft in hopes of finding something there.

If Hollywood ever makes another film about lost mines or treasures, this site would be ideal. It's hidden at the end of a rugged canyon and is perched high on the steep slopes of the mountain. It's difficult to see from below, so one would never suspect a shaft was hidden there unless he or she came upon the site accidentally and looked behind the trees. The spot is also surrounded on three sides by sloping banks. Thinking back, we cannot remember seeing a vehicle in the vicinity, and often wondered how the three got there. Perhaps the doctor brought them out, and then returned each week to see their progress. However, they did have a tent and supplies near a tree.

141

Yes, these hills and others still hold unsolved mysteries. Perhaps the individuals involved in sinking this old shaft were following a small silver vein, and it pinched out in depth.

Most mines in this area are located well below the mountains. It's rare that one would be discovered so near the summit of the hills, but that old saying, "gold is where you find it," may also apply to silver.

Another interesting point: the Lost San Pedro Mine is supposedly hidden in the same vicinity as the old shaft. Could they be one and the same? And did it once hold a portion of the vast treasures hidden by the padres from Tumacacori? If it is the San Pedro, I can see why it could have been missed all these years, until found by the doctor. If he did remove a treasure from its depths, only the surrounding mountains know.

Chapter 33

THE MAP

W e knew this treasure game wouldn't be easy, as many more experienced than us have searched, only to come up empty handed. We had climbed, slid and explored many desert mountains for almost eleven months. The only items found were: a cutlass, one rusted antique gun and a small buckle, but we never became discouraged.

In our possession we had an original Spanish map that was a complex puzzlement. It contained numbers, directions in Spanish *varas*, signs, crisscrossing lines and no doubt hidden clues known only to those who penned the old document several hundred years earlier. It gave detailed directions to all the mines of Tumacácori, but deleted their names from the map. Looking at the mine location at the upper right hand corner, it could either be the San Pedro or the Isabella Mine. This map was a maze of crisscrossing lines leading to different mine sites, with measurements in *varas*. If one could decipher this riddle it should eventually lead to all the mines once worked by the padres from Tumacácori.

Say you found the San Pedro Mine, and definitely knew its location on this map. Directions are given to the Guadalupe Mine from this site. It then would be quite simple to measure off the correct distance and discover the mine. Sounds easy, but it's not.

You measure the distance on the map then hike to that site, expecting to find the mine. Nothing is there but flat terrain with no signs of mining activity. Are the measurements on the map correct, or are they to be divided or multiplied by some other secretive number somewhere on the ancient map? Other strange symbols on the document are mystifying and meaningless, except for those knowing the clues. These padres were masterful at concealing their treasures and used many tricks, especially in laying out their maps and directions.

We eventually discovered the legendary Isabella Mine, and still could not locate any others from its location. The directions would say something like: 1800 *varas* in a southerly direction you'll come upon, say, the Guadalupe Mine. Following this we'd find ourselves near a sheer drop-off, or mountainside that hasn't changed since year one.

This entire game is like a detective mystery, a clue here, a clue there, misinformation and leads that go nowhere. But still you push on searching for that missing clue that eventually will solve the mystery. It's a fascinating game of cat and mouse, if you have the patience of Job. If any treasure is ever found it will be a combination of long research, hard work and old Lady Luck.

Chapter 34

THE HIDDEN CHAMBER WITHIN CERRO PELON

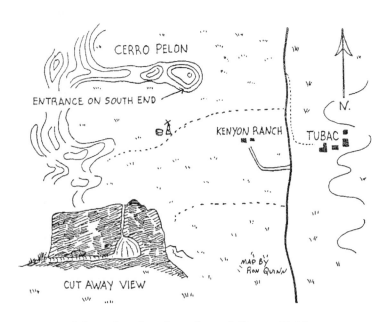

Map showing interior of Cerro Pelón.

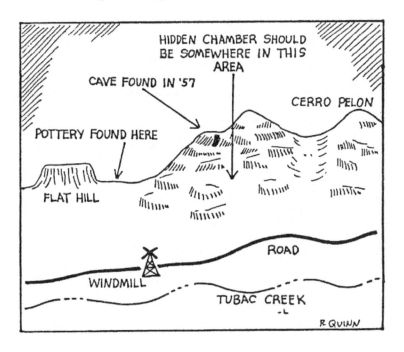

"Relentless Search" map

Cerro Pelón near Tubac, AZ.

Southern Arizona Trails, Vol. 3, No. 46, September 01, 1987, page 17

Just two miles west and a little north of Tubac stands a lone pile of sun-baked volcanic rock. It's located at the tail end of a long ridge protruding from the Tumacacori Mountains, and is called Cerro Pelón [Bald Hill].

This small hill can be seen just north of the old windmill which is located on the dirt road that runs parallel with Tubac Creek. At one time, Indians lived within the chamber that's located inside this rugged hill and its entrance is concealed in such a way one could pass the opening and never notice it. This camber also has a natural chimney that extends from the dome-shaped room to the outside, some 12 to 15 feet above.

My partners and I first discovered this well-hidden entrance in 1957, while in the area searching for a large stone wall that runs across the summit of another ridge; but that's a different story.

Chuck and Roy explored the vicinity below me near the cliffs. In a short while I came upon a small natural crack in the rocks that snaked its way downward. The opening was about 18 inches long and perhaps 5 to 7 inches wide.

Picking up several fist-sized rocks, I rolled one down the opening to see if I could determine its depth. I heard the first rock clattering off the sides but never heard it hit bottom. I did this a couple of times with the same results.

Chuck called from below and I walked to the edge. He asked what I was doing, as they both heard a few light thumps coming from inside the mountain. I told them about the opening and dropping the rocks. Roy said to drop another, and again they heard the faint sound of the rock landing.

They were standing about four feet from the face of the cliff, near some desert shrubs that grew beside it. Both looked behind the bushes and spotted a small tunnel about 2 ½ x 2 ½ feet.

As I rejoined them, Roy had half his body inside the opening looking around. Chuck remained outside as Roy and I removed our packs and crawled in.

The opening was the same size all the way through and we both made our way slowing along. At various points along the route, other natural small chambers could be seen on either side, some large enough to accommodate one adult. Remnants of old straw were visible, indicating these were used as sleeping quarters by the previous occupants.

After crawling several more yards we reached a dome-shaped chamber, some five-to-six-feet high and perhaps seven to eight feet across. It was near noon and the sunlight was shining directly down the chimney and onto the dry dusty floor. The rocks I had dropped could be seen scattered about.

I turned toward Roy and said, "Everything is here but the treasure." Can you imagine if there were a pile of gold bars in the center with the sun shining on them? It would have been a scene right out of some adventure movie. All kidding aside, it would have been a perfect place to hide a treasure.

After emerging from the tunnel, we told Chuck what we had found. Afterward, we searched the entire area and discovered bits of pottery and some broken arrow heads. Roy found a number of large pieces of pottery on a long shelf. There was no doubt in our minds that Indians had lived here at one time.

We guessed the hidden tunnel and chamber could accommodate five or six persons. We checked the surrounding rocks for signs of Indian petroglyphs but didn't find any.

As I said, all this took place in '57. Perhaps some of the older residents in the area, especially the ranchers, might still know of its existence today. If the shrubs are still in front of the entrance, one could pass by and never realize a tunnel was concealed behind them.

When we made the discovery, there were many pieces of pottery scattered about, but that was 29 years ago. There's a very good possibility that others have found this spot and carried off any remaining fragments.

It's only a short distance from the highway, and would make an interesting trip. If for nothing else, just to visit the chamber hidden within the mountain.

While there, we saw no evidence of animals using the place as a den. If you decide to visit this place, be careful, carry a flashlight and look out for snakes. Also if you fear being in a small enclosure, don't crawl in — the passageway is long, dark and narrow. Good luck.

THE RELENTLESS SEARCH

Southern Arizona Trails, Vol. 3, No. 56, November 10, 1987, page 23

y article, "The Hidden Chamber Within Cerro Pelón" appeared in the Sept. 1, 1987 issue of *Southern Arizona Trails*. I hadn't been back to the area mentioned since we first found this chamber on April 1, 1957. The entry in our diary is under this date, and reads as follows:

We took off for Tubac to see Breezy, [a friend of Roy's] about a cave in the mountains. He gave us directions, so we drove on over. We found a lot of caves all right, but nothing was in them. Ron found a tunnel that twisted into the mountain for 30 feet and ended at a large chamber. A small opening ran to the top of the hill. We crawled in and out of several for the better part of the afternoon, but found only pieces of pottery and some arrowheads. It was another hot day.

Over the years I have been under the impression it was discovered on the southern slopes of Cerro Pelón, since my story appeared, several people have searched for this tunnel. One was Dean Yedica, Jr. of Green Valley. I had met him while visiting A. J. Allan in Arivaca, and he seemed interested in the story.

As of this writing, Dean has made perhaps two trips into this rugged county and failed to locate the hidden chamber. This of course was not his fault. Bill Conley, another treasure hunter I know asked if I would show him the tunnel and chamber. A few days later we left, with me full of confidence I could walk directly to this hidden passageway. Unbeknownst to me at the time, the "Thunder Gods" were about to play their old tricks. After an hour's drive, and a half mile hike we stood before Cerro Pelón.

I realized at once it was the wrong location, as the few cliffs scattered about the slopes didn't resemble the ones we had searched in '57. The nameless peak just west of this mountain looked somewhat familiar, so our search began there.

After three hours of climbing, slipping and poking our heads into anything looking suspicious, we could not locate the tunnel, the crack above on the flat or the large cave Roy and I found. Also missing was the oval shaped small cave I happened to stumble upon while taking a rest.

I had taken several pictures in '57, and these I had with me. One shows me sitting beside this small cave. The others were of Roy standing near the entrance of the large one looking out across the valley. Everything outside was overexposed as I set the camera for the dark interior, [but] you could still make out a faint image of a mountain off in the distance, and this Bill and I were trying to recognize.

Try as I may, absolutely nothing was found that looked familiar. While on the mountain, I hiked around to the west side and Bill searched in the opposite direction. As I inched my way around a dangerous area, I glanced up for a second and stopped in my tracks. Off in the distance rising from the ground stood a small lone hill with a flat top, and high cliffs could be seen on its southeast side.

Immediately I recognized it as the hill we all hiked toward after leaving Roy's jeep in the vicinity of the windmill. By now I was somewhat fatigued, and I guess Bill was also from our relentless pursuit, searching for both the cave and the hidden tunnel. We decided to return at a later date and continue our search from this point. There isn't anything of monetary value out there, but it's the challenge now, I know that tunnel is lurking somewhere among those cliffs, and I'm determined to find it.

Oct. 19 found us again on our quest. The area below the flat hill was carefully searched but no caves. Bill, however, did find a small fragment of pottery nearby. We again checked the photos and saw the similarity between the faint image and that of Tumacacori Peak's eastern slope. They matched perfectly from where we stood. The large cave then would have to be somewhere in the general vicinity.

As we paused beneath some mesquite trees for a rest, Bill happened to look north and spotted an opening high on the south side of the sister mountain west of Cerro Pelón. The tall narrow entrance sloped at the same angle as the one discovered by Roy and me. It looked as though it was perhaps half a mile away, and located on a steep rocky incline.

After climbing the rugged hillside and being raked by catsclaw bushes occasionally, we arrived at the dark opening and stood peering into the entrance. It was definitely the same cave we had discovered 30 years earlier. The cool confines of its interior offered a welcome relief as the temperature was in the high 90s. We took a number of pictures and also some with the flash unit. Later we duplicated the photo of Roy pointing out toward the mountains, with Bill standing in.

The opening of this cave can only be seen from a certain angle. If you happen to be too far east or west, the dark entrance appears as nothing more than a shadow on the face of the cliffs.

After finding it I would have bet my life that hidden tunnel was nearby, but after searching a while, neither it nor the crack above could be found. Talk about being frustrated. I sat looking around in hopes of spotting something that might jog my memory, but nothing did. I apologized to Bill for my failure to find the elusive tunnel, as I knew he really wanted to see it. He said there's no need to as it's been 30 years since last being here, and besides we did find the cave, so this is the right area. I can retrace my steps to everything we discovered over these past 31 years without referring to a map, but for some strange reason I have a mental block when it comes to this one little location.

When nothing of real importance was discovered at the site but some pottery chips and arrowheads, we never returned. So I naturally put the incident out of my thoughts. Even Chuck and Roy couldn't recall where our hiking had taken us during that April afternoon. They just remember walking north toward some cliffs, and many are located in the region. It's quite possible we explored several different locations in the same vicinity where cliffs are prominent. If this is the case, I have been under the impression the pottery, caves, and tunnel were all discovered at the same site.

Bill, Dean [Yedica] and I will venture forth soon and make another attempt in finding this elusive passageway. I have doubts the tunnel has caved in. Even if it has, that crack above should still be visible. I promised Bill I'd show him the site, and I've never failed before in similar projects and I'm not going to start this late in life.

From now on, it's total war between me and the Tumacacori Range. Come to think of it, it's always been war between us over the last 31 years. If you let your guard down for a moment while climbing about them, these devilish hills will reach out and grab ya, or change some of the country around while you're not looking, just to confuse you.

Of course the above is said only in jest, but these mountains can be quite dangerous to those that do not take them seriously.

This desert range is made up mostly of lava, eroded down over millions of years to form canyons and valleys. Nothing mysterious lies within them (I hope), but at times you think these dark menacing hills are out to get only you. Several times they almost succeeded, but that's another story.

FORT BOWIE / DOS CABEZAS ADVENTURES

Chapter 35

BUFFALO SOLDIERS LOST SILVER MINE

Southern Arizona Trails International, Vol. 3, No, 25, April 7, 1987, Page 1, 8, 21

Between 1891 and 1892, a detachment of black troopers (called Buffalo Soldiers by the Apache) were stationed at Fort Bowie, Arizona. [7] This well-known fort was built to protect the populace of the area and settlers passing through. Most used "Apache Pass" and Fort Bowie was located just south of it, near the eastern entrance to the famous pass. This was the country of the dreaded Chihuahua [Chiricahua] Apache, under the leadership of Geronimo and Cochise.

A group of hostiles had been raiding along the Sulphur Spring Valley and would always ride off toward the northeast after a bloody raid on some unsuspecting lone traveler or rancher. Each time the cavalry gave chase, they lost the hostiles among the numerous canyons in the area of the Dos Cabezas Mountains.

A small patrol of these Buffalo Soldiers were returning from another mission, when they spotted a medium size band of Apaches heading toward a narrow canyon on the western slopes of these mountains. They followed unnoticed, then tracked them on foot a short distance. The Apaches climbed a long ridge, dismounted and disappeared among a large clump of trees and rocks.

Looking through some field glasses, the sergeant noticed they had a small camp hidden there. One Apache was observed fetching water from a small spring, which is quite rare in this part of the desert county. Returning to Fort Bowie, the sergeant filed his report then retired to the barracks.

Several days later, orders came down for an early morning raid on this encampment. A company of Buffalo Soldiers was selected. At three in the morning they arrived unnoticed at the mouth of the narrow canyon. From here on out it would be on foot. In less than an hour and a half, they had completely surrounded the ridge and went unseen by the lone Apache on watch.

One trooper, whom I shall call, Jones, as his real name has been lost in the retelling of this story, was located about twenty yards below the encampment. The attack would commence when the Captain gave the signal, just after dawn.

While sitting on the rocks Jones happened to notice an odd black vein of mineral cutting through the face of the rocks. Removing his bayonet, he broke off several pieces. In the twilight before dawn the new brake glistened like silver. To his surprise, it was pure native silver with small veins of gold zigzagging across it. It would be another two months before his enlistment was up, so Jones put the samples in his pocket, took in the lay of the land and remembered various landmarks.

Fifteen minutes later the action began. There were perhaps 20 hostiles hidden among the rocks, and most put up a good fight. Thinking of the rich silver he had discovered; Jones wanted to live long enough to

---

[7] The 24th Infantry (one of the Buffalo Soldiers regiments) was stationed at Fort Bowie from October 1891 to June 1892 according to Fort Bowie National Historic Site historian Larry Ludwig.

enjoy it, so he didn't attempt any heroic actions. The skirmish was going well for his company, so he held back some of his firing. He didn't want to attract too much return fire in his direction. The foremost thing on his mind at the moment was living through the battle so he could enjoy some of the good life the silver would provide. The conflict lasted a little over an hour or so, before the Apache surrendered. Out of 20 hostiles about 12 were killed. His company lost a few and several had minor injuries.

A few days later, Jones told his close friend Wilson about the silver. Wilson would be mustering out a couple of weeks after Jones, and Jones said he would take him in as a partner as there was enough silver for both. He showed the samples to Wilson and said it was located near a spring, above the valley on the western slopes of the mountain toward the northwest. It also was near a natural amphitheater with high cliffs above.

After leaving the cavalry, Jones headed for Tucson to purchase supplies. He informed Wilson he'd meet him at the main gate of the fort the afternoon of his discharge. That day came and went with no sign of Jones. Wilson waited a few days then traveled to Tucson, looking for him. He checked most of the mining supply stores and one storekeeper did remember selling equipment to a large black man. There weren't many blacks in Tucson at the time, so remembering him came easy.

Wilson searched for his friend but he was never seen or heard of again. An old rifle was discovered, along with some mining tools in the late 20s near the Dos Cabezas Mountains that very well could have belonged to Jones. He might have decided to return to the ledge and sample it more before meeting Wilson. Blinded by the discovery of this new wealth, he might have let his guard down momentarily and it cost Jones his life, as the Apache were still on the prowl. Wilson searched for the landmarks Jones mentioned for a short while; then left the territory, never to return.

In late 1950 my brother and I met a retired geologist in Southern Arizona that was here for his health. Prof. Moore [A. C. More] was in his late 70s and lived with son, Bob, in a small community of Continental [now part of Green Valley], some twenty miles south of Tucson. We would stop by occasionally to visit and get his advice on various ore samples we had found. He was old, but still sharp when it came to anything concerning geology.

We told him during one of our visits we had planned to move camp over to the Dos Cabezas area, south of Willcox and do some prospecting during the fall months.

Prof. Moore had spent a considerable amount of time in this area during the 30s, doing some geologic work for the mining company he worked for in either North or South Dakota. There are two very large faults that cross each other beneath Dos Cabezas, and these can be traced for hundreds of miles. He was making a study of these and also checking for mineral deposits in the area. There were some mines on the western side of this mountain which produced some gold and silver, but nothing like the vein Jones had discovered.

Prof. Moore told us while we're over there we should search for his native silver he found while climbing about the hills. The find was accidental while looking for the source of some aragonite crystals he had discovered in a small tributary. He traced them up the slope to an area beneath some cliffs. The silver was found nearby as he dug for more crystals. He broke off several large pieces and was amazed at the richness of the ore. Little veins of gold could be seen throughout the specimen he held.

The discovery was made on an active mining claim, so he placed the samples in his pocket and moved on, but not before covering the discovery site. He thought he'd keep this secret and return on his own sometime in the future, and see if the claim was still active. If not, he'd file on it himself.

Chuck and I heard the story of the trooper discovering the same type of silver, so it was obvious both had found the same outcropping. Prof. Moore also mentioned it was near a large amphitheater, and on a flat above his discovery there was evidence of a spring which had long since dried up. He told us exactly how to find the silver outcropping. After we arrived in the area, camp was set up near the mouth of a rocky canyon, and it was also full of snakes. Using his directions we still could not locate the landmarks. No cliffs, no amphitheater or spring.

We returned to Continental and informed him of these facts. His first words were, "If I could climb I'd go over and put a flag on it." He still insisted we were in the correct area, and to return and search again. We did, again and again but couldn't find a thing he spoke of. Prof. Moore did indeed find the silver, as when he was visiting an associate back east years later he displayed one of the large samples. A friend of this associate happened by and after seeing the fine ore asked if he could show it to his wife, who remained in his car. He did, and it was the last Prof. Moore ever saw of this remarkable piece of silver. The friend drove off with it.

Many years later, Prof. Moore heard that this "friend" had used this beautiful specimen to swindle over $50,000 from a group of investors, just on the strength of this single sample. He must have told one convincing story.

We came to the conclusion, Prof. Moore's story is true, but being in his 70s and spending nearly five months in the area, he just got two or three of his stories overlapping one another and was confused. He had found the silver but placed the location in another area. His son, Bob, told us his Dad had been doing this for several years now, getting things confused. No matter how we tried to explain this to him, he wouldn't hear of it. Time after time we returned and informed him there wasn't any amphitheater or high cliffs in the area he sent us to. At times he'd become a little annoyed and say, "We needed glasses," or "If that silver had teeth it would jump up and bite us on the ass."

Prof. Moore passed away several years later, and his son Bob never was interested in mining or searching for this elusive silver ledge, so we put the story on a shelf for awhile. One thing we never found out was why he didn't return while still young and file on this claim, if it was open.

Years later we tried our luck again, but we moved further south. Only then did we start to see the similarity between this country and both stories. Search as we did, and I mean covering every slope beneath any cliffs we happened to come upon, the silver or aragonite crystals were never found. If we located a flat ridge, there wasn't any amphitheater. If we came upon something that resembled an amphitheater, in our definition of the word, there weren't any cliffs or ridge nearby.

Before writing this story, there were only three others besides myself that knew of Prof. Moore's story. We believe this rich ledge is still out there on some rocky slope above the valley, and yes, we still search occasionally for it. If you want to give it a try, be our guests. Again we have a tale about two individuals finding the same silver about 50 odd years apart, and both discovered it by accident. One disappears after leaving the fort, and Prof. Moore never returned until years later when he couldn't climb four steps without help. I'm quite sure it'll be discovered again. Maybe not in my lifetime but someday a prospector will be climbing about those hills and stumble right over it.

The problem we had was, after all those years being away from that area, Prof. Moore was confused when it came to telling us the correct location.

Chapter 36

THE GUMP BOYS

Just north of Camelback Mountain nestled in the valley sat Willcox, Cochise County, Arizona. After searching for the "Moore Ledge" [A. C. More, see previous chapter] as we came to call it, we decided to remain in the vicinity for awhile and prospect other areas. Several mines were discovered and worked in the late 1880s south of Willcox.

While obtaining gas at the local service station, Jeff, the proprietor inquired where we intended to camp. "South of Camelback," Chuck answered.

Looking up, Jeff said, "Be careful you don't wander onto the Gump's land. Those idiots might take a shot at ya."

We asked Jeff to explain as we followed him into his office where a wiry looking toothless individual by the name of Hank, sat in a beat up chair with the stuffing hanging out. He heard our conversation and said, "Them Gump's are a crazy lot, especially the four sons. Nothing but a bunch of sons of bitches, them Gumps!"

Jeff sat down and continued, "No one knows where they came from. Just arrived one day, bought ten acres and built a dirt floor shack. Moved in, and dug a well. When they come to town, about twice a month, the old man sits in their flatbed truck staring straight ahead, while the sons do the shopping. The four would walk around in a tight group, not saying a word to anyone." Jeff opened a soft drink, offering us one and continued, "If anyone accidently brushed against one, all they'd hear is a low grunt."

Hank cut in saying, "Not a soul around these parts say a word to them. I doubt the sheriff would go out to their place alone. Hell, he'd call in the National Guard if there was trouble. That gang wouldn't come peaceable." This Hank was a character, like others we had met in small hamlets across the state

We regretted never having seen the Gumps in town. Jeff did say we had missed them by one day the last time in. Chuck said jokingly, "We should drive out and pay them a visit."

Hank again spoke up, "That old bastard could walk but he never left the truck. Guess he thought somebody might steal the damn thing. Also, two rifles hung under the rear window. That old man sat with a large black brimmed hat pulled low around his ears—had a face like old granite, all rough and everything."

After listening to all this, I said, "If they never caused trouble, why all the bad mouthing? There are folks that enjoy being alone and basically are unfriendly."

Chuck, looking quite serious came up with this bit of witticism. "Maybe they're shy and waiting for somebody to say, hi neighbor, welcome to the community."

Even the postman said the Gumps received little mail. Perhaps two or three letters a year. By now I began feeling sorry for them. They never caused any trouble, yet were being put down.

Nobody knew where their money came from, but all bills were paid. They didn't work a mine, do odd jobs around town or work cattle. I thought perhaps they found "Moore's Ledge,"—a possibility but far out. Several times we passed the road leading to their place. Chuck suggested we drive up waving a white flag.

Later we learned they were just simple country folks who kept to themselves, not wanting to bother with city slickers. Willcox back then was a tight knit community. The Gump's just didn't fit in. With their odd ways, rumors began like in most small towns when strangers arrive and keep to themselves.

We helped two of the Gump boys by pulling their truck out of a ditch, one afternoon. They were quiet and polite, thanking us in a low voice. Like they say, "You can't judge a book by its cover." I'll have to admit, though, they resembled character from that old movie *Deliverance*. They looked to be in their late thirties, stood over six feet, wore bib overalls, had a six-month growth of beard, several teeth missing and eyes cold as steel.

I often wish I could have taken a picture of all five. It would have been another interesting photo for our collection of memorable characters we met during our journey through Arizona.

Upon returning to camp we were surprised to find Roy there. "Hell," I said, "we expected you'd be sailing the Orient by now." He said he couldn't find a good ship so decided to return for another month.

Chapter 37

A CRACK OF THUNDER

Base camp on the Willcox dry lake bed.

Thunder storms usually occur in late afternoon during the summer months. Occasionally, one would come rumbling in before dawn. About 4:00 in the morning one crept in, hitting without warning. A crack of thunder hit above our tents like an artillery shell, awakening us from a sound sleep. We leaped from our cots, as Roy came charging in from his tent shouting, "Batten down the hatches and clear the decks. This is one hell of a squall mates."

Camp was in a narrow canyon, and the wind came rushing through like an express train. Peering outside, lightening could be seen dancing horizontality across the menacing clouds, while several bolts struck nearby mountains. Rain came quickly, filling the arroyos with rushing water.

We always camped on high ground, so there wasn't any danger of being washed away. Roy's tent was shaking wildly but stood its ground. We took turns holding onto the center pole supporting ours. The side facing the wind buckled and swelled throughout the raging storm and it shook violently. Roy kept saying, "Is my tent still with us?" as thunder rumbled above and lightening continued flashing across the skies.

Luckily we had closed the jeep windows. If not, the interiors would have been soaked by the driving rain. As the storm raged on we sat around joking. Roy said, "If the wind gets much stronger, this tent and us will suddenly be airborne."

Nature's fury lasted almost half an hour before slowly moving on. Afterward, we stepped from the safety of the tent to survey any damage. Roy's tent held up, but was partly open allowing the rain to soak his sleeping bag. Two camp chair and two buckets were blown away but later found in the brush. A towel Roy had hanging from a tree was long gone.

We had experienced several bad storms, but nothing like this one. It was quite devastating to a few homes and ranchers in the area. Later we heard on the radio the storm had gusts of wind approaching 65 miles an hour and ravished portions of south Tucson 70 miles west.

In our letters home we never mentioned any dangerous situations as Mom worried enough about us crawling around the wilds of Arizona. In her letters she would mention her prayers were always with us. During that intense storm, they were answered.

Chapter 38

FORT BOWIE

Chuck at Fort Bowie.

While in the vicinity of Bowie, Arizona, we decided to visit the ruins of this historic location. The site was perhaps a mile due south of camp, just over a ridge.

After making the long climb, we arrived at this once thriving fort. Only crumbling adobe walls remained of the barracks. Other foundations could be seen throughout the region. What I believe was the stockade stood intact as the building was made of stone.

Near a slope, Roy and Chuck discovered one of the three known garbage pits. Rummaging through, we found numerous discarded items. Old bottles, buttons, and what resembled small medicine bottles.

For almost half an hour we wandered throughout the ruins, taking pictures. No roads led into the fort at that time, so it wasn't visited much. The only visitors that day were us, a gentle breeze blowing across the abandoned site, and a lone horny toad seeking shade.

This once proud fort was now reduced to crumbling adobe under the harsh Arizona sun. Many battles were fought from this lonely outpost against the Chiricahua Apache. It was established after the 1862 Battle of Apache Pass, depicted in several motion pictures. The commanding officers residence was a two story wooden structure. The fort finally closed October 17, 1894.

I believe it was dismantled and moved to a military establishment somewhere in California.

As we returned to camp I stopped for no apparent reason. Turning, I took a wide shot of the ruins below with the camera. Many years later I saw a photo of the fort taken in 1894. To my amazement, it was taken from the same spot as mine—give or take a few yards. I had never seen the old print before, so it wasn't my subconscious mind coming into play. Was this a coincidence, or something bordering on the paranormal? Some believe ghosts still linger among the ruins. Perhaps one influenced me in taking the picture.

The fort is now a National Historic Site, and visited by those taking the time to see this notable location that once helped guard settlers crossing the pass.

On the west side of the pass there once was a sign erected near a large clearing. It read: Site of Wagon Train Massacre 1861. Last time through the pass I don't remember seeing it. The site is located some 15 miles south of Interstate 10 near the small community of Bowie.

Chapter 39

THE LAWHON RANCH

W hile prospecting south of Apache Pass, we'd have to drive into the town of Bowie to fill our water barrel. Near the eastern entrance to this pass, stood an old ranch built during the 1800s. Later we learned it was the famous "Lawhon Ranch," a renowned part of Arizona history.

We stopped by to ask if it would be possible to obtain our water there, as it would save us a long dusty round trip to Bowie. An elderly lady answered the door. After introductions, Chuck asked about the water. "Of course," she said inviting us in. She was Anna Lawhon, owner of the ranch.

**Anna Lawhon c. 1934,
long before meeting Ron & Chuck.**
Courtesy of Mrs. Janice E. Grizzle

Mining was mentioned and this interested her. Anna told us of some foothills north of the house we should consider exploring. Many years before, when the place was a working ranch, some cowhands happened upon a small cave among these hills. Upon entering, they discovered large clusters or crystals throughout the interior. Some measured over seven inches in length. Most were transparent, while others had a yellowish hue. Gathering several they returned, displaying the oddities to her husband.

At that period little interest was shown, as round up time was nearing. No other trips were made to the cave. In the following years the location was slowly forgotten. Stepping to a window, she pointed toward the foothills harboring the cave. If found there was a market for such crystal specimens.

Anna gave us permission to search, as the hills were located on her ranch property. This was old homestead land covering many square miles. Anna was quite well known and pure frontier stock. Born in 1876, I believe in Saint Louis, Missouri, her family moved west by covered wagon. She married a Joseph Lawhon in 1897. Anna had that rugged outdoors appearance, brought about by years of hard living. Upon the passing of her husband she had run the ranch herself since 1929.

159

The ranch had been around since the turbulent times of Apache raids. Picking up a framed picture she handed it to us. It was a photo of a young girl standing beside a well; nearby stood two Indians. We blinked in disbelief, as the one nearest the girl was, none other than the notorious Apache, Geronimo.

Anna stated the girl was her. During that time, around 1883, Geronimo would occasionally stop to water his horses. Settlements and outlying ranches were often under attack by his band of hostiles. For reasons unknown, he never harmed those at the Lawhon ranch. Either the photographer was already present at the ranch or knew of Geronimo's forthcoming visit.

This friendship was never fully explained. But most likely came about by some mutual trust. Perhaps the Lawhon's helped some needy Indian one time.

Many times under the cover of darkness, Anna would see his band silently ride up and draw water from the well, then move out as silently as they arrived. Several weeks would pass before making another appearance; no doubt returning from their frequent raids into Mexico.

During our visits, Anna told us fascinating stories of her life on the western frontier. They made our two year adventure seem like "a walk in the park." Numerous articles have been written about this proud lady of the west.

One day we decided to hunt for the crystal cave. After traveling overland a mile, we hiked the remaining distance. After hours of relentless searching, no cave was discovered; the reason most likely being that over the years sand and rock cascading down from above eventually covered the entrance. It might take years before the opening would once more appear through the process of erosion. What cannot be found one year, might be discovered the next. The area was mostly limestone, where caves have a tendency to form. Perhaps many were just yards below us, ranging in size from 30 feet to several miles in length.

Occasionally while hiking we'd get into one of our silly moods. This time, we stopped atop a hill for lunch. It was quite windy as it usually is in the Sulfur Springs Valley. Chuck found a piece of ocotillo bent like a Shepherds staff. He began quoting from the bible and acting somewhat like a fool.

While we were having a sandwich the bread began drying due to the wind. Looking toward Roy, Chuck said jokingly, "Hey brother, come break bread with us this day."

"Your damn right!" Roy's answered. "It's dry as hell from the wind."

With staff in hand, Chuck continued with his biblical portrayal saying we were the Three Wise Men. "Hell no," came Roy's response. "We're the three wise guys." That title remained for years to come. One thing led to another and this foolishness continued clear back to camp.

Many large caves exist within this region including the Colossal Cave east of Tucson. Another cave is located near the border town of Portal. It's been searched very little and numerous deep chambers remain unexplored. Some suggest it extends clear into Mexico.

Several years ago, another cave [Kartchner Caverns] was found near Benson, Arizona. It's discovers kept the site secret many years before revealing its location to the state.

Chapter 40

RIGGS RANCH

T he four of us were prospecting several large quartz veins near Helen's Dome, a lofty oval peak west of the ruins of Fort Bowie. These enormous veins stretch across the country and several can be traced for miles. This region is known as "pocket country." After discovering a deposit of gold and removing a substantial amount, the vein suddenly disappears.

Chuck and I were in the process of examining one vein while Walt was off exploring another. Roy was below us with pike in hand, pounding on some worthless andesite. It was quite windy and the sound was echoing throughout the hills.

Roy knew the treasure business, but little about prospecting. When striking andesite, it makes a tinkling sound as it flakes off the dry surface, while gold being malleable makes a solid thud when struck. Hours later we found Roy behind some boulders. Looking up, he said in disgust, "Damn country! Too much tinkle, tinkle and no thud." Walt's luck was no better, so we returned to camp several miles away as the sun began setting.

Upon arriving at camp we found a note on the tent. It read: "This is private land belonging to the Riggs Ranch. Please move."

The following morning as we prepared to break camp, two riders on horses were observed coming in our direction. It was Mrs. Riggs, owner of the ranch and her daughter who was leading her mother's horse. We apologized for camping, as we thought this was government or state land.

The old gal was blind, and like Mrs. Lawhon, was pure frontier stock. She was tall, lean, thin lipped and wore a black style Spanish hat and scarf, and looked mean as a hornet. They didn't want strangers on the property. Perhaps in the past they had trouble with squatters on their range.

Mrs. Riggs said quite firmly, she wanted us out. Chuck mentioned, we had camped on Mrs. Lawhon's land several weeks, and knew her quite well. This seemed to quiet her down some, but she still insisted we leave. A few moments later, both rode off.

Chuck said jokingly, "Let's remain and see what happens."

"Hell no," replied Walt. "She'll gather the ranch hands and ride roughshod right over us."

Roy's response was, "We sure don't want any range war erupting. Like that scene from *Duel In The Sun*, when Lionel Barrymore rode out with hundreds of hands to his fence line, daring the railroad to cross his land."

Roy had an exceptional memory when it came to western movies, and would bring various scenes up when the proper occasion arose. Later we learned the Riggs were another old established family which had been around since year one.

Another time Roy was attempting to adjust the carburetor on his jeep, as it was running rough. He was a great friend, but like prospecting, he knew little about vehicles. The more he tried, the worse it sounded. Finally in despair he came walking back mumbling to himself. "Lousy stinking four banger (meaning the engine) can't ever tune the thing." Walt rose, asking him to raise the hood and start it up. Within a minute, he had the motor running smoothly. Roy, jumping from the jeep said, "What did you do?" Walt's remark, "I'll never tell."

We all knew Walt's dry wit, and sometimes his annoying joking ways. Amusement like this occurred most of the time, especially while exploring. Roy seemed to always be the center of the jokes. With his easy going nature, Roy knew it was all in jest. Being close friends, nobody took this foolishness seriously.

One time Walt said to Roy while hiking along, "You better learn to fix your jeep. If you ever break down alone out here, your ass has had it." Roy, looking quite indignant, replied with this gem, "Well, ... if that ever occurs, please do me a favor. If you're hiking along and happen upon a pile of dry coyote droppings; please don't kick it aside, they might be me."

Before leaving this interesting country we stopped off to visit Mrs. Lawhon once more. How fortunate we were to have had the privilege of knowing this elegant lady.

PRESCOTT SUMMER BREAK

Chapter 41

HEADING NORTH

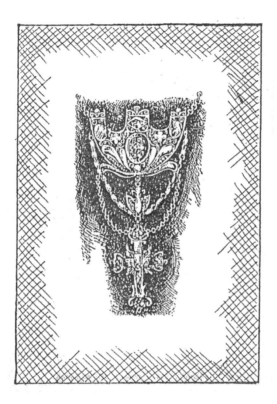

Perhaps the necklace would look like this.

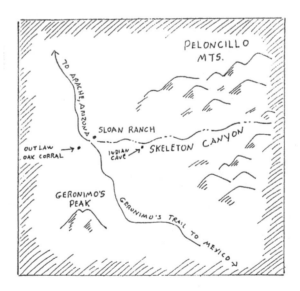

Original route of the Golden Necklace when it entered Arizona.

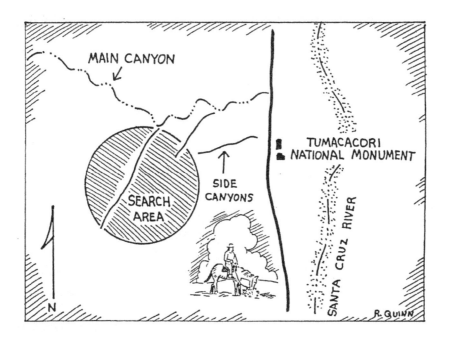

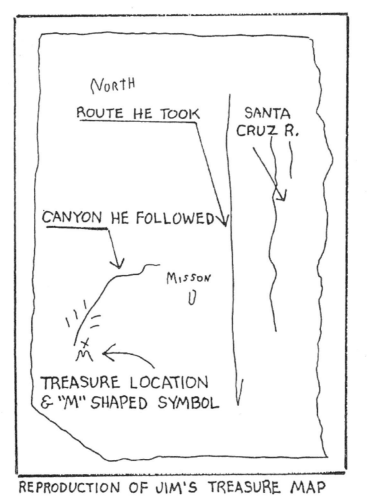

REPRODUCTION OF JIM'S TREASURE MAP

(Early Summer 1957)

T he desert was beginning to warm up, and Chuck and I didn't relish spending another summer baking on it like last year. We decided to head north to the cool country around Prescott, Arizona. Roy returned to the ships until August, and Walt wanted to visit old Pop.

Before leaving, Walt said jokingly, "Don't break down on your way Roy, as I won't be around to help you." All Roy did was to give him a dirty look. He knew it was all in fun, but with Walt's dry wit, you could never tell if he meant something or not.

After arriving in Prescott, we found an excellent campsite high among the mountains bordering the city. I believe it was named Union Peak, and was located several miles southeast. That evening I drew a map showing Roy how to locate us, and sent it off by mail several days later.
Prescott was Arizona's first capital from 1864-67. It had quite a history and many historic buildings, one being Henry Goldwater's Victorian style home located on Nob Hill and built in 1894.

At that time, 1957, Prescott was a rather small community, quite pretty with a large city park in the center. Whiskey Row, a famous street, was just west of the park. During the following months we did some prospecting, but little mineral was located.

Come September 20th, Roy arrived several weeks early. We spent many pleasant hours talking to the older residents that frequented the park. From them we heard many enjoyable stories of the area, but from a Tom Cooper, we heard a tale that eventually returned us to those haunting Tumacacoris.

1882 BANDIT LOOT— GOLD NECKLACE

Southern Arizona Trails, Vol. 3, No. 77, March 19, 1988, Pages, 1, 12-13, 19

At first I had second thoughts about writing this intriguing story as we occasionally search for this small, but fabulous treasure. Without elaborating, my partners and I made a significant find several years ago. I can now do my own thing, to quote our younger generation.

I thought, why be greedy and keep this treasure tale to ourselves? Why not pass the original story on, as it might offer somebody else the opportunity to perhaps discover something of great value?

Before relating this story, there were only three others beside myself, plus Tom [Cooper], who knew of the tale. We searched without success a number of times for the elusive treasure, but we still believe it's hidden out among the rocks where it was first buried sometime in 1882.

The mysterious item is a very large solid gold necklace, studded with precious jewels, and a "big diamond," measuring almost an inch across. Below dangles a gold cross, suspended from a gold chain.

The necklace originally came from Mexico from the turbulent times when puppet Emperor Maximilian ruled in 1865. During his reign, a robbery occurred at the palace. Jewelry and gold were stolen, one of the items being the necklace.

Most of this property was eventually recovered, but many fine pieces of jewelry were lost forever. The most impressive item, of course, was the mysterious gold necklace.

This no doubt had passed through several ownerships before falling into the hands of Mexican smugglers.

Through Skeleton Canyon wound the old Smugglers Trail from Sonora. It crossed a corner of New Mexico and into Southern Arizona.

There are numerous tales of blood, intrigue and murder associated with this canyon, and I'm quite certain an entire book could be written about these accounts.

American outlaws would occasionally ambush the smugglers and steal their cargoes. Many battles were fought among the rocks and cliffs that line the canyon and countless rumors of hastily buried treasures have been related around campfires and cocktail lounges throughout the Southwest.

One of these infamous outlaws was a William Graham. He and his partners would rob smugglers at times as they attempted to pass through this notorious canyon of violent and sudden death.

During one of these raids in 1882, a gang member discovered the necklace and succeeded in hiding it in his shirt—keeping it for himself. Several weeks later, the outlaw arrived in Tucson and approached a prominent businessman who dabbled occasionally in stolen contraband.

In the privacy of this gentleman's home, the outlaw unfolded a cloth, revealing the magnificent necklace. Our "pillar of the community" was taken by its exquisite beauty and offered his unshaven guest $5,000 (a steal), which he promptly displayed.

The unsavory character knew he hadn't been seen entering the businessman's home. Without giving his decision a second thought, he drew his knife, plunging it several times into the unsuspecting, very surprised gentleman.

With both the gold and necklace in his possession, the outlaw crept from the residence and rode south toward Mexico by way of the Santa Cruz River.

During his journey southward, our outlaw decided for some reason to hide the necklace before crossing into Mexico.

Reaching the ruins of an old Spanish mission (I would guess was Tumacacori), he rode "west" up a "twisting canyon," located in the vicinity of the church for a "mile or so." I'm almost positive it was the canyon located just northwest of the mission that winds its way behind Tumacacori Peak.

Dismounting, he looked about for a suitable location to conceal the necklace. Off toward the "south" almost a "hundred yards" he spotted a rock formation that was quite "recognizable," and could not be forgotten.

Upon reaching the site, the fleeing desperado dug a shallow hole near the base, burying the jewelry still wrapped in the cloth. After this was accomplished, he covered the spot with several rocks. Returning to the canyon "below," he continued his trek toward Nogales and vanished for nearly 34 years.

Around 1916 an old gentleman in rather poor health lived near Prescott, Ariz., and was about 72 years of age. Another younger man, known as Tom Cooper, looked after him for many years and had taken a liking to the old guy. During this time, the elderly fellow, whose name was Jim Wallace, related the above story to his benefactor.

He told how he had been in and out of various scrapes, both in Arizona and Mexico. One time he escaped from a Mexican prison with two others. The youngest of the three was later caught, and the other vanished near Chihuahua, Mexico, while attempting to reach Texas.

Jim managed to cross the border in 1887, but never tried retrieving the necklace he buried 34 years earlier for reasons he never mentioned.

There was a Jim Wallace riding with William Graham in 1882, but it's not known definitely if both were one in the same. To me it's obvious they were.

William Graham, alias Curley Bill Brocius, rode into Galeyville, Ariz., and was drinking with some of his men, including a Jim Wallace, a hired gun from back East.

A deputy sheriff from Tombstone happened to enter the same saloon where the rowdies were drinking. As he tried leaving after spotting them Curley Bill exchanged some rather harsh words with him and followed the lawman outside.

As the deputy mounted his horse, he drew and fired at Curley Bill. The bullet struck him in the neck and passed out his check, knocking out a single tooth, but causing no other damage. After healing, Curley Bill decided to leave Arizona forever.

Several months before dying, Jim tore a blank page from a book, drawing a rough map showing the approximate location where he buried the necklace. After Jim died, Tom made several attempts to find the treasure, but failed each time.

While in Prescott during the summer of '57, Chuck and I met Tom while camping south of town. Over a period of time we became close friends, and would sit in the city park swapping stories. He seemed quite interested in our prospecting and treasure hunting adventures.

One morning several months later he arrived at camp. That afternoon Tom told us the entire story revolving around Jim and the necklace. Reaching into his pocket he withdrew a folded piece of paper handing it to Chuck. It turned out to be the original map drawn by Jim himself.

Tom smiled and said, "These bones are too old to go climbing around the hills anymore, so maybe you youngsters can use the map to find the damn thing." He went on to say, "If ya do and it brings a good price, remember ole Tom up here."

Continuing, he said, "The way I've been feeling lately, you better find it soon, as I think I'm sitting in the shadow of that fellow in the black robe who carries that damn sickle."

The last we saw of old Tom was Aug. 17, the day before we broke camp and headed south to our old stamping grounds, the Tumacacoris, and the area the necklace was alleged to be hidden.

He told us to write him in care of General Delivery. We sent several letters during October, and one was returned. The way he spoke concerning his health, I suspect the old fellow went on "to his reward" soon after we left. He never told his age, but I'd say he was in his early 70s. Another one of those lonely old men that pass on unnoticed and now lays forgotten in some unkempt grave.

Chuck and I made several attempts to locate the necklace. We searched the terrain northwest of the mission, but neither of us could locate a rock formation that would be "recognizable" and not easily forgotten as mentioned by Jim.

Most of the rocky areas in the vicinity were carefully searched with our detector, but again nothing was discovered. As I stated in a previous article, I never had complete confidence in that machine, but unfortunately it was the only game in town. I often wonder how many things of value we missed.

Jim's crude map shows the mission and a canyon toward the west. Near this he drew an X, indicating the treasure's location. Beneath he drew a symbol, and perhaps this illustrates what the rock formation looks like, but nothing resembling it was found.

When Jim entered the "twisting" canyon there's a strong possibility he only followed it a short distance, then detoured up one of the branch offs. By examining a topo map of this area, you can see several tributaries emptying into the main canyon north of Tumacacori Peak.

Just west of the mission in township 25, there is a small branch located in the lower southeast corner that extends into township 36. Another one starts at the southwest corner of number 30 and extends into the northeast section of 36.

Both are possibilities but lack interesting rock formations. Also, Jim related this story 34 years later, and memories can fade after this length of time, especially at his age and being ill.
While in Los Angeles in '67, I had the paper the map was on analyzed for water marks, etc. I discovered it was made during the early 1900s. A reproduction of this accompanies the article.

Perhaps some reader will venture forth and make a diligent search for this buried necklace. I believe it's still hidden west of the mission in the vicinity of this canyon.

It's not located deep within the mountains where hours of hiking might be involved but in an area that can be reached with a minimum of effort.

It would make an interesting weekend project during our cooler months, and there is always the possibility of finding this elusive treasure. Just because we searched and failed, doesn't mean it's not there.

I feel Jim might have left out some crucial details that would have simplified discovering the correct spot, but doubt this was intentional. Lapse of memory and his advanced age could have been the contributing factor.

So, here we have a story entirely different from most treasure yarns. It hasn't been "beaten to death" over a hundred years by the continuous recounting of the story. This usually changes the facts around to such a degree that it becomes almost impossible to find.

The drawing that accompanies the story is not of the original necklace, but resembles it.

If there are any adventurous souls out here who are willing to give it a try, the rewards might well be worth the effort.

I'm 99 percent certain this story is factual and such a necklace is indeed hidden near some group of rocks, if they can be located. It's also possible the treasure site might sit high enough to overlook the nearby freeway.

What Jim's interpretation of the word "recognizable" is might be the clue that will eventually lead some searcher to the hidden spot. After digging a short way, he will reach down and pick up the gold necklace, studded with precious stones and one big diamond.

RETURN TO CLIFFORD WELL & OUR PARTNERS

Chapter 42

WALT'S BACK

fter our unsuccessful hunt for the necklace, we moved back once more to Clifford Wells, our old stamping grounds. Arriving in Arivaca, we spotted Randall Hill and Tata Ellis relaxing at Townsend's store.

Old Tata shook his head, saying, "Damn, their back again." Randall thought we had given up and returned to Washington. "Hell no," I said. "We're just getting started." Tata grinned and said, "You three sure are a glutton for punishment, living on this God forsaken desert all these months." It had been exactly 19 months since our trip began.

We related how we first went to Willcox searching for the "Moore Ledge," then moved to Prescott to escape the summer heat. Randall mentioned that Walt had returned and was looking for us, but nobody knew our whereabouts. He believed Walt was camping somewhere in the vicinity of Ruby, the old ghost town. As dusk approached we told Randall, "If Walt returns, tell him our camp is at Clifford Well." A week later, Walt came rolling in.

Walt told us old Pop was in critical condition and wasn't expected to live much longer. A month later Walt received word Pop had passed away. This really hit Walt hard as he liked the old gentleman. Luckily I had taken a picture of him during our first introduction last year.

After visiting Pop for the final time, Walt had left for Palm Desert and then into the area of "Pegleg Smith's Gold." His camp was west of the Salton Sea near the Borrego Badlands. This terrain resembles the surface of the moon, some of the most barren, inhospitable country in Southern California.

He came upon several buttes as described by Smith, but they had been recently searched by others as evidence was seen. A few weeks later, Walt moved further south and then searched west of State Highway 111. This area was limited as several military gunnery and bombing ranges are nearby. The area is slowly being taken over by these ranges. Walt now believes the three buttes discovered by Pegleg Smith are within one of these ranges.

While in the region Walt heard two rather amusing tales concerning these ranges. The first supposedly occurred on the range near Gila Bend, Arizona, and is related here with tongue in cheek. These stories were written up by me and published in *Southern Arizona Trails*.

THE GUNNERY RANGE CAPER

Southern Arizona Trails, Vol. 3, No. 74, March 8, 1988, Page 19

Τhis rather short but amusing tale supposedly occurred on the gunnery range near Gila Bend, Ariz., and is related here with tongue in cheek.

About 14-years-ago, some unwelcome guest entered the range in the dead of night. Objective to retrieve the brass casing of 50-cal. Cartridges dropped by the Air Force during practice runs over the desert. Of course this is quite illegal and can lead to serious trouble if caught.

During one of his nightly ventures into this forbidden zone our "public enemy number one" came upon an area well peppered with casings. With flashlight in hand and peering over his shoulder for any uninvited military personnel, he went about stealing the government's unwanted brass.

It was a cloudy evening, and occasionally the moon would peek out from behind a cloud above, the only witness to the illegal activity being perpetrated.

As he was collecting the contraband, our scavenger of the night spotted a coin near a small wash that cut across the area being pilfered.

Reaching down, the intruder picked up the glittering coin. It was of Spanish mintage and a little smaller than our old silver dollars. Several others were scattered about and some half hidden within the dirt.

As he searched for others, he spotted a light approaching off in the distance. Suspecting they were the "night owls of the range" out looking for possible intruders that might have entered their sacred domain, he abandoned his sack of brass and fled the area with the five golden coins clutched tightly in his fist.

If our night raider ever returned to search for more, it's not known. The mystery is, where did the gold coins come from? Most likely some Spaniards were camped in the immediate vicinity of the find and buried a cache but died before recovering it.

Through years of erosion it's possible they were brought to the surface, and the night prowler happened upon some as he crept about looking for illegal brass.

If the Air Force knew the identity of this American citizen, I'm quite certain he would be made an example of. Life imprisonment at hard labor and, of course, forfeiture of all the gold coins. I guess these would go into some Air Force general's private collection.

I would not advise anyone to ever think of entering these gunnery and bombing ranges, of which Arizona seems to have an abundance. First, it's illegal and second, it's quite dangerous. Much unexploded ordnance is scattered about. If some curious party would happen to touch one, "BOOM," ashes to ashes — dust to dust.

It's also quite frightening if you're caught by their dreaded "security force." I heard of one incident involving a group of gate crashers. They were surprised as they crept about the "off-limits" parcel of desert land.

A shiny black helicopter rose slowly from behind a hill. Dark tinted glass covered the front and from a loudspeaker, a somewhat unemotional young voice said, "You are on a restricted military range—do—not—more or attempt to flee. Stand—where you—are and place your hands on your head. Any hostile move WILL bring appropriate response."

All the while they stood peering up into the barrels of two modern-day versions of the old Gatlin guns, mounted on either side of the hovering machine.

When their hosts landed, they were dressed in dark tight-fitting clothing, and wore black helmets with tinted face visors. All meant for your entertainment and intimidation.

I heard the two above stories several years back, and have no idea how truthful they are. They are retold here mostly for your enjoyments.

Chapter 43

A FIST FULL OF COINS

Southern Arizona Trails International, Vol. 3, No. 33, June 2, 1987, Page 20

B ack in 1966 I was told a rather interesting treasure tale, from a friend [George Bell] that vouches for the authenticity of this story.

A gentleman by the name of Ray Fisher lived in Oklahoma as a youngster. The time, around 1916. His Uncle Bob was doing a year in prison for some minor infraction of the law. While there he met this weather-beaten old-timer by the name of Jed. His last name must have started with an "O" as everybody called him, Jed O. His face resembled old leather left out in the Arizona sun for a season or two. He was in his late sixties but still walked straight and tall.

In a short period of time the two became friends. Jed liked Bob as he wasn't the typical run-of-the-mill prisoner going in and out of the prison gate. One day while having a conversation, prospecting and gold came up, and Jed told Bob he would tell him an interesting story before he was released.

About a week before being set free, Jed and Bob were sitting in the athletic yard watching some convicts playing a rough game of baseball. Jed tells him that he had been in and out of jail most of his adult life, and no doubt will die in one. He said he liked Bob, so told him this story of robbery, death and gold.

In 1886 Jed and his partner, Will, held up a stagecoach outside of Yuma, Arizona, but across the river on the California side. They got away with a strongbox full of gold coins but as they rode off, the fellow riding "shotgun" must have had another rifle hidden beneath his seat. He fired several times, one shot hitting Jed's mount. He managed to ride a few more miles before the horse gave out. He then doubled with Will along with the strongbox. In a short while both knew they couldn't make it riding like this, so they stopped near the edge of the sand dunes that cover a great portion of the area. Opening the box, each grabbed a handful or two of twenty dollar gold pieces. Jed then looked around for a suitable spot to hide the remainder. Looking south he spotted an "anticline" near the edge of the sand (An anticline is a rock stratum or group of strata forming a bend with the convex side upward.)

This landmark could never be forgotten due to its unusual shape, so the strongbox was buried about thirty feet north of it in the "blow sand." With one riding and the other on foot they kept moving south toward Mexico. They crossed the border and remained there for several months. During that time they kept on the move until Jed thought it was safe to cross back into the Arizona Territory and retrieve their loot. For some reason, Jed decided to pass by Arizona and cross at a point near Signal Mountain, which is located south of what now is the Imperial Valley, in Southern California. He didn't like being too close to Yuma as we will find out later.

That evening they made a dry camp beside some boulders and settled in for the night. That evening some "crazies" as Jed called them, spotted their fire and came in shooting. His partner, Will, got hit behind the ear and in the side, and dropped like a brick. Jed got two shots off before he caught a slug in the upper arm and another grazed his neck. Thinking both were dead the crazies went through their pockets taking any cash they could find. Afterwards they stole the horses and rode off.

Next day, Jed managed to make it to the stage route just north of their camp, and then waited for any help that might come his way. The bullet went through his arm and Jed managed to stop most of the bleeding. The neck wound was nothing more than a scratch. Later that day a stagecoach came rumbling down the dusty road and stopped. Luck abandoned him at this point, as the destination of the coach was Yuma.

While being patched up somebody recognized him as being wanted for another crime, and went for the sheriff. Five years later, after being released from jail, Jed worked a few months for a rancher, then drifted slowly back toward the dunes in hopes of retrieving his gold.

The sand dunes had moved some, changing things and the anticline couldn't be found. Without that landmark all the surrounding country looked alike. (No doubt the marker was covered by the ever moving sands.) After spending a few days looking, he left and rode north and got another job. Once or twice a month, he'd ride south in hopes of finding the rock, but still he couldn't locate it.

After that he moved slowly eastward, getting in one scrape after the other, until he landed in prison for breaking and entering, and there met Bob. Jed told Bob, if he ever had the opportunity to head west, he should search for this landmark and the gold. He kept reminding him that the guidepost to the gold was finding this geological formation and that the box was about thirty feet north of it. Bob was released a week later and never heard of ole Jed O. again.

Ray grew up hearing this story, but his uncle or father never made an attempt to search for the gold. It wasn't until 1950 that Ray did have the opportunity to visit the area while on vacation. He never knew the area was that big, but he did spend quite a number of days driving his jeep around searching for the rock. But the anticline was never found. After that little adventure Ray got bitten by the "gold bug." While in Tucson during the fall of 1964, Ray visited the library at the University of Arizona, as he was interested in the legendary treasures of Tumacácori Mission, and was doing some research on the area.

How he happened upon finding this particular book is unknown, but somehow it found its way into his hands. It was a copy of a journal written by some government surveyor that was studying the area near the dunes for a possible route for the railroad. He made a daily record of his findings, and while thumbing through its pages out of curiosity, Ray came upon an entry describing the anticline, which the surveyor happened to come across. The odds of this happening, especially to someone that was searching for this very rock formation are about a million to one. The location was briefly described and anyone with some knowledge of map reading could locate it. Ray left Tucson early the next morning with this information, a topo map and "hope." Within two hours after arriving in the dune area, Ray found the rock. About three feet of it was protruding above the blow sand. Not having a metal detector at the time, Ray dug at various locations thirty feet north of the rock. He finally found it at a depth of only one foot.

I wonder how many times the wind has uncovered the box, only to cover it again after another wind storm, and they do have some awesome sand storms in that area. After carrying the strongbox to the jeep, Ray opened it and found 287 twenty dollar gold pieces and a large sack of 200 ten dollar pieces. At the price these coins were selling for that year, his find was a sizeable one.

Several years later I heard an elderly gentleman was walking his dog in the dune area, but quite some miles north of Ray's find. He found a strongbox sticking halfway out of the sand. Opening it, he discovered the box was full of gold coins. Wells Fargo's name was on the box and I believe they still have a main office in Texas. This gentleman calls them and says, "I believe I've found something that belongs to you." His reward, two hundred dollars.

It seems this dune area was a popular spot for outlaws to hide their ill gotten loot. Oh yes, by the way, would you have called Wells Fargo???

176

Chapter 44

TRASURE HUNTERS HOPE

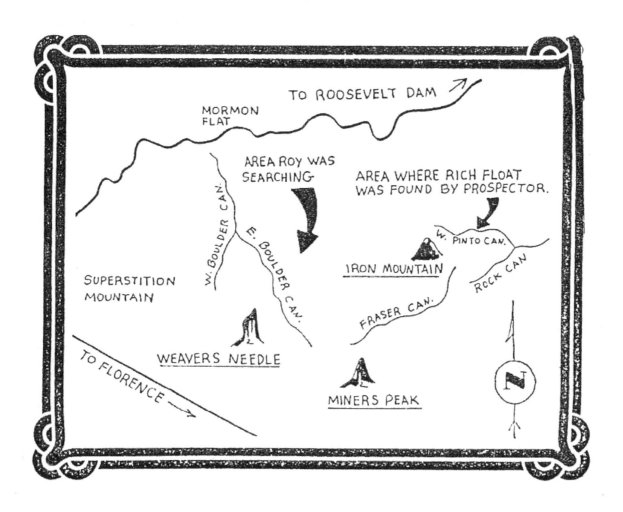

NEW APPROACH WILL SOLVE AGE-OLD MYSTERY

Southern Arizona Trails International, Vol. 3, No. 37, June 30, 1987, Page 22-23

W hen it comes to lost mine and buried treasure stories, "The Lost Dutchman" seems to dominate all the rest. Countless stories have been written about it in books, magazine and newspapers. A story so popular needn't be beaten to death, so I won't relate the tale again. Instead, I'll concentrate on my own experiences and those of my partners, in hopes of engendering in readers a new perspective or approach towards this hoary old legend.

Upon our arrival in Arizona in early 1956, my brother Chuck and I had read nearly all the standard books available on hidden treasures supposedly buried in this picturesque state. The majority of these books contained an account of the Dutchman's mine, and the author's opinion about this famous discovery.

Desert Town

A year or so before we met Roy, (one of our partners), he had spent a considerable length of time in Florence, Arizona, a small desert town due south of the Superstition Mountains. He spent most of his time crawling around these hazardous mountains alone, which was very foolish. It's quite easy to injure oneself in the harsh environment of this particular mountain range. Numerous bodies have been found up there, and all the deaths weren't attributed to natural causes.

But Roy was a hearty devil, and the ghostly stories about the Superstitions never seemed to bother him. Roy spent a lot of time searching the rough terrain two to three miles north of and between Weavers Needle and Miners Peak, two well-known landmarks.

Several weeks later he checked out of the motel in Florence, had lunch and bought gas at the local gas station before heading south back to Tucson. While filling up, he noticed an old Indian gentleman near the restrooms eyeing him. A few moments later he walked over to Roy and said, "I see you on Superstition last week standing on slope of hill worth million dollars."

Perhaps this was his way of telling Roy he'd gotten close to something of great value. Roy tried to pin the Indian down on the exact area, as he was exploring numerous slopes and canyons. But the old fellow just smiled, shook his head "no," then shuffled off toward a waiting truck hitched to a "horse trailer." Roy naturally asked him why the Indian was alone in such a remote area. Could he have been guarding something? If this elderly man was indeed watching over something and spotted Roy in the vicinity, why would he mention seeing him? That would only arouse suspicion that something was hidden in that particular area. But maybe the temptation of teasing Roy was too great, and the old Indian figured his hint wouldn't be of much use. If true, though, the clue does narrow down considerably the area to be searched.

The Old Prospector

Another of our experiences dates back to late 1957. We were introduced to an old prospector through a close friend of his while in the mining town of Superior, Arizona. The old-timer looked as though he had just stepped out of makeup for some Western movie. His friend, Frank, told us the old fellow claimed a relative of his once resided on the outskirts of Florence, during the time of the Dutchman's discovery, and had obtained a sample of the gold found at the Peralta mine from Waltz himself. He reached into his pocket and brought out a rather large piece of gold, which was worn smooth in places from carrying it around. The rich specimen consisted of 20% "rose quartz" and 80% raw gold. It was two-thirds the size of a large egg.

I must admit feeling a strange tingling sensation throughout me as I rolled the gold between my fingers, knowing I held an original piece of ore from the Dutchman's hidden mine. We had read enough about this legend to know the gold was carried in a vein of rose quartz.

The Findings

The old man also said he himself had discovered several rich pieces of gold float with the same quartz interlaced throughout it. His find was made in Pinto Creek, just east of Iron Mountain. He compared the sample that supposedly came from the Peralta diggings with his, and they matched perfectly, both in the color of the gold and quartz. Although the old prospector searched for many years, he never discovered the source of the rich float. He heard from others who claimed the lost mine is definitely located somewhere near the west branch of Pinto Creek. But still others insist the mine is hidden north of Weavers Needle. One has to remember, though, the Peraltas had eight working mines. I doubt if all were within shouting distance of each other. There is a strong possibility several were located quite a few miles away, and one could very well have been in the Iron Mountain District.

The only point dumping cold water on this theory is the lack of rock house ruins in this area resembling those in the Superstitions, which were built to accommodate miners.

I believe the deposit shown to Doc Thorne and the discovery made by the two soldiers in 1880 are one in the same. Both mine dumps were located in a canyon, not a mountain slope. Also these parties stated the gold was found north of a tall, sharp peak, which was most likely Weavers Needle or Miners Peak. Its possible several Peralta mines were accidentally discovered over the years, like the one the soldiers stumbled across during a journey through the mountains. After hearing these stories, most people jumped to the conclusion the discovery had to be the same as the Dutchman's mine.

Hidden or Earthquake

The earthquake that rumbled through the area sometime in the 1880s may have forever sealed several of these mines. But, on the other hand, the quake may have opened a few concealed by the Indians after the Peralta massacre. It's also believed by some that Jacob Waltz would deliberately head into the Superstitions, as it was easy terrain to lose anyone that might be following. He would then leave this region and head toward Iron Mountain. In doing this, he placed the idea in people's minds the gold was somewhere within these mountains. If he carried out the shrewd maneuver, it would be quite simple to take East Boulder Canyon south then follow Fraser Canyon on up to Iron Mountain.

Gold Stash

There is some speculation that Waltz only visited the original mine several times. It's quite likely he removed enough gold to stash in various locals, and from these hidden caches he obtained the gold that was later sold in Florence and Phoenix. If by chance pursuers had succeeded in following him, he would have led them to one of the smaller sites, not the original discovery. While in Mesa, Arizona, we happened to meet another elderly gentleman who was well in his 90s. He informed us that about a mile north from downtown Mesa one could see the mountain containing the Dutchman's mine, if you looked through a pair of binoculars in the direction just north of Goldfield. The trouble here was that the old fellow didn't know exactly which mountain top you should look at.

Over a thirty year period we have explored a great many mountain ranges in Arizona. Out of them all, the deadly Superstitions take the grand prize as the most rugged and mysterious. Water is at a premium; snakes wait in shadows; high craggy cliffs dominate the skies above; and there is always that uncertain gut feeling you are being stalked and watched. Perhaps at times you are. Hearing the numerous tales about his strange mountain—including the idea of sudden wealth and the unsolved murders—you seem to sense something unfriendly behind every rock.

Did Roy ever return to the Superstitions after his brief encounter with the elderly Indian? Yes— in fact, we met Roy some eighteen months after the encounter, and upon hearing his interesting story, we all decided to make a trip back there in November. We left both trucks at a local ranch and hiked in on foot from the west and for a three-day search. We established camp near the intersections of East and West Boulder Canyon. Chuck and I were the youngest, so we carried most of the gear. Roy was in great shape and kept up with us during the long trek thorough the rough country. We didn't mention it much, but during this time, we kept an eye open for anything out of the ordinary, like some movement among the boulders or a glitter of light off something in the high cliffs.

Our purpose on this short but interesting trip was to try to figure approximately where Roy might have been when spotted by the Indian. It became like a detective story, as we tried to pinpoint where he may have been through the process of elimination. Roy had spent three days in this rugged area the week he was observed. For some reason, he kept insisting the Indian fellow mentioned "Thursday" during their short conversation, but wasn't sure. He remembered on Wednesday he was searching the slopes and canyons northeast of Weavers Needle, and in the area of Bluff Spring Mountain Canyon. Thursday, his last day there, he climbed around the slopes of Black Mountain. From there he followed La Barge Canyon, crossed a low spot into Needle Canyon then headed south toward his main camp. He did most of this hiking along the canyon floors. So he wasn't on a "mountain slope" during this period of time.

Beginning of the Search

The only area left was the slopes south of Black Mountain. We began our search there. We checked every place that might conceal the entrance to a mine or cave. If there was an entrance somewhere, it was no doubt well concealed. This was our first of several trips into the menacing Superstition Mountains with its maze of dark canyons, broken rock and harsh terrain. The area is unbelievably rugged, and I could see why this mine has remained lost all these years. To undertake a serious all out search, it would require quite a number of years of complete dedication. Base camps would have to be established, water and supplies hauled in and horses either bought or rented—although rangers patrolling the wilderness area might take a dim view of such an operation.

We never approached the search with this dedication, as other ventures rated higher on our priority list. A few of our searches did prove successful many years later. But there was always that tugging at our souls to search again for the famous gold mine that had eluded rediscovery to this day.

I called the Tonto National Forest Headquarters in Mesa, and received the following information:

The superstitions and surrounding vicinity are a "wilderness area." Permits are not required for visits to the 159,780-acre wilderness. Permits are required, however, for any type of guiding and/or outfitting service that is not on a total cost-share basis. The wilderness area is now closed to mining except on valid mining claims. Other claims that prove to be worthless (no commercial mineral in place) are being closed.

An application for a treasure trove permit will be accepted, but it must include evidence linking a suspected treasure to a specific location.

Issuance of a permit will depend on the reasonableness of this evidence. The permit fee is $250. A reclamation bond is required in most cases, and the amount is dependent upon the extent of the "resource disturbance" permitted. Applications for treasure trove permits in the wilderness areas must be approved by the Regional Forester and may take up to six months or longer to process.

Perhaps the gold supposedly hidden deep within these mountains will never be discovered. But the legend will live on for years to come, and be retold around cracking camp fires.

If this famous lost mine is ever relocated, the desert mountain range will lose some of the mystic hold it has had over many who dared enter its domain.

Fortunately, there haven't been any reports of violence in these mountains in several years—unlike the way it was many year ago. At that time, people who searched the lonely canyons and slopes, hoping to find a storehouse of gold, often only found lead from the business end of a killer's rifle.

Chapter 45

THE HOAX AT CERRO RUIDO

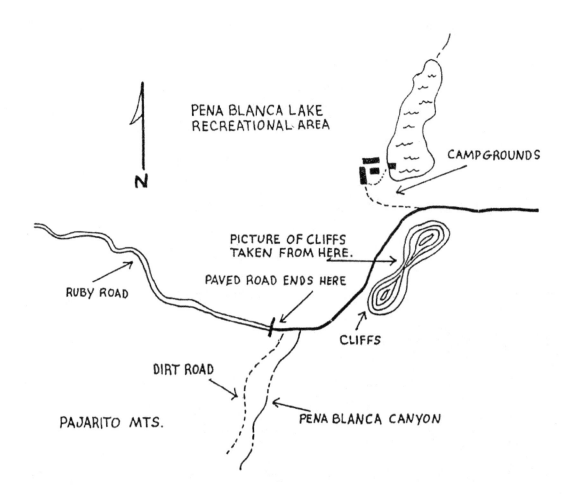

Southern Arizona Trails International, Vol. 3, No. 24, April 1, 1987, Page 2, 24

T reasure hunting is difficult enough even when you have most of the facts relating to the one you're searching for. Others involve trying to separate the fact from the fiction, and this too becomes quite perplexing at times. When some individual deliberately writes a treasure story which is a complete hoax, and causes people to spend time and money to search for a figment of this person's imagination, that's when I decide to do something about it. As they say, "Stand up and be counted."

The story which I have in mind has been written under numerous titles: "Lost Silver of the Jesuits" and the most famous, "The Mystery of Cerro Ruido," which appeared in the October 1945 issue of *Arizona Highways*.[8]

This is by no means meant to discredit this very fine magazine, which I still enjoy. The editors cannot always check each and every article for its authenticity. I must admit though, the author of this article could indeed tell one convincing story.

Ever since 1956, when we first embarked on this long odyssey of treasure hunting, we've heard countless stories and "tall tales" of lost mines and buried treasures. Most were told by local residents from the immediate area these treasures are alleged to be hidden. Some were factual while others were just "stories," and one could determine this quickly after listening but a short time.

I'll give you a rather condensed version of the "Cerro Ruido" story, which I will prove was indeed a hoax from the very beginning.

A prospector known only as Dave was exploring the region near the Pajarito Mountains located just northwest of Nogales, Arizona, in the early 30s. His camp was established in the vicinity of Cerro Ruido, a large peak nestled within these mysterious, legendary mountains. His partner's real name has been lost in the pages of time, so we'll just call him Jim. Both were searching for high-grade outcroppings of native silver, reported to be in this area in old Spanish documents.

Just south across the Mexican border, the famous "Planchas de Plata" silver slabs were discovered sometime in the fall of 1736. They ranged in weight from 25 to 300 pounds. One was reported to weigh close to 1200 or 2500 pounds but the vein was never found. It's believed they eroded out of the vein and rolled into the canyon below.

One day, Jim who was away on personal matters returned to camp. That afternoon, Davie arrived back at camp very excited, and explained to his partner that while prospecting a new rugged area he discovered an old Spanish silver mine. Reaching into his pocket, he displayed several samples of rich silver ore.

Also located near the mine were the ruins of a "small mission" or "visita." Davie always carried a camera and told Jim he had taken a number of pictures. One photo was of some high cliffs, the mission and one supposedly showing the entrance to this ancient mine.

Jim was again leaving for Tucson, so Davie gave him the camera an asked him to have the film developed. Placing the samples in a paper bag he also instructed him to have the ore assayed. Jim would be returning in less than a week and Davie would return to his discovery and put up the necessary location papers.

As Jim approached his truck which was parked a distance away he heard a rumble and looked back, and spotted a thunder storm moving in from the south. Taking Davie's camera he took a picture of it then drove off.

A week later, Jim returned and found the damp completely washed away by a cloudburst, and presumably, Davie along with it as his body was never found.

---

[8] The article credits the author as Norman G. Wallace and "Photos by the Writer and by the Principal Characters in the Story."

The pictures that were developed revealed the mine entrance, the front of the "mission" and another from a different angle. The remaining two were the high cliffs, probably located in the vicinity of his discovery and the picture of the approaching thunderstorm.

We heard in 1965, this entire adventure was manufactured on the back porch of a ranch located within this area. The instigator of this elaborate hoax once worked for the railroad in Mexico, and took numerous pictures during his trips across the country.

The others involved were ranch hands, and most had heard the tales of lost mines, supposedly hidden by the Jesuit padres of nearby Tumacácori Mission. They all thought it would make great sport to fabricate some story about prospectors finding a lost mine and mission, out in the Pajarito Mountains, which at that time were very inaccessible.

Pictures were selected from his large inventory, but they needed one showing some mysterious cliffs that could be a possible "guide post" to the imagined lost mine and hidden mission.

First, the photo of the small mission or *visita*, [accompanying the article] actually is located in the San Blas area of Mexico. The mission that appears in this picture was constructed of stone only, and is very well preserved. The second photo is supposed to be the same mission, but here we see only adobe bricks and no stone work. As one can notice quite clearly, these are the ruins of a large mission, and not a small *visita* as claimed in the story, and are in the last stages of erosion.

At the rear of this picture one can also see the arched entrance and again, no stone work is visible like in the first photo, which reveals the elaborate stone carvings around the doorway. These two pictures are undoubtedly not of the same mission.

The picture of the mine entrance could very well be one of the hundreds that are so plentiful in this area, as they dot the entire landscape. This one however is quite unique, as it's dug into some uplifted sedimentary rock. It also looks as though it might be located beneath the level of the canyon floor. If correct, this tunnel would have been filled in long ago by sand and gravel during the local "monsoon" seasons, when these canyons become roaring rivers. In my opinion this picture looks rather suspicious and could very well be a recent dig.

Next comes the final "proof of the pudding," the photograph on page 35 of the October 1945 issue of *Arizona Highways*. This was the last picture needed for the "big Hoax." Being the ranch was quite near the old Ruby Road, this person drove along its route until he discovered a wall of cliffs, a hundred yards or so south of the road. They are located near Pena Blanca Canyon, which today is "Pena Blanca Lake and Recreational Area."

We have driven this road numerous times and have noticed these cliffs, but never really paid much attention to them. One afternoon, Ray [Roy Purdie], a partner was returning to camp and happened to look toward them. Perhaps it was the way the light fell across them, but at that moment they looked rather familiar.

Stopping, Ray noticed the similarity between these and the one pictured in the magazine, especially the contour near the bottom. He made a sketch of the outline and returned to camp. We found the issue the cliffs appeared in, and compared them. To our surprise they were identical but the one in *Arizona Highways* was in reverse. Around noon the following day we all drove out to the area of the cliffs and took several pictures.

What apparently happened was, after taking the picture, our instigator reversed the negative before printing and tilted it about 15 degrees, and printed the section near the bottom of these cliffs.

Our photographs show the cliffs as they appear from the road, and one in reverse. As the saying goes, "A picture is worth a thousand words."

If the individual would have taken the time to locate some cliffs further back into the mountains, there's a strong possibility this hoax would have never been uncovered. So here his laziness caused the eventual downfall of this once believable story. Knowing they were quite near the road, he thought he would just reverse the picture and tilt it some, and nobody would be the wiser, and his little deception would go unnoticed. It did for almost 35 years.

During several of our trips into this area, we came upon a few parties searching for these very cliffs. After relating our version and displaying the pictures, they immediately lost interest in their venture and mumbled some "unprintable" words toward the instigator of the original tale.

One gentleman, a retired Army officer had been searching for this several months out of each year for some time. Upon hearing our tale, he refused to believe it. I told him the cliffs were a ten minute drive away, and he should go see for himself. At that time we hadn't brought the pictures along, so couldn't show them. He said, no, as he was fatigued from hiking all day. Chuck, my brother spoke up and said, "Climb in our jeep and we'll take you there." He again refused, so we dropped the subject.

I suppose he had believed this "fairy tale" for so long and had put so much time, effort, sweat into the search, that his mind just wouldn't allow him to believe the whole thing was a hoax. To him, our cliffs just didn't exist.

Yes, this entire tale was nothing more than a hoax, hatched into life back in the late 30s. I find it difficult to fathom that some "halfway" rational person would deliberately tell a story like this, then vouch for its authenticity. I also wonder how many other stories like this one are floating about. I would also like to know how many "poor souls" have spent time and money they perhaps couldn't afford, searching for nothing but a hoax concocted on the back porch of some ranch in the early hours of the evening.

Chapter 46

INTERESTING TALES

D uring our lengthy trip we occasionally came upon interesting and mysterious sites. Most are still shadowed in mystery to this day. The following are several of the most fascinating. Sardina Peak, the highest in the Tumacacoris dominates the northern extension of these mountains. Several Spanish mines are believed hidden within the shadow of this peak.

Stone Cabin

While exploring below high cliffs located on the western side of this jutting peak, we happened upon the ruins of a stone cabin. It was nestled among trees and boulders and difficult to see. If it had been made of adobe, it would have long since returned to the earth from which it came. Nearby were the rotted remains of an old cottonwood and cut deep within its dry surface was a perfect cross.

Later we asked Louie Romero what he knew of the site. He said the cabin had been there long before he was born. Nothing was known of its occupant or when it was built. Most believe it was [built] during the early 1800s.

If the facts were known it probably was constructed by somebody seeking the old Spanish mines as it's in close proximity to two, the San Pedro and Isabella mines.

Just north of the cabin several sections of the Carreta Road are still visible where it crosses the arroyos. The cross upon the tree was no doubt another trail marker cut by the mission fathers.

From another reliable source we learned that during 1906, an old Spanish cup was discovered within the cabin. Is it possible the stone structure wasn't built by modern day treasure hunter, but by the padres from Tumacácori Mission? Perhaps it was some kind of a way station located along the old Carreta Road. That's what I have always loved about this region. It's so full of mysteries.

The Isabella Mine

We discovered the Isabella Mine in late '57, after obtaining documents furnished by Don Page. It was difficult to locate, hidden among brush beside a hill northwest of Sardina. The hill had collapsed into the mine workings, completely burying the interior.

The remains of a "chicken ladder" (a large log cut with notches and used for climbing from one level to another) were found nearby.

According to several Spanish documents, no treasure was concealed within this mine. So, it was decided not to undertake the project of clearing out the tunnels. It would entail months of dangerous work, digging perhaps several hundred feet. The Isabella produced low grade silver ore, and wasn't classified as a prominent mine.

Indian Stones

Another time Louie told us of some Indian signs he once found. They were carved on nine or ten black stones the size of bowling balls. These were placed in a semicircle, located at the junction of Murphy and Apache Canyons on the hill just a short distance toward the northeast. The stones had stick figures cut into them along with animals and other petroglyphs. He first discovered them during 1945, and last saw the stones three years later while rounding up cattle.

One afternoon we drove down Apache Canyon, shortly arriving at the junction. After climbing a slight rise we searched but found no stones. Perhaps Louie was mistaken, so we checked the other hills, but again nothing. There weren't any rock formations consisting of dark colored stone in the vicinity, only broken lava. It's possible the stones were carried from another location and placed at the site for perhaps some religious ceremony. Some hunters or others might have stumbled upon the site and hauled the stones off. It's a shame that those who find these bits of history have removed them for personal use. Perhaps they are decorating someone's flower garden. This occurs quite often, and is the reason I haven't publicly revealed the location of the mysterious stone wall.

Chuck's Lost Canyon

While searching Carreta Canyon, Chuck decided to climb the low hills south of our location. While he explored elsewhere, I followed a narrow canyon cut through solid rock. At its head I came upon an opening partly filled with dirt. The top portion resembled a mine entrance, but later we discovered it was a natural formation caused by erosion.

Chuck had been gone perhaps half an hour. Glancing up, I spotted him approaching, carrying a set of deer antlers. While on the opposite side of the hills he found a canyon and entered it. As he walked along its rocky bed for five minutes, the sides became steeper. Not finding a way to climb out, he retraced his steeps and found the antlers as he emerged from the canyon.

A few days later Chuck was still curious about the canyon, so we returned. The terrain was mostly rolling hills with small arroyos scattered throughout, but no canyon. Try as he may, Chuck couldn't relocate it. He had only been gone a short while, and his wandering couldn't have taken him too far. We searched in all directions and still nothing resembling his canyon was located. Later we checked our Topo map of the area and found no deep canyon as described by Chuck.

While visiting the same region with Roy and Walt, we often kidded him about his phantom canyon. Chuck did find the canyon and the antlers, but where did his hike take him during that 30 minutes? No canyon like it is within a square mile of the area. For years Walt would jokingly say Chuck had no doubt entered the "Twilight Zone." Perhaps he did!

The Cement Floor

Another tale concerns a cement floor hidden near Sopori Wash, just south of the Arivaca Road. The time period was early 1910. The occupant that once resided at this cabin managed to save a considerable amount of money over the years. Where it came from is not known. Not trusting banks (like Tully) the cash was buried beneath the dirt floor. It's estimated he had approximately $2300 in gold coin.

After his sudden death, the cabin sat vacant for several years. Finally another party took up residence in the old cabin which needed repairs. Not liking the dirt floor, it was covered with cement. Several years later this occupant abandoned the property and moved on.

Over the years the adobe slowly eroded down until nothing remained but the floor. No one knew of the money buried beneath it. In time the floor cracked and deteriorated from the elements, weeds grew over its edges and the place was slowly forgotten.

Most treasure hunters will check any floors they happen to find during their searching. Being no different, we came upon the floor by accident one afternoon during '57 and to our surprise a large hole was dug squarely in the center and reached a depth of about 18 inches.

Louie said, a local rancher once told him, he had seen two men in that area during 1954. They were searching the vicinity with an old army mine detector.

Little treasures like this are scattered across Arizona and other states, hidden down old wells, beside rocks, trees and corners of old homes. Since the popularity of modern detectors many of these small unknown treasures have been discovered.

We heard the story of the gold beneath the cement floor from a party that once lived in this area in 1915. The story regarding this gold never became public until long after it was found.

TUCSON ADVENTURES

Chapter 47

THE IRON DOOR MINE

There have been many stories drifting around concerning the famous "Lost Mine with the Iron Door." A few of these tales are somewhat believable, while others stretch the imagination to the limits.

The most widely accepted version involving this lost mine, centers around two prospectors. Sometime during the 1800s while crossing the Santa Catalina Mountains, located just north of Tucson, they claimed to have discovered a hidden valley deep within the high rugged range. Scattered around were the old remains of a large settlement and evidence of extensive mining operations.

The two spent considerable time exploring, and discovered a mine tunnel well concealed near an outcropping of jagged rooks. Its entrance was covered with a huge iron door, plus several *arrastras* were found nearby.

On the morning of the second day, both headed for Tucson. Upon their arrival they approached a merchant they knew and told him of their discovery. If he would grubstake them, they would split any gold found at the old site. They were out of supplies and would need enough for several months, also some dynamite, as they planned on blowing the door from its hinges. They were most anxious to discover what was hidden on the opposite side.

With visions of great wealth dancing before his eyes, the merchant agreed. He grubstaked the pair once before and they had found gold, not much, but a profit was made.

With their mules heavily loaded with provisions, the two left early the following morning, and slipped into the dusty pages of history. Neither was ever heard of again. Rumors and accusations claimed the pair had made up the tale to obtain another stake. After leaving Tucson, they were supposedly last seen in the San Pedro Valley heading north and no doubt out of the country.

Don Page and several colleagues once visited Cañada del Oro, which winds its rocky way down the western slopes of the Santa Catalina Range. There they discovered a number of old stone ruins on a small flat overlooking the canyon.

Roy, our partner, heard the following from Don Page:

They dug and discovered that two different Indian cultures had once lived there before the stone structures were built on top. The dwellings were undoubtedly erected by Spanish explorers that were working a mine somewhere in the surrounding vicinity, as several *arrastras* were found later. Don and his friends made the discovery sometime during the mid 1940s. Don also claimed the "Mission of Ciru" once stood at this location. If he's correct, it would make the settlement older than Tucson. Most historians disagree with his findings, with some saying there never was such a mission. Take my word for it, there was.

Roy had obtained Don's notes, so we made our own search of the region. We never found the *arrastras*, but Don had stated they were located east of the ruins. Also, a faint trail led toward the towering mountains, but was lost after a mile or so. Don always believed there was a hidden mine somewhere in the area and that it was once worked by the residents who occupied the small village. But, he also felt no "iron door" would have covered the entrance.

One just has to turn this idea over in their mind for a moment to realize how foolish it sounds. These people had more to occupy their time than to undertake the enormous task of making an iron door, and for what purpose, to cover a mine? Some have suggested it might have been shipped from Spain, but I find this unlikely too.

During our search of the site, we did locate the ruins and the area where Don claimed the small mission once stood, but found no trace of its remains. The area is now designated as Catalina State Park, and the ruins and mine, if one does exist, might fall within its boundaries. I believe the ruins do, as the park covers some 5,500 acres and most of Cañada del Oro. No digging or collecting is allowed.

Several years back, the mayor of Kearny, Arizona supposedly found a sealed mine or tunnel in this region. He wanted a permit from the state to excavate the site, as he believed it "might" contain one of the treasures hidden by the Spanish padres. If it was unearthed, he was willing to split with the state 50-50. His request was denied.

Soon afterwards, a state official said that if there is such a treasure, it should belong totally to the state. Did the mayor discover the Iron Door Mine? We will never know, but he isn't the only one to claim finding a sealed mine in that area.

Walt, our second partner, heard an interesting story from a rancher that once lived in this vicinity:

A family arrived in Tucson with their son for a two week vacation at an uncle's. The boy had never read any literature concerning Arizona's lost mines, but he was raised in the country and knew the outdoors.

One day he asked if he could explore the canyon nearby, which happened to be Cañada del Oro. The lad was about 17 and was given permission, but told by his uncle to remain in the canyon as people had been lost in the rugged terrain. He agreed, so off he went with a full canteen.

After hiking and looking the country over for awhile, he decided to climb from the canyon floor. From his vantage point the young lad could make out a portion of the highway, perhaps two miles away, also, several rooftops could be seen reflecting sunlight. Breaking his word about not leaving the canyon, the adventurous lad began exploring the terrain. When he left the canyon it's not known if he climbed to the left or right.

An hour or so later he came upon some leaning flat rocks. In the narrow opening separating the two he spotted an old wooden door with an ancient padlock hanging from it. Near the entrance were several rusted mining tools and the remains of a blunderbuss, an old fashioned short gun with a large bore and flaring mouth. The wooden stock had long since rotted off. Not aware of the countless tales of lost mines and treasures, the youngster didn't become overly excited at his discovery. To him, it was nothing more than some old abandoned mine.

Upon his return the boy told what he had found while out exploring. He did so before realizing he was admitting he left the canyon. After a brief chewing out from his parents the uncle asked if he could again find the location. He answered, "Yes." The discovery of the blunderbuss had triggered his uncle's interest. In the ten years of living in the area, the uncle never heard of anyone finding a site as described by his nephew. Later that evening the uncle told the story surrounding the "Mine with the Iron Door."

Early the next morning all three began the long hike up the canyon, following the boy's tracks that were still visible in the soft gravel. After a few miles the group climbed from the canyon's bed and began their search. They looked for well over two hours, but the youngster became confused after awhile and couldn't relocate the leaning rocks. Occasionally they came upon his tracks in some soft earth, only to lose them again. The mine was never found, even though the three made frequent trips before the family returned home.

What the boy apparently found was the diggings worked by the residents of the small settlement perched atop the flat hill. The blunderbuss could date the mine, as they were used during the 1700s and even earlier. Why it was left outside is unknown unless a guard was posted there and was killed by Indians that hated the invasion of the Spaniards. Also the remaining miners could have been run off or killed by the same group of hostiles. What lies beyond that wooden door could be nothing or a king's ransom in gold.

The boy's story is intriguing, but questionable in two ways. First this area has been searched for countless years, and why this lone site near the leaning rocks was never found boggles the mind. During the Great Depression many individuals worked the gravels along this canyon. Enough gold was found to help keep body and soul together. Undoubtedly these same men searched the surrounding country for the source of the placer gold being discovered in the canyon. If the entrance to this mine was not concealed, as the boy stated, surely it would have been found.

Also questionable is that this tale is strikingly similar to other tales of the Southwest. Somebody accidentally stumbles across something while hiking the desert, but doesn't realize at the time what he has found. Later he relates the story to another who is familiar with the area and its stories. When informed what he might have discovered the party can never retrace his steps back to the site, and another tale is added to all the rest creating more confusion.

Personally I don't quite believe the two prospectors who are credited with finding the Iron Door Mine. Instead, I think they came upon these stone ruins and *arrastras* near Cañada del Oro, and then concocted a tall tale about finding a mine with an iron door and the large settlement in some unknown valley. Their purpose, of course, would have been to obtain another stake from the gullible merchant, as some people suspect.

Even if this assessment is correct, a mystery still remains. The location of the hidden mine Don Page felt was associated with the Cañada del Oro *arrastras*. The mine he suspected could easily exist, and it's possible the young boy happened upon it, sealed with a wooden door and an "iron" padlock.

EVIDENCE OF EARLY SPANISH MINING

Southern Arizona Trails, Vol. 3, No. 84, May 17, 1988, Page 19 & 22-23

T he following information has been taken in part from Mr. Don Page's various correspondence and documents now in possession of this writer.

February 4, 1929, "Tomé [Augustíne Tomé] hunted around until he unearthed a small piece of smelter slag and said when he was a boy he used to find many large pieces in the vicinity just north of the San José de Tucson Mission. This type of slag comes from one thing only, the reduction of ore.

May 31, 1929, Charlie Bell another associate and Don Page drove out and found abundant indications of a large Indian village. Bell discovered several arrowheads and a large piece of "furnace brick" together with a good-sized piece of "slag."

June 5, 1929, Tomé and Don again drive out to the mission location, and he tells Don that about five years ago, the daughter of a family that lived in a "jackal" (hut) just north of the old road dug a hole in the ground and unearthed one side of a large copper pot that contained gold.

The ruins in the Cañada del Oro, also known as the Mission of Ciru, are mentioned by Archbishop Jean-Baptiste Salpointe in his writings. Just east of this old Spanish settlement several *arrastras* were uncovered by Mr. Page. (They were not used to grind corn.)

Some of my own evidence includes:

1) A small well-hidden Spanish tunnel in the Tumacacori Range.

2) The old Cerro Colorado Mine, located just north of the Arivaca Road. This was an ancient Spanish silver mine before it was abandoned by the fleeing Jesuits. It later was rediscovered by Mexicans and worked rather crudely until Samuel Heintzelman obtained the mine and worked it for many years.

3) The ruins of an old Spanish mine just south of the old Paul Bell place. It was either the legendary Sopori Mine or the San Pedro. Paul informed us back in '56 that several ancient "chicken ladders" were discovered within it. These ladders were used extensively by Indian miners in climbing from one level to another.

4) The old Canez *arrastra* located just north of the Las Guijas Wash.

5) The well-hidden Spanish shaft concealed on the southern slopes of Tumacacori Peak. Many have dug at this site in search of treasure or the silver vein the Spaniards might have been following.

Many will point at this evidence as inconclusive, saying, "It doesn't prove a thing." If the Jesuits never engaged in extensive mining activities, how come such a large amount of adobe smelters and *arrastras* have been found within the areas surrounding their missions? These crude works were never used by the early American miners in their operations. Also, the American miners dug ample-sized tunnels to work in, not the small "mole holes" Indians were force to labor in.

Our disbelievers also refrain from mentioning why the Indians rebelled during 1680 and again in 1751. It was because of the treatment they endured under Spanish rule.

Their leader, Luis Oacpicagigua, saw how fast the Spanish mining and ranching frontier was advancing, and he knew that more and more of his people as well as those of friendly neighboring tribes would be subjected to the "injustice" of forced labor.

On November 20, 1751, the second rebellion began with the killing of 18 Spaniards who had been partying with Luis at Saric, again fact.

There are many who will never believe the Jesuits were engaged in any type of mining, even if undisputed evidence was presented before them. It's like politics and religion. Some will never change their beliefs, no matter what.

A number of these debunkers of Spanish mining wrote their articles around 1889 or thereabouts. Long before historians like Don Page and others entered the scene with fresh evidence indicating the padres were indeed mining some "rich ores" in the surrounding hills.

Of course, tall tales about the Jesuits burying large amounts of bullion sprang into existence around various American mining camps. This began when several old Spanish workings were found and some traces of gold and silver were discovered nearby.

Over the years, the value put on these treasures has increased to enormous proportions. A couple range from $80 million to $200 million. It's up to the seekers of these mines, etc., to separate fact from fiction, and Mr. Page was quite skilled at this.

The mission that now sits on the Tumacácori Monument grounds is not the one mentioned in old Spanish documents. This was built during the 1800s.

The first small mission was supposedly built near Calabasas. From there, its location was moved further north and to the east side of the Santa Cruz River, then to the opposite side of the bank directly toward the west. The ruins of the last and final mission are now located within the structure east of the present church on the monument grounds.

One author of "mission treasures" wrote there once were "two" Tumacácori Missions. The upper and lower—the upper being located on the southern foothills below the Sierrita Mountains. This is pure fiction, and the writer was doing his readers an injustice by making this claim. A small Spanish mining settlement was located in this general vicinity, but no mission occupied the site.

My advice to those wanting to search for these lost mines, etc., is: "Do your research well." Much of the information you seek is hidden away on high dusty shelves in libraries and in the Arizona Historical Society.

You will not find any old maps pinpointing these locations, but many papers have been written on this subject. In reading through these works, some clues will surface. In all the years I've been at this treasure game, I'm quite certain I haven't found all the documents available on these legendary treasures.

Chapter 48

THE GEM BED

W hile visiting several gem shops in Tucson with samples of the geodes, fire agate and thunder eggs (a cryptocrystalline variety of quartz formed in egg-shaped nodules) found near the mysterious archway, one particular owner showed interest.

She said she'd take a number of geodes, and perhaps a hundred thunder eggs. She cut several open with her diamond saw and liked the various colors within the eggs.

Chuck with geodes.

Three days later Chuck and I found an overland route to the gem bed, saving us a mile of hiking. We spent two days making two trips a day packing 40 pounds each down the uneven canyon floor. It was a grueling walk. After gathering around 190 pounds of material, we returned to base camp.

Randall stopped by one afternoon soon after the trip to the gem bed. The rear of his jeep was piled high with slabs of snowflake obsidian, a hard black colored volcanic glass often used as a gemstone. He had discovered the outcropping near Apache Canyon. He offered us several pieces in trade for some of our eggs and one geode.

We told him of our deal with the gem shop. We said he should try selling them some of the obsidian, and told him that during our first visit we had left a number of samples with the owner.

A day or so later, Randall went to Tucson, showing his obsidian and leaving some samples with the same gem shop. Later that week we arrived with her order.

She had changed her mind, saying she couldn't use ours. Not knowing we knew Randall, she pointed toward his samples, saying, "Now if you had several hundred pounds of this, we could use it."

Our haul for the day.

Reloading our gemstones we returned to Arivaca, a little on the angry side. Two days later while in town we spotted Randall. He informed us while at the shop, the owner didn't want his, but pointed at our samples, saying, "If you had several hundred of these thunder eggs, I could sell them."

When Randall heard what she told us, he couldn't believe it. She didn't care for his obsidian, but liked our samples. While we then hear she liked his but not ours.

Over a period of time we discovered most gem shops were difficult to deal with. One of their ploys was, "I'm not interested, but where did you find it?" They are hoping to get a clue from you. You really have to be careful when dealing with them. We learned fast.

We kept several of the larger geodes and thunder eggs and eventually sold many, but the majority were given to friends whose hobby was lapidary.

The gem bed still sits high on the side of that steep hill leading to the archway. Beneath the ground must be tons of these oddities of nature. We only removed what was on the surface. To date it hasn't been found by anyone. The reason, it's located deep within these rugged mountains where few venture.

197

PECK CANYON & CALABASAS ADVENTURES

Chapter 49

PECK CANYON POINTING ARROW

Southern Arizona Trails, Vol. 3, No. 53, October 20, 1987, Page 23

During one of our informative conversations with Louis Romero, whom I have mentioned many times in other stories, he told us a rather interesting tale about finding a large arrow, some 20-feet in length. It was carved into some cliffs in the vicinity of Peck Canyon.

This canyon cuts through the widest of the mountains, and is the boundary line between the Tumacacori and the Atascosa Ranges.

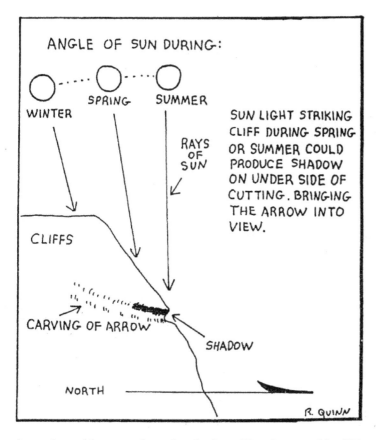

He also remarked the shadow of the arrow could only be seen during a certain time of the year and only during a particular time of day. It was carved at a 45-degree angle and pointed west when viewed from the north.

I believe what Louis had seen is called "open camouflage" and was employed by the Spaniards for the concealment of some of their treasures throughout the New World.

The signs were made quite large so they could be seen from a distance, and were cut into cliffs facing north. These signs could only be seen during the summer months and near high noon when the shadow would be most prominent.

During this time of year the sun would be almost overhead and would cast a shadow along the cutting-edge, bringing the sign into view. In the winter the angle of the sun is lower in the southern sky and would not produce the shadow. The sign would still be there, but would not stand out as much.

Louis had seen this marking several times and believed it was during late spring or early fall. He looked for it during the winter months, but it didn't appear on the cliffs from his vantage point about 200 feet away. He couldn't remember exactly where these cliffs were, but said they were near Peck Canyon around six miles west of the Tucson-Nogales Highway.

The arrow could have long since disappeared if it was cut into andesite. The light volcanic material has the tendency to flake off over the years. We've seen it happen at other locations. Water seeps in between the small cracks during the winter and when it freezes large thin portions flake away. It wouldn't take very long until the signs on the surface would be completely gone.

THE ABOVE ILLUSTRATION SHOWS WHAT THE ARROW SHOULD LOOK LIKE ON THE FACE OF THE CLIFFS.

R. QUINN

If someone did happen to find the correct area and it wasn't the right time of the year, the sign could go unnoticed unless one examined the cliffs carefully. It would also be difficult to see if the cliffs had hundreds of cracks running in all directions as most do.

What the arrow represents is not known but it could be pointing toward the entrance to some hidden mine, or to that one little word that turns most head when spoken, "treasure."

When the great Pima uprising began in 1751, the padres wouldn't have taken the necessary time to cut a 20-foot arrow showing the way to their buried wealth, not with Indians out looking for their scalps. The arrow could have another meaning and was no doubt carved long before the rebellion.

Again, to see this sign you would have to be at the right spot at the correct time, to see it slowly appear as the sun climbed higher.

During our many trips back into the remote area, we always kept a watchful eye out for this elusive arrow. Each set of cliffs facing north were examined carefully, but nothing resembling an arrow was ever found.

Louis did hear a tale, however, from another *vaquero* during the early '40s, when some men arrived from Texas and began searching the vicinity around Peck Canyon.

The group was looking for a rich silver mine once worked by the padres from Tumacácori Mission. One of the guideposts to its location was an arrow pointing toward the hidden entrance.

The four searched the area over a period of several months, then departed but returned the following year. After another futile attempt, they left the locality never to return.

When Louis first discovered the arrow, he didn't tie it in with the story concerning the four treasure hunters. He never was one to believe all the tales drifting about concerning lost mines and mission treasures. He never gave them much thought until meeting Chuck and me. Only then did he start remembering all the stories he had heard over the years.

It was too bad they didn't have portable tape recorders then—1956—as Louis was a walking book of knowledge when it came to this area.

I know we missed much by only taking notes at times, relying on our memories years later.

There just might be a hidden mine in or near Peck Canyon as Chuck and I did discover that single nugget of pure silver while digging into a small outcropping of caliche clay back in '57 in the area of this canyon.

I believe the story about his arrow is not well known, as I've never heard it mentioned by another individual during our 31 years of rainbow chasing here in Southern Arizona.

Chapter 50

ELEVEN BARS OF GOLD

Southern Arizona Trails International, Vol. 3, No. 32, May 26, 1987, Page 24

CALABASAS GOLD BARS

Southern Arizona Trails, Vol. 5, No. 244, July 16, 1991, Page 15

After the big crash of '29, a gentleman by the name of John Allen left New York and headed west. He traveled by car over the back roads of America, stopping at various towns for short periods of time; then moving on. He eventually arrived at Calabasas, AZ, a small village located some 15 miles north of the Mexican border.

At that time the population of this desert community was around 80. There was a general store, school and a cemetery just to the south.

John arrived about mid-fall and was surprised at the warm mild climate for so late in the year. After all those freezing winters he spent a New York, this was indeed a welcome treat. He decided to stay awhile and see if he could "thaw out" those cold winters from his bones.

There were several empty adobes in livable condition. After chasing a variety of desert varmints from one, he rented it on a month-to-month basis. In a short time he began to meet the other residents, and before long he was playing cards and checkers with the older population.

During the evenings they'd sit on the porch, swapping stories and discussing local gossip. One evening a Mexican gentleman in his late 70's, body wracked with arthritis, happened by and struck up a conversation in broken English. Pointing to a caved-in well, the old man told John that some outlaws had come through town in the 1880s and hid their stolen gold at the bottom of it. He told John that four years ago he met an old friend that once lived here as a boy, but left with his family and returned to Mexico.

It was this friend that witnessed the outlaws concealing the gold. The boy was afraid to mention what he had seen to anyone and kept the secret. His family remained in the village another year or so after the incident, and the boy kept an eye out for the strangers that hid the gold. He never saw them return for their ill-gotten loot.

While living in Mexico, he grew older, married and had a family of his own. Because he worked hard to support his family, he never had the opportunity to return and see if the treasure was still hidden. It is not known why his friend didn't return with the old man and attempt to retrieve the cache after telling him the story. Perhaps he was too old and sick to make the trip.

The crippled Mexican assumed the treasure was still in the well, which now was cluttered with rubbish, as some families has used it as a garbage pit. He couldn't dig due to his arthritis and when he tried to enlist the help of some local residents, they only laughed at his crazy tale. Some people said that if anything of value was there, it would have been dug up long ago.

Famous last words.

When somebody new arrived in the village, the old man would approach him and made his pitch in hopes they would help open the well. Most listened but politely turned him down, as they had their own work to attend to.

After hearing this most interesting story, John said he'd think it over. That night he decided to give it a try, as there was something in the old man's voice that convinced him that he might be telling the truth. Besides, the weather was cool and it gave him a chance for some needed exercise. Also, that nightly game of cards or checkers was starting to get a little stale.

A few days later, some residents spotted John building a windlass across the top of the old well. Some laughed and said, "So the old man got you to believe that crazy yarn."

John didn't mind the joking and kidding that was going on at his expense, so each morning he could be found digging away. The most difficult part was removing all the junk that had been thrown in over the years. Each day he'd be a little deeper and the joking would continue in a friendly way.

Some of the local cowboys heard of "John's Folly," as it came to be known, and would ride by, take a look, laugh and ride on shaking their heads.

The old Mexican would stop by and watch the proceedings from an old rickety chair, no doubt wishing he could lend a hand. Nobody would offer to help for any length of time, but some residents would happen by and turn the windlass to bring up several buckets of dirt. Most of the time John would have to climb up and do it himself, but he was in good shape for a man in his mid-fifties. Throughout his daily hours in the well, a head would appear above and someone would laugh and say "We told you so," or "Had enough, John?"

When he reached the 15 foot level, water began seeping in and turned the bottom to mud, making his work more difficult. After hitting water, he believed he had finally reached the bottom of the well.

A small pick he was using was beneath the mud near his feet. When he reached down to retrieve it, he felt something hard. After washing the mud off the object, John discovered a three pound bar of gold. A yell emerged from the bottom of that hole like a devil howling from hell.

By that afternoon, most of the village was standing around the well opening. On the ground before them were eleven bars of gold and several dozen gold coins. The old Mexican, who was home at the time of the discovery, now moved slowly through the crowd. He stood there with a tear in his eye as John offered him half the loot. John left Calabasas a few weeks later and drove off into the pages of history. The old man died several years later, after a good rich life and the last laugh.

There was still a substantial amount of money left after his passing which has never been found, as the old man didn't trust banks. The balance of this small fortune is believed buried somewhere within sight of the village as the old Mexican couldn't walk very far.

Like I have said many times, the gold from the earth is only given to us as a loan, and the earth will always get it back in the end. In a way it's true. Look at all the billions in lost treasure that has been buried back within the earth over the centuries: the Aztecs golden idols; the treasures of the ancient Egyptians; and the loot of a lone outlaw who hides it beneath a rock in hopes of later retrieval, who then rides of into the night never to return.

Chapter 51

THE HIDEOUS FACE

nother haunting story occurred on the western slopes of the Santa Rita Mountains located east of Tubac, Arizona. These rugged granite peaks rise abruptly from the valley floor. Many have been lost among their deep twisting canyons.

This tale was told to Frank Salcido by two brothers. Both were born in the region and grew up hearing stories of alleged treasures being hidden by the fleeing Spanish padres during the great Indian rebellion.

At times the two would explore the Santa Ritas in hopes of discovering one of the long lost treasures. During one such trip into these harsh mountains, one brother happened to slip, and slid down a small incline. As he came to an abrupt and jolting stop, he noticed an object protruding from the ground beside some rocks. To his surprise, it was an old revolver like they used during the Civil War. It was cap and ball and its cylinder still held several cartridges but the wood handle had long since rotted off.

Spotting his brother, he called telling him of the discovery. Checking the area carefully they found a narrow opening to a cave hidden behind some trees. With flashlight in hand both entered slowly, searching for any signs or sounds of rattlesnakes.

Bringing their light slowly up, the beam fell on a large statue, perhaps three feet high, of some Catholic saint. Its right arm was raised, and attached to the hand was a knife. On the dusty floor nearby were many old leather bags filled with gold nuggets.

Being Catholic, themselves, they figured whoever placed the statue there with the knife, hoped it would ward off any superstitious individuals that might stumble upon the cave. But the frightening display didn't disturb them.

As they searched around with hearts beating with excitement over their discovery, their light again fell on the face of the statue. At that moment another face, an ugly face, appeared over the statue's features. Its red eyes glowed from black holes, and a hideous grin appeared.

Both fell backwards in terror. The apparition's mouth slowly opened revealing its rotted teeth. Both scrambled from the cave, and ran, slipped, sometimes falling down the rocky slopes until reaching their truck.

One had unconsciously placed several gold nuggets in his pocket while there. These were later shown as proof of their discovery.

A month later, one returned to the area of the cave, but never again located the hidden site. Others have searched but never succeeded in finding the golden cache.

Was this their imagination or did some evil spirit appear on the peaceful face of the statue?

It also would be interesting to know what occurred at the site regarding the gun found there. It's not known whether the brothers had the weapon or left it behind during their mad scramble to flee the scene.

Perhaps others had discovered the gold, had a dispute over it and killed one another, leaving their blood spilling out on the unfriendly earth, along with the revolver. If so, where is the other weapon? It's just speculation but something deadly happened as nobody would deliberately leave their gun behind.

Perhaps the sneering face was the spirit of one of those that died during the argument over the treasure and his ghost now guards the fortune he believes rightfully belongs to him alone.

Chapter 52

THE STONE CHAIR CACHE

Southern Arizona Trails, Vol. 3, No. 161, November 7, 1989, Page 22

Since 1956, my partners and I have heard numerous tales of lost mines, buried treasures and various other hidden items of great value. This story is completely new and came to light about a month ago while visiting with friends. Their neighbor, Bill, stopped by while we were discussing the lost mines and treasures, supposedly hidden within the confines of the rugged Tumacacori Mountains.

After listening for a while, Bill told us a rather interesting tale of buried gold near a "natural stone chair," located in or near a canyon in a remote corner of these mountains.

Instantly, I remembered coming across such a stone chair while prospecting with my brother Chuck during the spring of '56. He had even taken a picture of me sitting in the chair before we moved on.

This is the story Bill told.

Sometime during the late 1800s, two Mexican bandits were returning to Mexico after a successful robbery on a group of travelers. They made off with approximately $6,000 in gold coins.

After a few days ride, they crossed the rolling hills north of what is now the Tumacacori Range.

They headed for a gap in the mountains just east of Bartolo Mountain. The area is known as Apache Pass, and not to be confused with the famous Apache Pass located near the ruins of old Fort Bowie.

As darkness closed in, the fleeing bandits decided to camp beside the canyon they were in.

As the sun peeked over the ridges the following morning, the two decided to bury most of the gold. If a posse was out searching for them, they didn't want to be found carrying such a large amount of money, which would surely cast suspicion on them as being the guilty party.

Each kept around a hundred dollars and buried the remainder near a natural stone chair they happened upon while looking for a suitable hiding place. It was rumored both died in Mexico in a shootout before returning to reclaim their ill-gotten loot.

That evening I searched through our old pictures trying to locate the one of me sitting in the chair, but no luck. After 33 years, I had most of the photos taken during that time, but a roll or two of negatives and some pictures were missing—no doubt lost during our many moves.

Next, I checked our old diary of 1956 and discovered the stone chair was found on April 9. But no clue was given to its exact location. Chuck's entry read in part, "We worked an area about three miles west of our base camp."

At that time, our camp was located at Murphy Well. This would place the location of the chair somewhere south of Bear Grass Tank. I remember we drove down the old ranch road near the tank that winds its way southward over the hills toward Apache Pass.

After 33 years, I find it difficult remembering exactly where Chuck and I stopped our jeep before heading out across country.

It was during this short prospecting trip we came upon the stone chair. It was located on a flat near a canyon surrounded by large trees and other boulders. Later that morning while returning to the jeep, we again passed the chair. At that time it was nothing more than an odd curiosity, and we paid little attention to its exact location.

It stood between six or seven feet in height, and about three feet wide. The seat itself was around five feet above the ground. It had short arms and a small backrest.

A few days later, I related the story to Bill Conley, another treasure hunter I've known for several years, and plans were made to make a trip into the region. I wanted to see if I could again locate the stone oddity after all these years.

We left Tucson on the morning of Oct. 7, arriving in the area around 11:00. Several spots looked vaguely familiar, and I expected to see the chair at any moment. We hiked a little over a mile down one rocky canyon without finding it. Afterward, Bill and I returned to his 4 x 4 and drove to another location, but still no luck.

Two weeks later we again ventured back in search of the elusive stone chair, this time arriving in the general vicinity about 8:30 a.m.

It was overcast and a fine rain was coming down, but this didn't hamper our search. Two other regions were carefully explored but again nothing. A number of locations resembling the spot, as I remember it, were found, but no chair. Not being discouraged, Bill and I returned a third time on Oct. 27 and searched several different locations. One particular area fitted the description perfectly.

Everything was there, the wide flat area beside a canyon, tall overhanging trees with large boulders scattered beneath them. Everything but the mysterious stone chair.

I know we're in the correct location, but it's difficult to remember where our wanderings had taken us that spring morning 33 years earlier.

Chuck and I both agreed we came upon the chair shortly after leaving our jeep. Also the entire round trip that day hadn't taken more than two or three hours. Upon returning to the jeep, we drove into Arivaca to check on the mail and purchase some needed supplies.

I'm quite certain we'll eventually find it, but it'll take several more trips and numerous hours of hiking

This is just another treasure tale, with no documentation, but it's still worth the time and effort to search, as the story just might be true.

I'm sure of one thing—the stone chair does exist. Even if no gold is discovered, I would again like to find that natural stone chair, if for nothing else, just to satisfy my own curiosity where that oddity is located.

Chapter 53

UFOs?

Southern Arizona Trails, Vol. 3, No. 44, August 18, 1987, Page 17-22

Another time while waiting for my partner Roy to arrive from San Francisco, I made camp west of Calabasas near Peck Canyon, and informed Roy by letter where I'd be. He wouldn't be arriving until sometime Monday, so I passed the time hiking about, doing target shooting and some reading.

Saturday morning around seven I heard the loud rumble of several trucks approaching. Three trucks and a car came into view then stopped a short distance away. People began pouring out of every door until there were perhaps 14 or so scrambling around.

Some old gal seemed to be in charge, and she started shouting instructions like a sergeant major. Spotting me she came over and said, "How long have you been here?"

I said, "Since Friday morning. Why?"

"Oh," she said, "then you must have seen it come down last night?"

Somewhat bewildered from all the sudden activity going on, I frowned slightly and replied, "Seen what come down, lady?"

This rather overbearing individual seemed surprised at my question and said, "Why, the UFO! It landed somewhere in this vicinity late last night, and the group and I are going to search for it." She asked again. "You positive you didn't hear or see anything strange?"

Some fellow way back yelled out, "Maybe the authorities already got to him, and made him promise to keep his mouth shut."

By this time I was becoming a little annoyed. I told her the only sounds I heard were some hungry coyotes out on their nightly hunt.

The group consisted of about eight men, some women, several children about 13 or so, and a few older folks. Anyway, it was quite a gang.

Most had packs on while others carried cameras, binoculars, canteens, and believe it or not, one guy had a Geiger counter. He was swiping the area with the instrument and keeping an eye on the needle. For a moment I thought this was all a dream and I was still asleep in the jeep. If this was so, I was hoping to awake soon.

Most started up the canyon while others climbed the nearby slopes like an army of ants. Comments, suggestions and idle chatter were going on among 'em.

Throughout the day, when the wind was right, I could hear some voices up canyon and occasionally I'd see a few in the distance on the rocky slopes.

Late that afternoon the small herd began filtering back. Most looked pretty well fatigued, especially the older ones. Reaching the vehicles, the raggedy group dropped in the shady areas and rested. Most had disappointment written across their faces, especially the old gal. By their conversation, they couldn't understand why the UFO hadn't been located.

I walked over to one fellow nearby and said, "How was your luck?" A few in the immediate area looked up, shook their heads "no" and returned their gaze to the ground.

After resting awhile, they started putting their gear away while a few others took pictures of the activities. One youngster even snapped one of me beside the jeep. Guess I'm in somebody's album somewhere.

I asked another gentleman how they knew a UFO had landed. He said a friend of theirs was in the service and stationed at Davis-Monthan. He had overheard several officers discussing a report about a UFO landing in the Peck Canyon area. Also, radar hadn't picked up any object taking off, so they assumed the UFO was still there. This individual had called several group members and informed them about the incident.

A short while later they all left, leaving the canyon once more to its peaceful solitude. I have to say, though, they did pick up all their litter before departing.

That evening I again heard only the sounds of the desert night. No pulsating lights were radiating up from behind any hills, and no humming sounds were coming from the dark canyon. I do have an open mind when it comes to unusual tales, and often wonder if there was any truth to that serviceman's story.

After Roy arrived I told him the entire story, then we left for an area north of Tucson.

Chapter 54

THE GUADALUPE MYSTERY

Southern Arizona Trails, Vol. 3, No. 68, January 26, 1988, Pages 19, 23

T he majority of the gold and silver accumulated by the padres of the Tumacácori Mission was supposedly hidden within the Guadalupe Mine. Its location: about one league (2.5 miles) southwest of the mission.

This legend was first told around open campfires by Indians living in the vicinity. When it finally reached the white man's ears, the search was on and has continued to this very day.

The treasure's total value has been greatly exaggerated, but if such a cache exists somewhere within these desert hills the amount would be quite sizable.

Most tales centering around this well-known treasure, claim there are 2,050 mule loads of silver and 905 loads of gold bullion concealed deep within the hidden tunnel.

With their crude mining and smelting methods, I doubt this much precious metal could have been extracted from these hills in a hundred years.

The story goes, some white man befriended an Indian and he described the mine and its location to this individual. The old Indian also claimed he was taken to the mine once as a young boy. If this white man was ever led there by the old Indian, I'm not certain.

In old Spanish writings, this mine was called "La Virgen de Guadalupe" and belongs to the string of rich workings that were operated by the Jesuit padres of Tumacácori.

It was located one league from the entrance of the church to the south and from the water of San Ramon toward the left in a northerly direction some 1,800 *varas*. The mine was in operation from 1508 to 1648.

Two hundred *varas* before arriving at the mine there is a dark rock marked with a cross and the letters CCDTD on the underside of the stone. This information was supposedly copied from old documents found in Spain.

There are persistent rumors that some treasure has been removed from Tumacácori Mission. These consisted of bullion, both gold and silver, crosses and various altar fixtures made of silver. It's also rumored that several smaller tunnels were discovered while excavation was under way at the monument, but this is, of course, denied by monument officials to this day.

When the treasure was hidden within the mine, two mountain areas were "off limits." It was then the "Baca Land Grant #3" and the owner never gave permission to anyone to search this property.

I understand its changed ownership and Rio Rico Properties of Nogales now owns the land. I'm quite certain you wouldn't have much difficulty entering and searching, but I would first contact them before trying.

Several individuals also claim most of these lost mines are located just below the border in the vicinity of the famous "Planchas de Plata" discovery. I'm sure this silver was found long after the discovery of the Tumacacori Mine, as it was discovered sometime during the fall of 1736 by a party of Indians; then later worked by the Spanish.

It's estimated some of these huge slabs of native silver weighed in at 2,500 pounds.

It also has never been determined where the first mission of Tumacácori was located, but I'm reasonably certain it was within a league of the present and "new mission." The measurements that were given in locating the mines were taken from the "old mission," not the one that stands on the monument grounds today. If it was built further south, there's a strong possibility most of these treasures are located just over the border in Mexico. As you can see, there are numerous probabilities, and this is what makes searching for these treasures so difficult. They could exist in three or four different locations, with two hundred years of erosion helping to conceal their entrances, and with very few clues, if any, on the surface.

If somebody could actually discover one of the landmarks referred to in these documents, one would have a definite starting point, and perhaps locate one or more of these old Spanish mines. Even if no treasure was found, it would at least shed some light on these endless stories of hidden treasures.

So you can see how frustrating this treasure hunting can become. Like I jokingly told some recent new treasure seekers I met, "If you don't enjoy hiking rugged terrain for hours on end or have the patience of Job, leave it alone and take up another hobby like ping-pong or something." When the treasure was hidden within the mine, two mountain peaks were supposedly blasted down over the entrance, but this I find somewhat difficult to believe.

The trouble with this story is that there are numerous version and countless ideas where the mine might be. Some claim it's not located in the Tumacacori Mountains, but southeast toward the San Cayetano Range. This sounds more logical as this area is well mineralized and several working minds have operated in the district.

The region 2.5 miles southwest of the mission is completely barren but a few diggings are scattered throughout the vicinity. We have explored portions of the area and, believe me, there isn't a thing there that would interest a prospector or geologist. A substantial treasure was located several years back, but it's believed to have originated in Mexico and later buried quite near the border on the American side. It consisted of 251 pounds of gold bullion.

I did hear once that some Indian showed a white man a single bar of gold and wanted his help in selling it. The agreement somehow went sour and the Indian became frightened and reburied the bullion. It's believed he hid it somewhere near the old rock corral, located beside the canyon of the same name. Where he obtained the gold is not known, but some believe it came from a small treasure cave in the immediate vicinity. Many have searched for this cache and it's rumored a man from Tucson did discover it and removed a portion of the treasure, but the remainder still is hidden somewhere among the surrounding hills. This individual went blind before he could return and claim the rest.

If I were to seriously undertake a search for the Guadalupe Mine, I'd first satisfy myself by making a token search near the head of Tinaja Canyon, located just southwest of Tumacacori. From this point I'd fan out and search in a northeasterly direction.

Afterward I would make a diligent effort to search the terrain northeast from the mission in the vicinity of the San Cayetano Mountain

THE SO-FAR FRUITLESS HUNT FOR GUADALUPE MINE

Southern Arizona Trails, Vol. 4, No. 229, February 26, 1991, Page 18

P eople have been searching for the lost Guadalupe mine and the incredible treasure alleged to be hidden within the old mine workings for countless years. One noted treasure hunter is Bob Pate, from Carmichael, Calif. I first met this interesting gentleman and his partners a few years ago through Bill Conley, another treasure enthusiast I have known for several years.

At that time Bob and company were searching for this elusive treasure southwest of the Rock Corral Ranch. His research indicated the old Spanish mine might be located beneath an outcropping of rock his partners had found.

After obtaining a treasure permit at the cost of $250 and putting up a cash bond of several thousand dollars, work began at the site. Bulldozers and a large backhoe were moved onto the property. After several weeks of extensive digging, no treasure was found.

A year later, Bob and his partners again returned and began peeling away the rock after obtaining another permit, from the old Workman claims located in Peck Canyon. Again no treasure, but they did receive some positive readings on their state-of-the-art detectors.

Their third attempt at unraveling this mystery occurred toward the end of last year [1990]. Again they were back in Peck Canyon, but several hundred yards west of their previous diggings.

Work was delayed through bureaucratic paper shuffling, and also Bob had broken his arm while in Nogales. Finally work began in February.

A long trench a few hundred feet in length and 40 feet deep at the center was cut through a hill where Bob guessed the treasure might be located.

No treasure or ancient mine workings were discovered, but a suspicious reading on their detector at the 40 foot level indicated something metallic might be buried below. It's quite common to receive false reading in these hills, known to many treasure hunters as "hot rocks."

Bill Conley, his son Bill Jr. and I drove to Peck Canyon and met Jay Hudson, one of Bob's partners. We then proceeded to the site after navigating the rugged road leading to the property.

We spent our time examining the area and interjecting our own comments about the site and the alleged treasure. Bill Conley also took pictures for his third story for *Treasure* magazine about Bob Pate's relentless quest for the elusive Guadalupe hoard.

On Feb. 13 a bombshell was dropped on Bob Pate's lap. The Forest Service asked him to cover up the excavation and be off the property by Feb. 15 and not to come back.

This strange turn of affairs occurred only a few weeks after work began. The permit allows the Forest Service to terminate digging activities at their discretion. Since then they have backed off and allowed work to continue.

I heard a group of hikers happened upon the diggings and complained to authorities about the "ugly scar upon the land." This could have triggered the action to terminate Bob's lease on the site.

Over the years other excavations were dug by Pate and company and no negative response was ever heard. These diggings were covered and seeded with desert growth when the property was abandoned. This time, however, tongues started wagging in protest

Could it also be possible the Forest Service and others believe the Guadalupe treasure might just be found this time and moved to prevent its recovery?

If indeed it was discovered, the flood gates would be opened and other treasure hunters, realizing the tales of Tumacácori's legendary hidden treasures are true, would swarm onto the land like locusts, digging and gouging away at the landscape in search of other possible treasures.

I can understand their concern about this possibility. The surrounding countryside would resemble an artillery range.

On the 16th, the excavation had reached the 51-foot level, but again nothing of interest was found.

I hope Bob Pate or somebody will eventually find this treasure, if in fact it does exist.

Documentation and years of research prove "something" is buried out among the rocky canyons of the Tumacacori and Atascosa Mountains. I also have doubts the total value of this hidden cache isn't as great as some might hope.

Will this treasure ever be found? Only time will tell.

There are also those who believe the Jesuits never carried on any extensive mining operations in this region. There are also those who like to hide the facts that they did.

Chapter 55

HOMEWARD BOUND

At this time camp was located in Carreta Canyon. It was decided to search once more for the elusive well, but after five days we gave up. Later, Roy left for California informing us where to meet him in Pasadena. Walt drove north to seek employment at the new Glen Canyon Dam being built on the Colorado River.

During the evening I stepped from our tent, like I did upon first arriving two years before. I looked around admiring this fabulous country we'd soon be leaving. A warm breeze brushed past my cheek, signaling the approach of spring. The rugged mountains we had explored stood silently against the sky overlooking the terrain below. It brought back memories of all the wonderful adventures we had experienced, from things we discovered and friends we had made.

Toward the east the light from the setting sun could be seen reflecting off the cliffs beneath Sardina Peak, as dark shadows crept eastward like a giant hand slowly enclosing over the land.

We had traveled Southern Arizona, discovering many places and heard countless tales; hiked some canyons so narrow and deep, their depth only caught sunlight several minutes during the cycle of a day. We met Roy and Walt, who became lifelong friends.

We arrived here over 23 months earlier in our quest for treasure, and lived a happy carefree life and gathered memories that would remain forever. Like Frank Sinatra singing, "I Did It My Way," we in turn did it "our way" with no regrets.

We had established some 19 different camps, met interesting people, found numerous sites seldom visited by man. Crawled through old mines and dangerous caves where ancient Indians once lived. Found an old Spanish mine minus the treasure and a strange wall surrounded in mystery. We also had the privilege of knowing the master story tellers, John D. Mitchell, and Louie Romero.

The following morning we broke camp and drove to Arivaca to bid goodbye to our new found friends. Even old cranky Tata hated to see us go. To us it was a sad day, as I felt as though I was leaving part of myself behind. On the other hand, I felt I was taking something with me.

As we turned onto the old Nogales Highway, I could see the Tumacacori Mountains through the rearview mirror. They slowly slid from view behind nearby hills. Our trip had ended and we were heading home.

After meeting Roy, we drove north to Washington. Roy wanted to visit his brother in Seattle before again shipping out.

Chapter 56

THE RETURN

U pon arriving home, we both obtained employment. After two years of freedom, the daily routine of working turned unpleasant as my heart was still roaming the mountains of Arizona. I kept searching for a way to return, and that opportunity presented itself three months later.

One evening Roy called asking if I'd like to accompany him on a search for the Lost Escalante Mine believed to be hidden somewhere within the Santa Catalina Mountains north of Tucson. Roy had obtained some documents from Don Page regarding this famous gold mine once worked by the Spaniards. I informed him I didn't have the necessary capital for such a trip. "Hell," said Roy. "Come on down and I'll pick up the tab."

That adventurous spirit once again stirred, so I accepted. The family thought I was crazy, especially Chuck. "Give up the ghost," he said. "We searched for two years and never found any treasure. What makes you think you'll find something this time?" I had a little savings for any unexpected expenses I might incur. I knew why Roy had called. He didn't like tramping these dangerous mountains alone as accidents do occur, especially when you're alone. Six days later I arrived at his motel on the old Benson Highway south of Tucson. We hadn't heard from Walt since last seeing him and I knew why. Walt wasn't much in corresponding. One day you'd turn around and he'd just be there.

After several weeks exploring the numerous canyons and high peaks in the Santa Catalinas we returned to Tucson for awhile. While driving on North Stone Avenue, I spotted a gray Willys heading south. As it passed, I shouted, "Turn around, it's Walt!" Three blocks later we caught up and began waving and yelling. Walt turned to see our two smiling faces. I thought he'd run off the road. Walt said, he tried acquiring work at Glen Canyon Dam, but discovered you had to know somebody first. Returning to Tucson, he found night work and entered the University of Arizona to study geology. When asked where Chuck was, I said, "He decided to remain home this time."

Roy and I spent three months scrambling around the high rugged Catalinas searching for the Escalante with no luck. However, we did locate two Spanish *arrastras* half buried beside the Cañada del Oro Wash, and the stone houses built by those working the mine. A month later Roy returned to the ships, and I drove on home. Before leaving, Roy handed me $300 to help tied me over until I found work. This I promised to repay, which I did a year later. Of course, Roy didn't want it, so it was pushed back and forth across the table until he finally accepted it. Walt continued attending the U of A for another year. This time I told him to keep in touch through our parents address.

Chuck and I returned to Tucson in 1963, making it our permanent home. All four of us were still a bunch of "worthless bachelors" as some friends called us, enjoying life to the fullest and having good times, and of course, still heading into the hills at times in our relentless search for treasures. Walt was still attending the university. He is what is known as a professional student. Roy was still on the ships but would be retiring soon. Occasionally he'd visit for several weeks then move on.

There weren't any more lengthy trips, but we'd spend a few weeks exploring other locations previously not searched. I was employed at KOLD-TV as news photographer until Chuck and I opened Aztec Film Produdtions, filming local TV commercials, travel films and medical photography.

OUR MAJOR FIND

Chapter 57

"MAYAN NUMBERS LEAD TO EVERY TREASURE HUNTER'S DREAM"

I'm pictured with our treasure discovery in 1984.

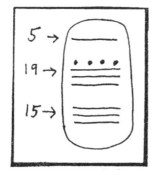

Mayan Number Rock.

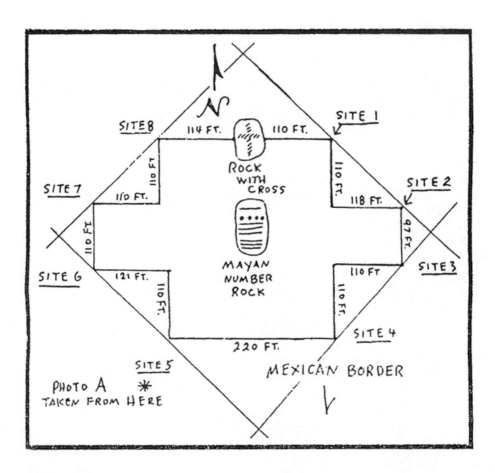

Diagram of treasure site.

Site 1 produced 27 lbs. of gold; Site 2, 16 lbs.; Site 3, 10 lbs.; Site 4, nothing; Site 5, nothing; Site 6, 19 lbs.; Site 7, nothing; Site 8, 10 lbs. of gold.

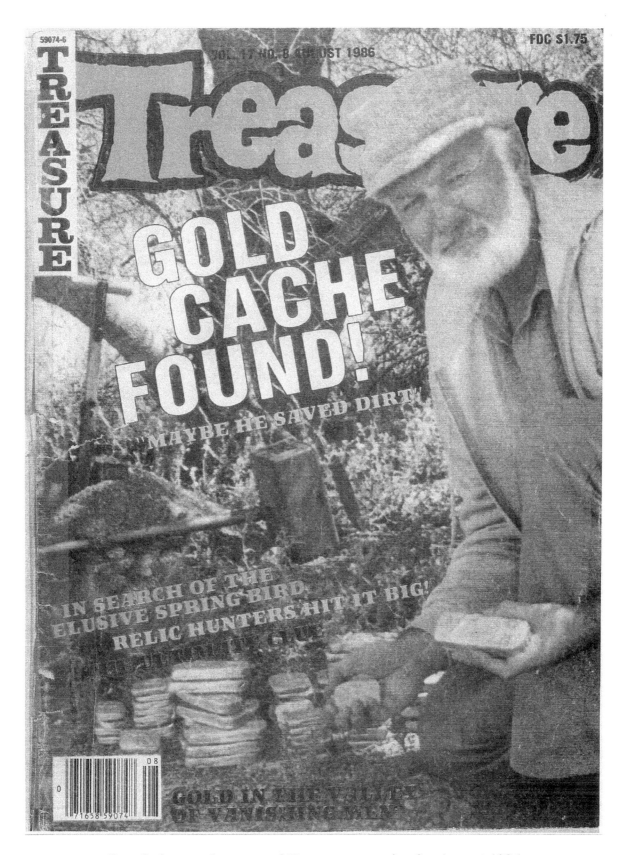

Ron Quinn on the cover of *Treasure* magazine for August 1986

TREASURE SITE

LOCATION OF DISCOVERIES
1. Cache Site #8 = 10 lbs. of gold bars
2. Cross on Rock located behind this hill
3. Mayan Number Rock located on top of hill
4. Cache Site #1 = 27 lbs. of gold bars

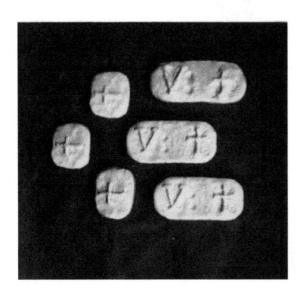

Gold bars found by Ron Quinn and partners.

FOUND! 82 POUNDS OF GOLD BARS

Treasure Magazine, Vol. 17, No. 8, August 1986, Pages 56-59, 61

Editor's Note: For obvious reasons, the author of this article prefers to remain anonymous, as do his partners, who bear fictitious names. Nothing else, including the location of the site, has been changed. The following article appeared in Treasure *magazine. It gives details of the treasure find by the four partners. Note: Dave = Roy Purdie, Ted = Walt Fisher, Jim = Chuck Quinn, Bill = Ron Quinn.*

[Ron Quinn's Discovery Story]

Since the mid-1950s, my three partners and I have been prospecting and treasure hunting in Arizona. Most of our trips have taken us into rough mountains and desert country of the southern part of this picturesque state. One expedition lasted a full 23 months.

During these odysseys across Arizona, we visited many desolate lonely sites. Most are one step away from being ghost towns; others barely maintain populations of more than one hundred. We have encountered many colorful, friendly old-timers residing in these out-of-the-way hamlets who have little to occupy their time save sitting in the shade swapping stories, which they wholeheartedly believe, while watching "Front Street" go by.

These cheerful, often witty, weather-beaten "ledge lizards" (Gold bless them) have spun us many tales of buried bandit loot, lost mines and Spanish treasure—including their values and current status, no matter how precarious. These stories floated about freely, with "facts" as varied as the tellers' personalities. Though we found their stories interesting, we have usually disregarded them because most lacked sufficient documentation to launch an all-out search.

Most treasure leads we followed had been well researched and documented. But, the problem encountered when searching many documented sites is their popularity. It seems that everybody and his grandmother have searched for them at one time or another. Some sites resemble old artillery ranges, with holes covering nearly every square yard.

While one of my partners, whom I'll call Dave, and I explored some interesting country near the Mexican border, during the closing weeks of fall 1983, we climbed a hill to get a better view of an area we hoped to prospect. Dave, finding himself near an outcropping of rock at the summit, called me over. He showed me some faint markings he had accidentally found on the soft volcanic rock. Although erosion had taken its toll, they were still visible if viewed from an angle. We'd come across many markings during our lengthy adventures, but nothing resembling these. They consisted of a single straight line about ten inches long, followed by four dots in a row, and three more straight lines beneath. About five inches further down there were three more line. I made a copy of the symbols and marked the site on our topographical map. On the next day of our overnight trip we discovered a flat rock marked with a cross a little over 100 feet north of the symbols Dave found the day before. As this was beginning to look interesting, we checked the area over again, took pictures and returned home.

Out came all our treasure-related resource materials books, maps, charts, and reference on known treasure signs and symbols. A week or so later Dave, our two other partners (Ted and Jim), and I returned to the area to begin gridding it out. We were certain these symbols had something to do with that one little word which turns everyone's head upon hearing—"treasure."

Jim and Ted worked the area near the rocks, using a length of cord to grid the site in 10-foot squares, then detecting within the squares. They did this around both markings. By working out to a distance of about 80 feet, they came fairly close to a couple of the caches without knowing it in the meantime. Dave and I visually searched all rocks within a two hundred yard radius of the symbols with great care but found nothing. Two days later and still no further ahead, we returned home to take care of other business ventures.

I kept thinking about the first markings we discovered, knowing I'd seen them at least once, but couldn't remember where. Commitments kept all four of us from returning to the site together, although some of us were able to make frequent visits there either alone or in pairs, always returning empty-handed.

During the fall of 1985, almost 22 months after finding the marks, I was looking through some books on ancient civilizations of Mexico and South American and turned a page. There in front of me were the markings, the Mayan numbers system.

We then went to work trying to figure the meaning of both the markings and the cross. Ted, the mathematician of the group, handled all the calculations. We all worked on the directions, and he checked our findings.

The same question lurked in all our minds. What are Mayan numbers doing in Arizona, near an undoubtedly Spanish Christian cross? The ideas we came up with in the next few weeks were far too numerous and confusing to describe here. The Mayan numbers were 5, 19 and 15. On large 11 x 14 paper, I drew the locations of both rocks and indicated north. Each sheet had its own various calculations and directions. Before we had finished, there would be well over forty separate sheets. The probabilities seemed endless.

Armed with these maps and a positive attitude, we all left for the site in two 4 x 4 campers. Three hours later we stood beside the Mayan Number Rock, as we came to name it. Camp was established about half a mile to the west, as the terrain was far too rugged, even for four-wheelers.

By the second day, the maps we'd prepared and Ted's calculations weren't working out. The rough terrain had caused us to take several spills, damaging one of the two detectors. Nevertheless we once again had come very close to one of the caches (Site 1) with our techniques without realizing it.

The following morning, as Dave checked due east of the cross, he received a strong reading on the detector. We dug less than two feet and bingo! Bars of shining yellow gold and 2-by-2-inch gold squares, totaling 27 pounds, were looking back at us! Our actions during the moments following our discovery defy description, but I can relate a lot of yelping, something akin to dancing, and laughing was involved.

After some of the shock wore off, we began to hope for other sites in the area. Ted, the least emotional member of our team, suggested we measure the distance from the cache at Site 1 back to the cross. It came out to almost 110 feet. Working with the numbers on the rock, Ted eventually derived the following equation: $5 \times 19 + 15 = 110$. Wondering if this was a magic number, we then measured from the cross 110 feet west and detected all along this line, including 15 feet on both sides. Bingo! We made another find at 114 feet—10 pounds of gold (at what we later called Site8). We went wild again, but Ted kept his cool.

As dusk approached, we packed the gold into three back packs and happily made the 15 minute hike back to camp. Our excitement remained fervent, so much so, no one got much sleep. We sat up until one o'clock in the morning passing the bars around, guessing their weights and wondering if anymore gold remained buried out there.

Next day before sunrise, we were again on our way. The gold from the day before, we hid in a hole east of camp to keep it safe, even though we hadn't seen anyone for days since turning off the main road. The country was so rough we hoped it would remain that way. It did.

Reaching our site, we started running our 200-foot line out from the cross in various directions detecting first those spots between 95 and 119 feet. We also searched along those lines completely and about fifteen feet either side, as we did before, but found nothing. Lady Luck would again be with us that afternoon, although none of us knew it at the time.

While having lunch near Site 1, I mentioned we should run lines and detect north and south from this point. The others agreed. First we tried north, and found nothing; then south and again found nothing. Dave suggested we next run the line east from the point we had just checked; which was about 110 feet south of Site 1. We did this and 118 feet out, found the third cache — 16 pounds of gold at Site 2. During this measuring and detecting, we all fooled and joked around some, while still keeping our minds on our work. After the discovery of this third cache, the fooling came to an abrupt end. It finally began to sink in that we really were on to something.

The next brainstorm was mine. I spoke up, "It seems like we're going in steps — east from cross 110, south 110 and east again 110. If we continue south, then west and south again every 110 feet or so, and do this all the way around, we would be making a cross." Ted caught the mistake and showed us my error. He noticed that, if a cross pattern were the key, then we would have to run out our line 220 feet (not 110) the second time we turned west. Only in this way could we work out a cross pattern that would take us back to where we had found the second cache, at Site 8.

Since it was getting late by this time, we put off running the line out until the next day. The following morning was cloudy and windy, and all of us hoped it wouldn't rain, as the sky looked unfriendly. Luck again was with us — not a drop of rain all day.

Using the sign of the cross, we ended up finding two more caches, 10 pounds of gold at Site 3 and 19 pounds at Site 6. Like the previous caches, they were buried only 1½ to 2 feet deep. We kept to the same count of about 110 feet all the way around. We checked each site carefully and even worked out quite a distance on all sides. When a site failed to produce gold, we ran out our 110-foot measurements in other directions. The sites yielding gold did not come out to 110 feet each time. The distances varied from 97 to 121 feet. The reason for this may have been the rugged country, where exact measurements were virtually impossible.

Needless to say we were not at all disappointed with the overall results. We had discovered the treasure through hard work, guesses, calculations, and of course luck especially in coming up with the cross design. Why some sites had gold and others didn't could have been planned that way to throw off those who stumbled on the area and tried searching. If they discovered one cache, they might have thought that's all there was and moved on. Or, maybe this was someone's "bank," and he had made three withdrawals.

Numerous other questions came to us. Who buried the gold and when? Why wasn't it ever claimed? Why such an elaborate layout when a simpler one may have been as effective? How did the person (people) concealing the gold know the Mayan number system, and why was it used?

After batting these questions back and forth among us, we came to the conclusion the gold must have been brought from Mexico because there are no mines, past or present, in the area that could produce such an amount of gold. Also no Spanish missions existed nearby. The caches could have been buried at anytime, but we think the most likely time span to be from the mid-1750s to the early 1800s. Why the treasure was concealed at this location is anybody's guess, but whoever supervised the elaborate undertaking was probably a highly educated, very clever and cautious individual. The cross on the rock was telling us, only in a whisper, that the treasure was buried in that shape. Like I told my partners—when the Spanish conquest began in Mexico [New Spain], first came the priest and the soldier, then the businessman. Since the latter invest, rather than hoard money, the person responsible may have been one of the other two.

If the gold did come from Mexico, the person who brought it may have previously visited some Mayan ruins and studied their number system, as many dwellings no doubt had it carved into stone to withstand the onslaught of time and the elements. Perhaps a descendant of the Maya civilization taught him. Spanish officer or priest, whoever it was, did a masterful job using both the cross and the Mayan numbers.

Studying the treasure afterward, we tried to determine exactly what unit of measurement the Mayas used. We called the Archaeology Department at the University of Arizona, but nobody knew the answer. One professor did say that no one has ever been able to come up with the exact measure they used. It certainly wasn't close to the unit usually associated with treasure in the Southwest—the Spanish vara, which ranged from 31 to 33 inches. If our magic number was the correct one, 110 varas would have placed the gold over 300 feet from the cross. Rather, the Mayan unit may have been close to our 12-inch foot, give or take a few inches either way, since our 110-foot line worked out so well for us.

In closing, I would like to reiterate something said earlier. Most treasure tales have been blown clear out of proportion, with the telling and retelling of the stories down through the years. We have heard tales of buried gold amounting to $50 million and $100 million here in Arizona. For instance, in 1951 a treasure was found in the Yuma area of Arizona. Stories had it valued around a million. I know for certain it was only worth in the neighborhood of about $90,000.

My advice to the weekend treasure hunter is, do your homework first, then check and recheck every lead. My partners and I spend 80 percent of our time researching and 20 percent in the field. One treasure in 30 years isn't a good track record, but we did finally locate one. Maybe this is the way it has to be, for those priests and Spaniards were a shrewd lot when it came to hiding their wealth.

Chapter 58

WHAT WE DID WITH THE TREASURE

Many have asked what we did with the gold after the discovery in 1984.
Roy had a friend in Portland, Oregon that dealt with various private collectors, etc. After contacting, Frank, as we'll call him, he wanted to see the items. Two days later we traveled north in Roy's large camper. During the journey I kept saying, "Let's not get in an accident. We don't want bullion scattered all over the highway."

Three days later we arrived in Portland and checked into a motel. After viewing the gold, Frank took several samples for analysis. Smelting was rather crude during the 1700s, the time we believed the gold was buried. There was a small percentage of copper within the bullion.

A price of $410,000 was agreed to. It was worth much more, but Frank had the contacts for its disposal, and he also was entitled to a nice profit. Frank said he'd have a cashers check by the next day. Walt, the quiet one among us, stood listening then spoke up, "No way. We'd rather have cash."

We all grinned but Frank looked somewhat uncomfortable. He replied, "I understand but it'll take perhaps forty-eight hours to obtain that amount." We took shifts going out for meals and other necessities, with two of us always remaining at the motel. We didn't want 82 pounds of gold sitting under the bed unattended.

As promised, Frank arrived carrying a brown attaché case filled with large bills. At times this trip resembled some scene out of a James Bond adventure film. After the attaché was opened, Walt removed several bills at random inspecting them near a light. To break the quietness which hung over the room, I said jokingly, "We have an over cautious partner here. You'll have to forgive 'em."

After the exchange was made we departed that afternoon with me once again saying, "Remember, drive carefully. We…" Roy cut in saying, "We know. We don't want money blowing all over the highway."

Upon arriving back in Tucson, we sat around the table counting out our shares. Roy, the comedian was seen "accidently" dropping extra bills into his lap. He'd pause during the counting and several more would flutter down. When called about this, Roy looked quite surprised saying, "Why I'm not doing any such thing." Then looking down he continued, "Now where did these come from?"

Turning toward Roy, Chuck said, "I think a little of old J.D. Mitchell has rubbed off on you." After the kidding was over we each had $102,000. The other two thousand was used for our expenses to Portland, some gifts and several nights on the town. It had taken us many years of searching, digging and numerous disappointments but we eventually discovered a substantial sized treasure. It was the high point of our lives. Chuck and I also had something else of value. Two of the best friends anyone could ever have — Roy and Walt. I was happy we found something before one of us past on.

Chapter 59

CONCLUSION

One evening in 1989 we received a call from Roy. While he and Walt were camping near Prescott, Walt complained of chest pains. Roy drove him to the Fort Whipple VA Hospital east of town. Soon after arriving, our friend of 33 years passed away from a heart attack. It was devastating to all as Walt was like a brother.

Over the years we lost contact with Louie since retiring from the Arivaca Ranch. Years later I learned he was living in Tucson at his daughter's and in poor health. I called saying who I was and that I'd like to surprise him with a visit.

As I walked into his room, Louie was a frail elderly man. At first he didn't recognize me until I showed him several pictures. His deep lined face lit up, asking which brother I was. I answered, "Ron."

We reminisced for hours about the good old days, Arivaca, the gang, Mitchell and our wild treasure hunting adventures. Before leaving he took my hand, thanking me for remembering him. The old vaquero had tears in his eyes. Smiling I said, "We don't forget our friends Louie. You were just a little difficult to track down."

His daughter walked me to the door saying, "Thank you so much for coming. Dad hasn't laughed that much in years. I know he really appreciated the visit. He has spoken of you boys many times." I told her Chuck was out of town and we'd pay Louie another visit upon his return. Several months later, Louie passed away at the age of 92.

During 1992, Roy stopped by saying he was heading back to Seattle for the summer. He never liked the heat, and when the first bead of perspiration appeared on his brow, Roy was gone. He shook hands saying, he'd return by mid-October. That was on a Monday afternoon.

Five days later, Ben a friend of Roy's in Tucson called saying Roy was gone. "I know," I answered. "He left Monday."

"No," said Ben. "I mean he died this afternoon." I asked how and was told Roy had been working on his boat and asked his brother Glenn for a tool and collapsed.

Glenn couldn't locate our number so asked Ben to call. This old man of the sea was like a brother to us. We had many adventures and shared hours of laughter. They often say if you have one true friend during a life time you're a wealthy person. Chuck and I had two of the best, Roy and Walt.

I'm the last survivor now. I still venture out among the desert hills, visit Arivaca, enjoy the great outdoors and witness many of Arizona's spectacular sunsets.

Bill Conley, a new treasure hunting partner will occasionally travel with me on short excursions. We visit old camps and I take him to various sites throughout the mountains.

At times when camping alone and hiking old routes and using my imagination, I can almost hear Chuck, Roy and Walt joking from across the canyons. Wherever I looked, memories were rekindled. Old camp sites were overgrown, and bits of debris could be seen among the vegetation.

In the evening as the sun slowly sank from view the mountain tips still caught sunlight and solitude once again settled over the land. Yes, we had great times during those years. To me it was more than just a trip. It was an experience I'll never forget.

Most of our friends, Hack, Tata, Nicho, the Lopez boys and all the others have long since passed away. One thing I'm grateful for is we finally discovered one treasure before losing Roy and Walt.

Are other treasures still hidden among the hills? Of course there are. Will some eventually be found? Maybe. Will I ever find another, perhaps, but I have my doubts. One thing for sure though, you'll always find me out there searching.

In 1991 Bill and I returned to Carreta Canyon. It had been some 16 years since last being there. In '56 we had left several empty cans wedged between some boulders. They were still there, but all rusted and full of small holes. As I looked at them I felt that old sentimental feeling creep over me.

Bill's oldest son was an electronic wiz, and developed his own highly sensitive detector. While using it in the vicinity of the hidden well, he received a rather strong reading. Our hearts jumped at the possibilities of what might lie below. After digging perhaps a foot we unearthed a ring of stones 36 inches across, and extending downward some ten inches. We had found the well.

We returned the following day along with Bill's two boys. We began the slow process of sinking a shaft. Ours was much larger, measuring 4 x 5 feet. The earth in the area of the well was mostly gravel washed in over the years.

After reaching a depth of seven feet we hit bedrock, but no treasure. What the detector responded to is what is known as "hot rocks," and is prominent in this local. We had come across this numerous times during our travels. It's caused by the high content of iron within the rock formations. Anyway, we finally solved the mystery surrounding the elusive well.

A treasure might still be located somewhere within the immediate area, but where? Perhaps Mitchell knew. The padres were quite ingenious when it came to concealing their treasures.

Bill ventured back several times on his own to search, but never found anything. Keep in mind, that cutlass was discovered near the site of the ox cart, so something definitely occurred there.

Later I met Mike Garrison, a young man full of enthusiasm toward treasure hunting. He like others was intrigued with the story surrounding the golden necklace. Mike called several times asking about the story and asked if I had other information. After numerous calls and ventures into the alleged area we finally met. Like us years earlier, Mike was captivated by the thought of finding this treasure and others.

I have to give him credit; he was persistent in his quest for the golden artifact. Winter or summer, Mike would be found searching various locations he believed the necklace was buried.

Months later I decided to give him the original map drawn by Wallace. His reaction was like he had just won the state lottery. He couldn't thank me enough. To have in his possession the genuine treasure map was overwhelming. Mike insists he will continue the search, and if the necklace is still buried somewhere among the rocky canyons he might eventually discover the hidden site. He believes there is a secret clue on the map also. For someone to devote this much time in the hunt, I decided he deserved the map. As far as I know, Mike still searches the barren foothills of the Tumacacoris in his long quest for the golden necklace.

Someday all four of us will meet again in that Big Lost Mine in the sky. Roy, Walt and Chuck will appear, telling me about some hidden treasure buried just beyond the next cloud bank. Perhaps old Mitchell will be there trying to sell new arrivals some mining claim. Louie will be seen riding across the open sky chasing cattle up a cloudy draw. The four of us will then walk off into the setting sun laughing, joking and remembering all the wonderful adventures we had. ONCE UPON A TIME IN ARIZONA, LONG...LONG... AGO.

SOME ARIVACA TALES, GOOD FRIENDS, INTERESTING CHARACTERS & SURVIVAL TIPS

Chapter 60

ARIVACA

Arivaca in March 1956.

**Hack Townsend with rattlesnake we accidently ran over on our way into
Arivaca several months after our arrival.**

D uring our stay in this quaint little pueblo of Arivaca, nestled beneath the Arizona skies, we came to know most of its residents, one being Harvey Riggs. As a hobby, he published a small 8 x 10 four page newsletter, *The Arivaca Briefs*. It contained various articles about the town, its people and the outlying districts. One could not keep a secret there. If something occurred, it appeared in the *Briefs* the following Sunday.

Harvey discovered I was a cartoonist when we first met at the cantina. Afterward, he invited Chuck and me over to his home. Within a week I was furnishing cartoons for the paper. Most were of local characters and various situations which happened around town.

The locals looked forward to picking up a copy. These were available at both stores and the cantina. They wanted to see who would be appearing in my cartoon column. I believe Harvey printed around a hundred copies each weekend.

One particular drawing they enjoyed was, John D. Mitchell sitting around with his pockets full of quick claim deeds. These were done in jest and no feelings were hurt. To make things equal, I drew several of Chuck and I treasure hunting. One drawing included the famous "Small Miners Meetings." This took up two pages.

Bill Brouse, the proprietor of the La Gitana cantina, asked if I'd draw some caricatures of a few locals. Several weeks later 24 caricatures hung behind the bar. Names were not included as most knew their identity. This went over great with the bar crowd.

Hack Townsend, owner of the second general store and half of Arivaca, rented out a number of houses including Mitchell's residence. Hack told us many times he was hoping old J.D. would make a mining deal, as he owed him for six months rent plus groceries. He'd carry him until Mitchell hit pay dirt. Eventually he would and all bills were paid. Then it began all over again. Mitchell would sit around waiting for the next victim, and several months later one would arrive. How the old fool managed to get away with his shady deals over the years we never knew.

Once I painted several large signs for Hack. In return, he invited us for Sunday dinner. Mrs. Emma Mae Townsend was a teacher and their daughter, Hacklene, was a student. They lived in Tucson during the week and returned to Arivaca on the weekends. They sure were great cooks.

After living on canned food most of the time, an old sit down dinner was appreciated. Beef, gravy, fresh corn, steaming potatoes, warm biscuits and pie. To Chuck and I, this was a banquet. We ate there many times over the months.

Others we came to know were. A. J. & Alice Allen. Being a long time resident, A. J. knew the country well, including all the stories of buried riches. Others were the Bells, and Gordon & Jenny Metz. These two I believe kept the cantina open. Most were decent folks, but like many towns, there were several bad apples.

Taking all into consideration, Arivaca was a peaceful, friendly community. Out of all the interesting places and little desert hamlets we visited, Arivaca captured our hearts and always drew us back. The old village still sits beneath the blue skies. It has grown some, both in size and population. That rough road has long since been blacktopped, but to us, the town isn't quite the same.

Chapter 61

J. D. MITCHELL

John D. Mitchell, standing near a grave with his hat in his hand during a Memorial Day ceremony in Arivaca. It is the only photo we ever got of him.

We visited John D. Mitchell over the months but refrained from mentioning how he tried deceiving us concerning Carreta Canyon. He was harmless enough if you didn't venture into any deals with him.

Most of the stories he wrote are basically true according to legends passed down by word of mouth. In flipping through his book, for instance, I was attracted by one chapter in particular featuring the story of "The Guadalupe Treasure." In it Mitchell claims there were two Tumacácori Missions, the upper and lower. According to Don Page's historical records there never was a second mission.[9] When Mitchell was confronted with these facts, and others, he would change the subject or insist his story was correct, and the others didn't know what they were talking about.

J. D., as most called him, was a superb story teller, gifted with a golden tongue when it came to relating these tales. Occasionally while visiting him, we'd find ourselves somewhat mesmerized by his uncanny ability to convince us, almost, that the story he was telling was true, even though it was obvious to all including J. D., that most of the tale was fictional.

In another chapter titled "The Lost San Pedro Mine," J. D. claimed an old Opata Indian known as Calistro, guided him to its location. After discovering the site, the story abruptly ends. Nothing is mentioned about returning or staking out a mining claim. We brought this to his attention, but never received a satisfactory answer.

J. D. also insisted he knew the location of several lost mines, like the San Pedro, but always gave us an excuse why he couldn't return and open the mine up.

The Opata Indian appears in another story, and J. D. stated many of his facts came from this mysterious Indian nobody ever met or heard of.

We found the area where J. D. insisted the San Pedro Mine was located. But nothing was discovered indicating a mine was ever there, no mine dump or tunnel, just silence occasionally broken by the call of some desert bird.

Other stories we have doubts about include: "Pegleg's Black Nuggets," "The Lost Ledge of the Sheep Hole Mountains," and several others where he puts himself in the stories. In these instances, he had a habit of putting passages in that were a complete fallacy, to make them appear more interesting. Also, if some facts were forgotten or unknown, he'd add his own.

In this treasure game, where individuals spend time and resources in their quest for these lost fortunes, the writer, including myself, is expected to keep to the original story and stick to the facts as close as possible. At times this was not so with Mitchell. For this reason treasure hunters can use his stories as leads, but should also expect to do their own research. Otherwise, some of his writings send searchers off on "wild goose chases," like they did with us.

J. D.'s book, however, makes excellent reading if you are sitting alone some winter evening beside a crackling fireplace and looking for excitement. All things considered, this book *Lost Mines and Buried Treasure Along the Old Frontier* is well written and remains a treasure hunter's classic.

Yes, this gentleman was indeed a legend in his own time. I have to admit we enjoyed those occasions sitting around during the evenings, listening to his tales of buried treasures and hidden bandit loot. For

---

[9] Jesuit mission records record the first mission, San Cayetano de Tumacácori, was located on the east side of the Santa Cruz River. The present mission, San José de Tumacácori, was built by the Franciscans and is located on the west side of the river.

some reason you couldn't become too angry with him. If he needed the help of two strong lads, we of course, were always available.

One evening weeks later while leaving J. D.'s adobe, Chuck couldn't contain himself. Looking Mitchell in the eye, he said, "Oh, by the way, Louie showed us Carreta Canyon months ago. We checked the area out for weeks but couldn't find a thing. We did however discover an old Spanish cutlass where the ox cart once stood." Mitchell looked completely shocked. I do believe this was the first time old J. D. was lost for words.

Smiling, I said. "It's at the upper head of Lobo Canyon, which means *carreta* in Spanish." Chuck returned from our jeep, and showed him the sword.

The story went through Arivaca like wildfire. From that day forward, Mitchell never tried to B.S. Chuck and me again.

Then the rumors sprang forth:

We never did find the canyon.

We had found the treasure and were about to leave town.

The cutlass was purchased by us, not discovered at the site.

Some couldn't accept the fact we had found something they couldn't.

Chapter 62

OLD SAM & THE SMALL MINERS MEETING

Like most small towns scattered across Arizona, Arivaca has its share of memorable characters. Old Sam held the title— Granddaddy of them all. His last name sounded like (Tom-la-vitch). But to the community he was known as Old Sam Son-of-a-bitch. [10]

This colorful amusing old prospector looked as though he was in his late 70s, wore bib overalls, sported an unkempt beard and had devilish sparkling eyes.

Old Sam, Hack Townsend and Chuck in front of Hack's store.

When he danced into town several times a month, the place turned into a three-ring circus. We never saw him breathe a sober breath during our stay in the area. He could have been a stand-up comic in Las Vegas. Its difficult remembering all his one liners, put downs and endless array of jokes. The more intoxicated he became the funnier he was.

We first met Sam while outside the cantina, and couldn't believe the humor this fellow could generate. Anything said he'd turn into a joke. A while later he headed into the cantina with several friends.

Spotting Randall across the street we walked over to ask him some questions concerning a certain region we intended to search. A crowd began gathering near the post office, waiting for the day's mails to be put up. Moments later, Sam came staggering out, followed by other cohorts, and the fun started all over again. After

---

[10] Sam Tomalavitch was born in Lithuania in 1894 or 1895. He died October 9, 1976 in Tucson. His name also appears as Tamalavech, and Tomalavitch. Easy to see how he got his nickname.

checking our mail we returned to camp leaving Sam going through his antics in the middle of town.

Two weeks later, Arivaca had its "Small Miners Meeting" at the cantina. Hearing of these wild get-togethers we decided to attend. Miners, prospectors, mining promoters, etc., from far and wide came to this bimonthly ritual.

The meeting was held in the cantina's large back room, where some serious discussions were heard pertaining to mining and miners rights on government lands. Afterwards, the group which numbered 45 or so, retired to the open field across from the cantina for their weenie roast, eating, drinking and swapping lies among themselves. Fires were lit and a merry time was had by all.

From out of the darkness Sam's grinning face appeared, with bottle in hand and full of hell. You always knew his whereabouts by the laughter coming from that direction. Most became "high," but never were there any fights. Others arrived and joined the festivities, with Sam in the center of it all.

We learned one thing that evening. More ore was mined at these meetings than ever came out of the hills. Many were always "on the verge of striking it rich," or if the price of gold would increase they could work their claims profitably. Others would say they'd be "shipping high grade any day." Most lived in a dream world of finding sudden wealth. I suppose searching for treasures would place us in the same category.

Sam came over bumming a dollar for another bottle of wine. His was empty, and to him, that was a sin. Giving Sam a buck, he wobbled over toward others asking for change. Guess they didn't give him any because he stepped back and shouted, "If that's the way ya going to be, I'll piss on your fires." With these words he proceeded to unzip his pants. In the process he lost his balance, stumbling backward into the crowd. Knowing Sam's antics, most laughed his prank off, including several women. He was later taken under a mesquite tree to sleep it off, but was back in a short time.

These gentlemen were a breed of their own, and had their own rules. Having a good time, damaging no property, drinking and rising a little hell and damn what society might think of them. Most were happy with their lifestyle and loved living among the hills. They were a dying breed left over from the turn of the 20th century.

Soon after 1:00 in the morning the gang began breaking up. Some slept in their campers while others bunked with friends in town or drove home. Arivaca was like one big happy family. Most doors were never locked and friends came and went. As we returned to our camp my sides ached from all the laughter. Chuck often said, "If we never find anything during this adventure. Knowing this crazy town would be worth the trip."

Sam never wanted his picture taken, like many in Arivaca. Roy thought most were on the run from the law. One afternoon Sam was joking with Hack Townsend and Chuck. Retrieving my camera unnoticed, I yelled, "Hey Sam." As he turned I snapped the picture. Did I ever get cussed out, but all was forgiven weeks later.

Chapter 63

TATA ELLIS

Tata Ellis

Prospector Randall Hill, Tata's neighbor.

Randall Hill had a neighbor who lived nearby in his small trailer. He was known as Tata, which means grandfather in Spanish. This cranky old guy had lost a leg and hobbled around on a peg leg made from a water pipe. He drove an old beat up jeep that looked as though it went through several wars and lost. He acted mean and cranky, but this was all an act. Inside Tata had a heart of gold, and proved this to us sometime later.

He asked us if we'd like to check out his claim with our detector. It was located just south of Arivaca. Almost everyone in town had a mining claim whether they worked it or not. It was some kind of a status symbol. We climbed down the rickety ladder and examined the narrow vein. It contained lead, copper, silver and a trace of gold. Like most mines in this district, his deposit wasn't large enough for production. Afterward we returned to the surface from his 40 foot shaft. By its looks it hadn't been worked in years.

Before leaving, Tata asked if we'd search an area around some old tree stumps. One had a cross and bell cut into the bark. He never believed in treasure yarns, but wanted to search "just in case." Nothing was found but several rusty nails. I believe Tata was more interested in having us check this area out than having us look at his old mine shaft. Later we learned, a cross and bell were used as trail markers by the mission padres. The one on Tata's claim was in close proximity to the old Carreta Road and could have been one of their signs. Most of these old timers haven't a pot or a window to throw it out, but were always friendly and offered their help if needed.

237

Chapter 64
ANOTHER SMALL MINERS MEETING

The Lopez brothers: Manuel, Luis & Feliciano.

O ne day while in Arivaca we heard another Small Miners Meeting was to be held Saturday night. Roy and Walt heard us mention these rowdy parties and looked forward to attending one.

As the Arizona sun began retiring for another day, we departed in Roy's jeep hoping to arrive by dusk. As we rolled along the tortuous road, missing cattle that occasionally crossed our path, I noticed none other than old Sam [Tomalavitch] walking beside the road. As we stopped beside him, he recognized Chuck and me.

Mary & Harvey Riggs

Sam was heading to town for the meeting. To him, it was fiesta time. It was another three miles to Arivaca, so Sam squeezed in between us. After introducing him to Roy and Walt, we continued on. As usual, Sam was high on wine and his breath drifted among us.

Old Sam had a memory like an elephant and asked if we still had the picture I had taken of him. "What you want with that," Sam said. "I'm no damn celebrity." To many in town, Sam was a local celebrity as they enjoyed his none stop array of jokes and wild antics.

As we arrived in Arivaca, prospectors, miners and various no accounts were already drifting in. After giving Sam several dollars for the evening he walked unsteadily toward his watering hole, the local cantina.

Inside, others crowded around the long bar, talking assay reports, and anything relating to mining. The same old yarns were heard. All expected to hit "pay dirt" anytime. In the center of it all was, J. D. Mitchell spouting wild tales of how he almost found several lost mines, or what great mining deals were in the works.

Across the street, others were unloading wood for the traditional barn fires that soon would light up the sky. Walt said, "They sure are a rugged and wild looking bunch." Most were hard working honest men. Sure they had a "devil may care attitude," but never caused any serious trouble. They just wanted to do their thing, and occasionally kick up their heels, raise a little hell and visit friends.

The majority of them, no doubt, were on Social Security or some pension, as they always paid their bills. Most never mentioned their past or where they originated from. They just turned their backs on society to live among the hills, dreaming of making that big strike,

Most took up residence on abandoned mining claims, living in trailers or old shacks. They didn't have much but were some of the happiest folks we ever met. A rare commodity in today's high-tech fast paced world.

Others slowly arrived, including the Edwards brothers [possibly Harvey & Walt Edwards]. They lived just off the Ruby Road, south of town. Both were a little dingy but harmless. For years they had been digging through solid rock searching for a chamber full of treasure. They weren't as nutty as Crazy Davis, but close.

By now you might suspect the entire population of Arivaca was somewhat weird. On the contrary, most were levelheaded normal people. The merchants, Harvey Riggs and wife, Hack Townsend and family and countless others living within the town, moved there for the pure enjoyment of living in a small community.

Others who attended these meetings were the Lopez boys, Manual, Luis and Feliciano. They were half Yaqui Indian and resembled Mexican bandits seen in western movies. In reality they were kind, well mannered cowboys who worked for various ranchers.

One of my hobbies was card tricks, and I'd show them several while in town. These tricks fascinated them. They'd say something in Spanish; then ask to see the trick again. All three would watch with eagle eyes but try as they may, none could catch how it was done.

Throwing their arms upward, one would say quite loudly, "How you do that?" They were like kids at their first magic show. If they happened to see me around Arivaca one would call out, "You show more tricks?" Small bits of entertainment like this meant so much to them.

As the gang sat around flickering fires roasting wieners, drinking and trying to out-lie each other, we suddenly noticed Sam wasn't there rising hell. Bill found him sleeping it off in his patio beside the cantina. It was mid-April and the evening weather was comfortable. Not wanting to disturb the old fellow, Bill threw a blanket over him.

We returned to camp as the gathering began thinning out. Both Roy and Walt enjoyed themselves at their first Small Miners Meeting. Now it was time to return to our primary goal, trying to unlock the mysteries surrounding these lost treasures and mines.

Chapter 65

HOW A STORY GROWS

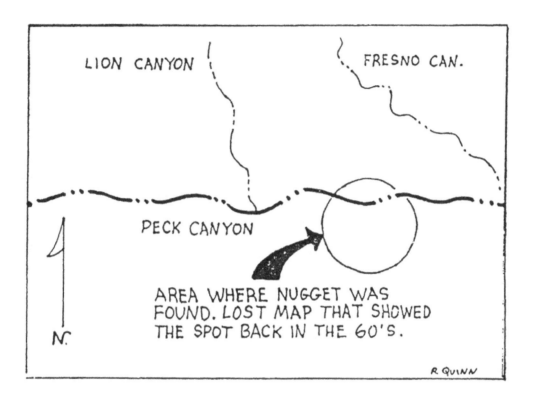

Southern Arizona Trails, Vol. 3, No. 42, August 4, 1987, page 18

In 1957, my brother and I found a large two-ounce nugget of silver while digging into a vein of caliche clay in the vicinity of Peck Canyon. We dug several more feet after the discovery, but found no more.

On our next trip into Arivaca, we displayed the impressive nugget to a few friends, and eventually ended up in John Mansfield's apartment, another acquaintance we knew that moved to Arivaca from Fallon, Nevada. The walls were rather thin and J. D. Mitchell, an author of several books on treasure hunting, was in the next apartment typing away.

The three of us discussed the find for several minutes. As John rolled the nugget between his fingers, he accidentally dropped it, and the nugget hit the tabletop with a nice solid thud.

At that moment the typing ceased. I guess when ole J. D. heard that sound, his ears perked up some. If he was listening, it didn't bother us none, as he saw the nugget a few days later. We kicked the story around awhile longer then departed for camp, which was located near the Tumacacori Mountains.

Four weeks later while selling some agate we had found to a rock shop in Tucson, we mentioned Arivaca. The proprietor said, "You fellows from there?" Chuck answered, "Yes," and the owner said, "Say...is there any truth to a story I heard about some young prospectors finding a rich silver mine down that way?"

Chuck grinned and replied, "That must be us, but we only found one nugget." I went to the jeep and fetched the specimen so he could see it. Of course, he wanted to purchase the nugget, but we declined the offer.

During our drive back to Arivaca, we both had a good laugh over the incident. If I had to guess, it was ole J. D. that started the rumor rolling about our find, and the story just escalated as it was passed along. One lone nugget became a rich mine in four weeks.

Three weeks later while returning from Nogales, we stopped off at the old Kingsley Ranch, which today is the Cow Palace, to have a cold beer before tackling the Arivaca Road.

At that time only a few miles were paved. It was nothing but holes and washboard, and our jeep didn't have the best suspension system. At times we thought the old wagon would come apart around our ears while navigating those twenty-two miles of (pardon the expression) "road." While at the bar, either Chuck or I mentioned checking for mail in Arivaca before heading back to camp. An old-timer nearby turned and said, "You guys from Arivaca?" My first thought was that he might be looking for a ride there, and I answered, "Yes."

Putting down his beer, he smiled and said, "Is there anything to that story about some miners from the Northwest finding a rich gold and silver mine out there? Heard the ore was almost pure silver, mixed with some gold." We answered no and said there was nothing to it — just a rumor.

This goes to prove how a story can be blown clear out of proportion, from one single silver nugget, to a "bonanza" in just seven short weeks. To me, that has to be a record. If we heard that story today, thirty years later, I'm dead certain I'd never recognize it.

If this can happen over a seven-week period, imagine a story that's been kicking around for well over a hundred years. If you hear a tale about some outlaws hiding their loot, and the story mentions it was worth, say half a million, deduct about 80 percent of the value and you might be close to the original amount.

The same holds with tales of lost Spanish gold. There are rumors that some of these local buried treasures are worth $40-$50 million, and sometimes even more. Another thing, these estimates were made most likely when gold was $35 an ounce. If these figures are correct, you can imagine what these treasures would be worth with gold (as of this writing) selling for around $400 an ounce.

If any readers happen to hear a story about some fellows back in '57 discovering a bonanza near Arivaca, the chances are it's us, and our two-ounce nugget of silver.

Oh yes, others have asked us if we ever returned to the area of the discovery to search for other nuggets. We made two more trips there, and after digging another four feet, the caliche vein pinched out.

Chapter 66

THE GREAT RABBIT HUNT

One afternoon Roy suggested we go rabbit hunting. Not the cute little cottontail rabbits seen occasionally near camp, but the giant "kangaroo" jackrabbits. Chuck balanced himself on the hood, anchoring his heels behind the jeep's bumper with rifle in hand. Roy drove as I sat beside him. Away we went over the rolling hills in search of our prey. Suddenly, one popped up from behind some brush and took off with Roy hot on its tail, and Chuck firing from the hood. The jack would dart, zigzag and change direction in its attempt to elude us—then disappear among the rocks. A moment later, another would shoot past and the pursuit continued, bullets kicking up beside the fleeing rabbit and ricocheting off flat rocks.

Chuck wasn't hitting any jacks from the moving vehicle but was blazing away at anything moving. We sat behind him laughing our foolish heads off as he attempted to hit one on the run. We bounced down one hill and up another, traveling about 25 miles an hour. If Roy had had to stop abruptly, Chuck would have been catapulted from the hood like an arrow in flight. But miraculously he held on like he was glued to the spot.

We drove in circles and flew down inclines and across narrow washes with Chuck firing all the time. Rabbits scattered in all directions but none fell to his onslaught of rapid firing.

I was hanging on for dear life and laughing so hard I couldn't see straight. Stopping, we'd scan the horizon while Chuck reloaded waiting for another to show. In a few seconds several would take flight, darting from the brush. Hitting the gas we'd take off over the rough terrain. I'm almost positive all four wheels were off the ground several times during the chase. Roy did the navigating from behind the wheel shouting, "As I turn starboard laddie we'll give 'em a four gun broadside. Keep ye powder dry mates." This horse play continued some twenty minutes before returning to camp.

Score: rabbits 1, treasure hunters 0.

We'd entertain ourselves to break the monotony at times with some nonessential activities like this. As Roy would say, "Hell, you only come around once in life. Have fun and the devil what others might say."

Foolishness like this occurred often, especially when Roy was around. Nobody was ever hurt, including the rabbits. In a way I was happy we didn't get any that day. During our travels there was a time for serious business and a time for fun and laughter. The next day we returned to the hunt—<u>treasure</u> hunting that is!

Chapter 67

NIÑO COCHISE

W hile in the Fort Bowie area we met, Niño Cochise, supposedly the grandson of the famous Chieftain. He was Apache and walked with a slight limp.

One time while visiting us, he sat with one leg across the other. In doing so his pant leg crept up, exposing his leg and sock. I glanced down; then looked again. While he was engaged in conversation I attempted to attract the others attention. Finally Roy caught my look, and I slowly looked toward Niño's leg, with Roy's gaze following mine. He then blinked several times grinning.

After Niño departed, I said. "Did you see that? His sock was tacked to his leg." We laughed as Chuck said, "Didn't you know Niño has a wooden leg? He often does that to keep his sock from falling down."

He was mostly seen around Willcox and Bowie, posing for pictures for a few dollars taken by weekend tourists. Many claim he was indeed a relative of Cochise, while others, including some historians disagree. It's possible this Indian was just capitalizing on the name.

Niño also appeared at Old Tucson, a movie set location and tourist attraction years later. Once he had a small role in the old TV series, *High Chaparral*, playing Cochise.

Chapter 68

JACK THE WANDERDER

A nother interesting character we happened to meet near Fort Bowie was Jack. He drove an old Conestoga wagon with rubber tires pulled by two mules, the type of wagon once used by pioneers moving west.

Jack appeared to be in his mid-50s, was tall with a long beard, and his companion was an old hound dog named Whiskey.

Jack could often be seen traveling along the edge of the road as cars sped by. Occasionally, he'd set up a table beside the highway, selling various items like post cards and making keys. If any passing tourists wanted a picture taken with him, like Niño, it was a buck.

Jack, Whisky & Chuck.

We purchased several things, and also took a picture of Chuck beside him. We'd stop at times to visit, and found Jack led quite an interesting life traveling the southwest, sleeping under the stars and visiting many out-of-the-way places throughout the west. He and Whiskey didn't have a care in the world and liked it that way.

In a way it sounded similar to us.

Most would look upon these wanderers as lazy rejects of society, but they were happy doing their thing. We came upon many following this lifestyle during our odyssey. I suppose by now Jack and Whiskey are traveling the heavenly highway.

Chapter 69

CHARLIE GERONIMO

C harlie was another interesting character and claimed to be Geronimo's son. During 1963 we met him through friends. He did resemble the old War Horse, and was the correct age, about 70. He insisted he had documentation verifying this but never displayed it.

The old fellow would remain around Tucson a while, then up and disappear. One time while returning from visiting an old army buddy in Santa Fe, New Mexico, I spotted an old Indian hiking down the lonely highway miles from nowhere. Stopping to offer him a ride, I saw it was none other than Charlie. He recognized me and was quite surprised. I asked what he was doing clear over in New Mexico. Opening a large leather bag, he displayed several pieces of fine turquoise jewelry. He was on his way to Albuquerque to sell 'em to a store. After dropping him off, I continued on toward Tucson. We never saw old Charlie after that.

Geronimo's family was killed by Mexicans below the border at his camp. That is why he had such a burning hatred toward them. It's possible he had other children afterwards. Old Charlie could very well have been one.

Chapter 70

MITCHELL — ALL OR NOTHING

While in Arivaca we decided to visit John D. Mitchell once again. We suspected the old fox knew more about Carreta Canyon than he was letting on. We came to this conclusion ever since Louie Romero informed us about how he kept asking where it was.

We found him sitting beside his adobe, relaxing in the shade; seemingly lost in deep thought. As we approached, Mitchell asked us to be seated. After a little small talk, Chuck came right to the point telling Mitchell how Louie had shown us Carreta Canyon, and about his relentless questioning of Louie concerning the location of the site. Mitchell looked somewhat uncomfortable upon hearing this.

We told him we had a strong suspicion he knew more about this story than he ever let be known. Mitchell said he was "only curious about the canyon's location and suspected Louie knew its whereabouts."

"We know the site's location, but believe you might suspect where to dig," I said. Mitchell had heard about us finding the Spanish cutlass, but we mentioned nothing of the well.

Our proposition was, if Mitchell would tell us what he knew, we'd split anything found three ways.

"No," said Mitchell. "You take me there first."

How easy it would be to direct us to the wrong spot! This statement alone proved he knew something. If a treasure wasn't there, Mitchell wouldn't go on any wild goose chase. He'd send us on one!

"No way," I said. "Then you'd know the location. If nothing was discovered, you'd say, 'Well, that's where I thought it was.' After several weeks or months, you'd return removing any treasure that might be found."

This old sly dog grinned saying, "Now I wouldn't do anything like that to you boys."

"Sure," Chuck said. "We've heard about your shady dealings. You can trust us, our partners do." No response came from Mitchell.

He wouldn't budge and no agreement was reached. No way would he share anything with anybody. If a treasure was there, he wanted it for himself. After years of searching, I suppose Mitchell believed it belonged to him and no other.

Numerous times we proposed the same terms, and received the same answer, "Take me there first."

Mitchell would not change his mind. That would show weakness on his part. Most mining promoters go by certain rules—their way or no way. If anyone would be taken, it would be you not them. They want the bees to come to the honey. That's when you get stung!

Another time while waiting for the mail, we met two others from California. They had been searching for the legendary Guadalupe Mine for several months. Funds were low and they decided to return home.

We engaged in conversation with them concerning various stories, and Chuck happened to mention Carreta Canyon. Mitchell was standing some twenty feet away. Upon hearing this he moved slowly in our direction hoping to overhear any clues.

Over the months Mitchell waited patiently for us to approach with a proposal favoring him. "Hell," said Chuck. "Two can play that game."

Several years later, the game ended. Old J, D. Mitchell passed away while living at his sister's home in Chandler, Arizona. If this shrewd old gentleman knew anything, it went to the grave with him. It wasn't in his nature to share. "All or nothing" was Mitchell's motto. It was the passing of a legend, as most in the "treasure circles" knew his name.

If such a treasure exists within this canyon or well, the secret would finally come to light 35 years later, while once again exploring this site with another close friend.

Chapter 72

CHARLIE AND HIS SILVER DOLLARS

By A. J. Allen as told to Ron Quinn
Southern Arizona Trails, Vol. 3, No. 52, October 13, 1987, Page 23

Years will pass but memories will linger on. It was early 1955 in the little mining town of Arivaca, Arizona. I had known John D. Mitchell for well over two years and after our evening meal, we would sit out under the stars and swap stories, and of course, Mitchell would do most of the talking.

A miner and explorer, he had worked numerous mines in old Mexico and other countries. John also wrote several books on lost mines and treasures, some of which are still in print.

C. B. Ruggles

I have been fortunate to know men like, Mitchell, C. B. Ruggles, J. Frank Dobie, and Chuck and Ron Quinn, real treasure hunters.

I understand a "big" find [11] was made down near the border a few years back, so I guess some of the treasure yarns floating around must have some truth behind them.

Getting back to the story… that evening Mitchell told me a tale about a "hermit prospector" he had known over in Death Valley who eventually moved into the Arivaca area after hearing about the gold strikes being made in the Las Guijas Mountains, located just north of town.

It was sometime during 1925, and he was known only as "Charley" as no one knew his last name. He built a small cabin on a ridge between two washes and "placered" for gold in the surrounding hills, but never sold any of the gold he found.

---

[11] This was the find by Ron, Chuck, Roy & Walt.

Charley would always pay for his supplies with silver dollars, and it remained a mystery where he obtained the coins, which he never seemed to run out of.

One day old Charley just disappeared, but left behind all his belongings, bedroll and all. Some of the residents thought he might have fallen into one of the many mine shafts that are scattered throughout the area, or met with foul play. No body was ever found, so it still remains a mystery to this day what happened to him.

He never came into town much so many locals never saw or even heard of Charley. One old pegleg by the name of Nicho, lived in town all his life, told me he once knew a Charley, but wasn't sure if he was the same individual that disappeared.

After all these years I told my wife Alice, the story and both of us decided to see if Charley had buried any gold at the old cabin site. I knew its location after Mitchell had described the place to me many years before. I had been prospecting in the area and found some pretty good placer nearby, and discovered the old place by luck while crossing the ridge from one wash to the other.

We packed our detector and other equipment into the truck and headed out of town. It was mid July of '87 so we left early to beat the heat, as temperatures would reach over a hundred by the afternoon.

We hoped we wouldn't run into other prospectors, as there are quite a few of them running around the hills. Its good nugget country and many individuals can be found out there with detectors, searching the numerous dry washes and hillsides.

Alice and I parked our truck just off the main road, to comply with the BLM rules not to "run over the grass." After removing our gear, we began hiking toward the area of the cabin. We didn't see any other treasure hunters and arrived at the site unnoticed. All that remained of the cabin was the stone foundation.

We began searching and soon Alice received a strong signal from the detector near one corner. We started digging and at approximately fifteen inches we came upon some old cast iron that looked like the side from an old wood stove.

Under this we discovered a large porcelain pan. The first thought I had was of that placer gold that Charley never sold.

After removing it we found the pan contained 19 silver dollars, some dated as late as 1923, but no gold. What a feeling knowing I should have searched that site many years ago, but I had doubts about the story from the beginning.

It sure pays to check out any leads, no matter how small or unbelievable they might sounds.

Alice remarked how that little "Mayan Detector" had paid for itself many times over. We of course took pictures, as we always do on our field trips before returning to Arivaca.

What happened to Charley and his gold will remain a mystery, known only to the mountains and deserts of Southern Arizona.

Chapter 72

THE MAYO INDIAN'S GOLD

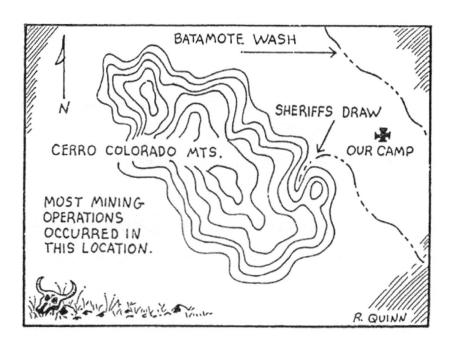

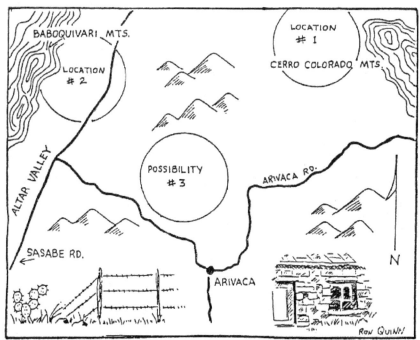

THREE LOCATIONS WHERE THE LOST SOPORI MINE MIGHT BE FOUND

Southern Arizona Trails, Vol. 3, No. 57, November 24, 1987, Page 23

D uring our first adventurous years of prospecting and treasure hunting here in Southern Arizona, my brother Chuck and I searched for countless lost mines and buried treasures. Out of all the ones we searched for, there were several that remain our favorites. High on the list, "The Carreta Canyon Treasure," followed by the "Tumacacori Treasures," "The Lost Yuma Ledge," Pegleg Smith's Black Gold Nuggets," and several others not as well known.

One that always captured our imagination was "The Lost Mine of the Blond Mayo." The original tale is quite lengthy, so I'll give you a rather condenses version.

Two Mayo Indian brothers, Juan Morales, the blond, and Fermín the youngest, came north from Sonora, Mexico. For a while they made their living panning gold along Arivaca Creek and other locations.

Juan quit panning for a spell and would venture off into the surrounding hills, as if he was searching for something that he knew was there. Several weeks later he arrived in Arivaca with his mules loaded down with rich gold ore.

The gold was interlaced throughout the quartz and was bonanza quality, so the tale goes.

The ore looked as though it had been mined many years before, as no fresh breaks were visible on the surface. In the months that followed, the two brothers made frequent trips northeast of town, always returning with their pack animals loaded with the precious metal.

Everyone knew the blond Mayo was a dead shot, so few, if any attempted to follow them to their secret diggings. If they suspected somebody was dogging their tracks they would vanish among the rocks, like the earth itself had swallowed them up.

The two prospered over the years from their mining activities, but soon settled down to ranching. It's believed by many they discovered one of the rich mines once worked by the padres from Tumacácori Mission. The location was believed to be near or in the Cerro Colorado Mountains. Also, many insist they found and worked the old Sopori Mine, considered one of the richest in the vicinity.

It's rumored the blond Mayo died while visiting his home in the Rio Mayo Valley of Sonora, Mexico. His brother, Fermín died and supposedly is buried in the Arivaca Cemetery. [12]

Many have searched for this rich but well-hidden lost mine, but none have succeeded in locating it as far as I know. I doubt if the mine entrance is still open, as if it was, this famous mine would have been rediscovered ages ago.

If the entire story is true, and I believe most of it is, I'm almost certain the Mayo brothers sealed the opening after removing enough gold to purchase a ranch and sustain a comfortable life in their later years. If one examines both the Arivaca and Tubac quadrangle maps, you will notice all the mining activity has occurred on the western slopes of the Cerro Colorado Range. This area is honeycombed with countless exploratory shafts, prospect holes and some mines that once produced large amount of rich ore, but most silver, not gold.

---

[12] Fermín Morales died November 29, 1944 and was buried by his family the following day in the Arivaca Cemetery according to Arizona Death Certificate #1531.

252

During our research and stories we heard from other knowledgeable individuals, we came to the conclusion this ancient mine could be hidden somewhere on the eastern slopes of this rugged mountain.

We moved our base camp during the closing months of 1956 to the area. We established our new encampment just off Batamote Wash, about two miles north of the Arivaca Road.

We decided to search for this elusive gold mine for five weeks, before heading up to Washington state for the Christmas holidays and a well needed rest.

The owner of the ranch who ran his cattle on this leased land didn't particularly care for strangers camping there, especially miners and prospectors We understood his concern, as many leave deep its behind for cattle to fall in. We did have several words with the gentleman, and once he accused us of leaving some of the cattle gates open, which we hadn't. We took this as being accused, tried, convicted and executed without having a fair trial.

We believed the lost mine was near Sheriffs Draw, or somewhere in the immediate vicinity. During our investigation of this interesting tale, we heard from a reliable party there was supposed to be the remains of an old cottonwood tree close to a canyon leading to the mine.

This same individual told us a dead cottonwood was seen around 1902 close to Sheriffs Draw, where it empties onto the flats. There is no sign of this tree today.

As we prepared to undertake our search, nature frowned on us and turned the weather cold and windy. But Chuck and I would still be found climbing around the windy slopes and cold canyons located in the region we suspected the mine to be.

Each day we'd enter Sheriffs Draw and begin our hunt. We would climb the dangerous rocky slopes, looking for evidence that would tell us the mine was somewhere in the area. During the third week, we both contracted bad colds and had to curtail our daily activities into the chilly mountains until we felt better. A week or so later we again tackled the rugged terrain, but never discovered a single clue indicating a mine was ever in the vicinity. We even extended our search area quite a distance, but still nothing. A few days later we broke camp and headed north back to Washington for the holidays, before returning once again to the harsh environment of the southwest deserts.

We never searched for the mine again, as our two partners, who had been out of state for awhile wanted to search the Dos Cabezas area for several months, and of course we accompanied them.

We're convinced the old ancient gold mine is hidden somewhere among the canyons near Cerro Colorado, but it's no doubt well concealed, after almost a hundred years and may never be found again.

Even today when I'm out among these mysterious mountains, I still wonder how many treasures, if any, are hidden among the craggy bluffs or sealed away in some long forgotten mine tunnel in the dark lonely shadowy canyons that stand out so vividly at sunset.

I'm quite certain many of these treasure tales are still discussed in the cities and small hamlets scattered across the state, and of course, with everyone telling a different version of the same story. How many are factual is uncertain, but most are quite tantalizing, arousing that adventurous spirit that lives within us all.

Chapter 73

SURVIVAL

During this lengthy adventure we learned to educate ourselves to the ways of the desert and its environment. When a thunderstorm is pounding the nearby mountains, you keep out of the narrow high-banked canyons and arroyos. It might be clear and sunny at your location, but the waters from the storm are gathering. They enter small tributaries which flow into the main canyons. If caught within one, a wall of churning water, perhaps several feet or more in height, will come around a bend sweeping everything away in its path.

Creepy Crawlers

Most creepy crawlers of the desert aren't dangerous, but several species are, including the deadly rattler, a small gray, thumb-tip size scorpion and the rare coral snake with its red, yellow and black bands encircling its pencil size body—this last guy is very dangerous. Fortunately, we only saw one in two years.

One night I awoke to find my left shoulder burning. I knew instantly something had bitten me. Below my cot was a desert centipede some nine inches long. It was orange with black legs and half dead. It had climbed the cot, and I must have rolled over on him. He bit me before falling to the floor. Their bite isn't fatal but will cause pain. I woke Chuck telling him of the incident. Upon fetching our first aid kit, I took both penicillin and codeine tablets. By morning the pain had subsided to just a dull ache.

During this time we had only seen two rattlers. One kept coming around camp, so we killed it. Hated to do so, as it had a right to live, but we didn't want to enter the tent and find it curled and ready to strike, or hidden among the boxes.

Old Mine Shafts

When hiking across country you will occasionally come upon several abandoned mine shafts hidden among the brush. If not careful, you'll find yourself falling into one. Most are over a hundred feet deep. While climbing you also learn where and where not to place your hands as some curled varmint might just be waiting for you.

Several times we spent the night away from camp. Searching we'd eventually find a cave or large rock overhang to spend the night. During such trips we would carry several canteens each, plus food, snake bite kit, matches, flashlight and other needed articles. Also, one should carry a sidearm.

The main thing is, always keep your wits about you. Don't rubberneck while walking. Stop, and then look around. Keep your ears open, a rattler might be shading himself nearby. Upon hearing you approach, he usually will rattle, alerting you of his presence. If you come upon one unexpectedly, there's a good chance he'll nail you just above the ankle.

Camp Day

About twice a month we had something called camp day. The tents were cleaned out, checking corners for any desert dwellers that wanted to take up residence. Sleeping bags were hung out to air and garbage buried. Our Coleman stove and lanterns were cleaned and tested. Oil and water levels checked in the vehicles, lug nuts tightened and tires checked.

When going into town for the day, we'd shave, clean up and change clothes. Just because we camped out it didn't mean we had to look like a bunch of grubby old prospectors.

When Roy was around he'd insist on doing the cooking. That didn't necessarily suggest Chuck and I were bad cooks, Roy just enjoyed it. He'd say, "When the old seaman's around, I'll tend the galley lads."

After many months living under these conditions in the outdoors it became routine, and nobody ever complained about the hardships we occasionally endured.

Lightning

One time while at Clifford Well, I was taking inventory of our supplies. Roy was again working on his jeep and Chuck was cleaning a bucket. The clouds above looked somewhat menacing but no storms were seen approaching. All at once a bolt of lightning struck nearby. It was as though someone had fired a flash gun off in my face. Chuck and the bucket went sky high, and Roy stood paralyzed beside his jeep. The bolt must have hit perhaps ten yards away.

The profanity which came from Roy is unprintable, and I'm almost positive it's still echoing throughout the canyon walls. It was a frightening experience, and dangers like this lurk around almost every corner in this threatening yet beautiful land.

Parts of Southern Arizona aren't true desert. The area south of Tucson is mostly rolling hills with mountain ranges scattered throughout the valley. I'd call the region something between desert and prairie. The terrain is easy to manage for those knowing the ways of the outdoors.

Usually trouble occurs when entering these hazardous unfriendly mountains, which always seem to beckon you. Their craggy peaks and desolate canyons have changed little since first viewed by the Spaniards.

Water

When exploring, water is essential, as little is found within these barren hills.

One time we climbed Government Peak near Bowie, Arizona. As we reached its summit, after an hour's climb, Chuck noticed an interesting rock formation far below. It was obvious we didn't have enough water left to hike there and return as the formation was almost a mile and a half below us in a rugged canyon. Not wanting to make a second climb with the necessary water, we decided to take the chance. It was early morning, slightly warm and overcast.

Several hours later the sun broke through, and the temperature rose. We estimated it was well over 105° in the sun, and even more in the narrow canyon near the formation.

During the long climb back our water finally ran out, and camp was perhaps two miles from the summit. As we pulled ourselves ever upward, the sun baked our brains and our mouths felt as dry as the rugged country around us. Remembering I had a roll of Life Savers, we popped one in our mouths to help generate some moisture. After several minutes we removed the candy, and discovered it was still dry. We realized our bodies were slowly becoming dehydrated, and it was getting hotter all the time.

Chuck and I became a little dizzy and our legs weakened as the menacing sun drew out our strength from lack of water. Chuck complained his throat was closing and swallowing was difficult. But we continued on, resting about every two hundred feet. We also knew every step brought us closer to water.

We finally stumbled into camp dropping exhausted beside our tent. Reaching for our water bag, we drank our fill, but slowly. In a little over an hour we had consumed almost two gallons of water between us. This thirst continued into the evening, and we didn't take a "leak" until early the following morning. If we hadn't been accustomed to this rugged life, I doubt Chuck and I would have made it out.

Many have perished trying to walk out from the desert after their vehicles became disabled. This occurs quite often, especially near the border. When traveling among these hills we always carried no less than four gallons of water, plus food in our jeep.

Rule

The rule is, never hike beyond your water supply. If you do, trouble usually rears its ugly head. We knew better, but had to learn the hard way. It never happened again. As I have said before, the deserts are unforgiving and wait patiently for the unwary to enter and make a mistake, especially during the harsh summer months.

TWO MORE STORIES

Chapter 74

SEARCH FOR SAN XAVIER SILVER TREASURE BURIED NEAR MISSION?

By Peter Pegnam
Tucson Citizen, February 25, 1989, Page 1-2A [13]

A Tucson man believes valuable Spanish church ornaments that may have been secretly buried in the 1860s could be a blessing in disguise for San Xavier Mission.

The cache — if it exists — could be worth several hundred thousand dollars, said treasure hunter Ron Quinn.

Quinn said he has a pretty good idea where the treasure may be and wants only a modest finder's fee if he locates the silver altar vessels.

The remainder could be used to help save the mission, whose eroding 200-year-old walls are the object of $1 million fund drive.

But the spot Quinn wants to search is on Indian land and he need permission to search and is trying to strike a deal with Tohono O'odham tribal leaders.

He is not confident of doing that. Quinn said he was told earlier that the tribe claims 100 percent of anything found on the reservation.

Most historians insist there never was a treasure of any kind at the mission.

But Quinn says one historian, Donald Page, was here in the 1930s and interviewed an old tribal member who remembered seeing silver ornaments and vessels on the mission altar.

Page wrote in a letter that the priests would use them on special occasions. And in 1880, many Tucson residents allegedly saw the treasure.

The silver was hidden when Army soldiers were pulled out in 1861 and Apache raids increased, Quinn said.

"They removed it, afraid that it might be stolen. And they hid it out there by that black mesa."

Standing in front of the mission, Quinn gestured to a dark-colored mesa about a mile to the southwest.

"That's a big one," he said of the mesa. "That runs way back. That's where they supposedly hid it.

---

[13] Permission to use from Mark B. Evans, Tucson Citizen.com, Sept. 7, 2011.

"In the 1950s it was rumored that some of the older Indians here supposedly knew where this altar treasure was buried," Quinn said. "They either passed the secret on or they died with it on their lips."

He believes the mesa also holds the legendary Esmeralda Mine. Silver from the lost mine allegedly was used in making the chalices and other items used at San Xavier. Quinn thinks the mine is where the treasure was hidden.

One version of the story is that the treasure was thrown back into the mine and the entrance blown shut.

"I kind of doubt that," Quinn said. "They'll hide it but they're not going to blow tons of rock over it."

Treasure tales of the Esmeralda Mine have placed it in various locations.

But, said Quinn, "The only place a mind could be hidden in would be this big black mesa.

"Notice how it's sitting out there all by itself? That shows that maybe inside there's a lot of heavy quartz holding that thing together. It didn't erode like the rest of the country."

Quinn said he has a few clues as to the location of the treasure.

He said he was snooping around on the mesa about 20 years ago and discovered an interesting pile of rocks.

He said that may be the starting point in looking for the treasure.

Perhaps a shadow of a stick placed in the center will point the way.

Quinn said he has been a professional treasure hunter for 33 years.

Chapter 75

THE TREASURE OF ÁTIL

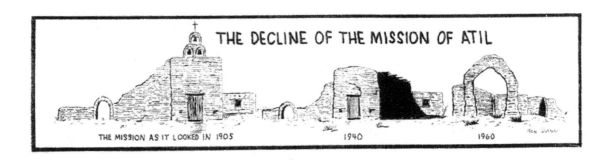

THE DECLINE OF THE MISSION OF ATIL

THE MISSION AS IT LOOKED IN 1905   1940   1960

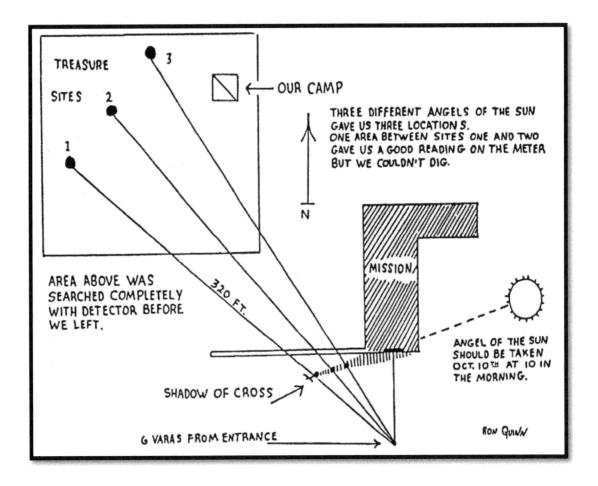

TREASURE SITES 3 2 1 ← OUR CAMP

THREE DIFFERENT ANGELS OF THE SUN GAVE US THREE LOCATIONS. ONE AREA BETWEEN SITES ONE AND TWO GAVE US A GOOD READING ON THE METER BUT WE COULDN'T DIG.

N

MISSION

AREA ABOVE WAS SEARCHED COMPLETELY WITH DETECTOR BEFORE WE LEFT.

320 FT.

ANGEL OF THE SUN SHOULD BE TAKEN OCT. 10TH AT 10 IN THE MORNING.

SHADOW OF CROSS

6 VARAS FROM ENTRANCE

RON QUINN

Mission Nuestro Padre San Francisco de Átil, old and new. NPS Photo

Chuck at Átil.

S ome sixty miles or so below the Mexican border lays the adobe village of Átil, also called Áti. In an open field northwest of the old mission (which no longer exists) a treasure is believed to be buried at a depth of six feet.

One of our partners, Roy, knew a gentleman by the name of Don Page from Berkeley, California. Don was an historian well versed in the history of Old Mexico, especially the Spanish Mission Chain. One of his interests was checking the authenticity of the "so called" mission treasure of Arizona and upper Mexico.

While staying with a friend in Mexico around 1923, Don happened to mention something about the treasures supposedly hidden by the Padres of these missions. His friend Rafael, walked from the room and returned in a few moments with a roll of very old parchment. Placing it upon the table he rolled it out.

He informed Don that just after the revolution, a cousin of his was working on the restoration of a church (believed to be the mission in Caborca). While working on a wall, he discovered a hollow space behind the first layer of adobe bricks. Looking in, he saw a crucifix, two very old knives and a roll of parchment. He placed the items in his work box and later that evening in the privacy of his home examined the artifacts.

The parchment mentioned something about a treasure buried at the village of Átil, located some 35 miles to the east. He became somewhat nervous upon reading this, so placed everything on a high shelf, and there it remained for several years.

When Rafael was visiting him in Caborca, he was shown the old parchment and asked by his cousin, Frank, if he would help in locating the treasure. Rafael advised him against it at this time, and asked if he could borrow and study the document first, which Frank agreed to. Several months later, Frank died in an accident. Again the document was forgotten until Don mentioned buried treasure, and Rafael remembered the papers which he still possessed.

There wasn't much information in the document concerning the history of the mission itself, but somehow the Padres came into possession of this sizable cache of silver and some gold bullion. The majority of the treasure consisted of silver altar item such as: cups, candleholders, pates and crosses.

The directions for locating the cache were rather simple, compared to most mission treasure. I do not have Don's notes with the exact working from the document, but it went something like this:

From the entrance to the mission, you measure six varas in a southerly direction and there drive a wooden stake into the ground. On October the 10th at ten in the morning, place another stake where the shadow of the mission cross falls. Sight along these two stakes and measure 320 feet. (Don worked the distance out from the measurements given in the document.) There the treasure was buried at a depth of two varas.

Don estimated the height from the ground to the roof of the mission at 16 feet. The bell arches were about 3 feed and the cross another 3 or 4 feet height. This would give a combined height of around 25 feet.

Don and Rafael did make a trip to Átil in search of the treasure, but digging was impossible due to the location—almost right in the center of town. They did, however, take measurements and pictures and returned on the 10th of October and checked the angle of the sun, along with the shadow of the cross. Again, we do not have Don's original notes, and I'm only guessing at the measurements on the drawings.

The measurements are important, but with a metal detector you could cover the entire field, as we did back in 1950. Our meter reading between sites one and two wasn't a sudden climb but the needle rose steady and held that position for a two foot swing of the detector, before dropping of sharply. We couldn't guarantee the reading was produced by the treasure, but we were in the correct area in relationship to the 320 foot distance.

The treasure was buried two varas deep or almost six feet deep. How much space this cache would occupy in height is unknown. If it was say, two feet we have a four foot overburden. I'm certain with today's modern detectors, should register a strong reading through four feet of earth. Our Fisher detector gave us a fair reading, and that was a 1960 model.

The road, and I say it with jest, leading to Átil begins at Sasabe on the border some 67 miles southwest of Tucson. We have traveled this "road" several times and believe me, it's a living nightmare, almost 60 miles of bumps, washouts and holes. It takes us well over two hours to make the journey, then you make a left before reaching the outskirts of the village of Altar, and the nightmare continues for another 45 minutes before arriving at Átil.

About three quarters of the way through the village, the old mission stood on the earth from which it came, but there still should be some evidence of it being there.

While there in 1960 they were building a new church beside the old ruins. One wall of this new mission had collapsed and I have no idea if they ever completed the structure.

As Don stated, the ruins were squarely in the center of the village, and digging was just as impossible for us as it had been for him. Very few Americans venture this way and when some do, like us, you're treated kindly, but also as an oddity. The people follow and watch you during your entire stay. It's not because they think you're after their treasure, as nobody in Átil knows of its existence.

You might say then, we should dig at night. Our camp was located on the open field, and once at two in the morning we began digging at the spot where we received the reading. Then minutes later three villagers came waling by carrying a lantern. They asked what the digging was for. Roy speaks fairly good Spanish and said, "It's a latrine."

The people of Átil had never seen a metal detector before, so when they asked who we were and what the machine was, Chuck told them the following, using Royal as the interpreter.

We were from the University of Arizona's archaeology department, and there was evidence that some ancient Indians once lived in this area in large encampments, and we believed one existed where Átil now stands. We wanted to locate some old pottery pieces for study, and the instrument was a (now don't' laugh) "pottery finding machine." Chuck also said, we were interested in the old missions of northern Sonora, and would be taking measurements and pictures of the old ruins down the street, before they were completely gone. We hated to do this, but we couldn't tell them the truth about the treasure, as you will learn later on.

On the third day the fun really started. While working in the field we happened to look down the main street and spotted a police truck with two officers inside. They stopped at the local cantina and went in. Roy's expression at that moment was like he had just bitten into a sour lemon. He said, "Looks like the jig is up boys, the village in on to us." Chuck quickly disassembled the detector and put it away. The two red boxes when clamped together could resemble a portable radio.

It looked rather serious at the moment because of our guilty conscience, as we didn't have a permit for either the detector or digging. As the officers returned to their truck, one spotted us and they drove over. They asked who we were and what we were doing here. I spoke up saying, we were putting a book together on the old missions of the area, and also interviewing the older villagers about these ruins. They believed it.

They weren't abusive but did want to look around some. One spotted the red detector box. Picking it up he said through a wide grin, "Radio?' We all smiled back in unison, "Si." A short while later they drove off down the dusty road. Roy's first remark was: "Am I glad I don't have loose bowels."

We found out later some rancher lost some livestock south of the village. Guess the police thought some poor villager here might have stolen them. Why they stopped at the local cantina to ask we'll never know. Perhaps it's the headquarters for all the contraband in the area, and the two officers were looking for their share.

If that incident with the officers would have turned into something serious, we were prepared to "repel all boarders" and make a run for the border, shooting all the way if necessary.

When you go into Mexico and have either guns or a detector, I hear you must register them at the border. This might be true but we never asked when crossing, as it would only make them suspicious and perhaps check us out more closely. It was also against the law then, 1960, to carry a .45 automatic into Mexico, as it was the official side arm of the police, etc. You guessed it, we had two.

If we had been caught there is a very good chance we'd still be cooling our heels in some "rant hole dungeon," and believe me they have some. When you have been running in the "treasure circles" as long as we have, you hear stories that would make the hair on the back of your head stand straight out.

We decided to leave the following day, as that encounter with the officers had Roy a little shook up as he doesn't like things like that. We couldn't blame him as it could have turned into something serious. We were going to leave anyway, as we couldn't dig with half the village watching.

When Don Page passed away during 1962, most of his research material went to some university. If I has to guess, I'd say Berkeley, It as a shame they received it and not Roy. Don had enough information of caches in Mexico to keep any serious treasure hunter hopping for years. Roy mentioned several times that Don had some good leads on two treasures that were much easier to remove than the one at Átil. He died before passing the documents on to Roy.

We often wonder who has all this vial information at the present, and how it's being utilized. If the truth was known, it's locked away in some library basement and hasn't even been inspected yet. What a loss!

It's one thing searching for treasure here in the states, but when you become involved below the border, the situation can get quite serious, if you don't have the permits or grease the proper palm.

I have to admit the stories you hear down there are very enticing but removing a treasure, if you happen to locate one and getting it out of the country can lead to Big trouble. We have been in Mexico numerous times, like the trip to Átil. Each time we never feel relaxed until we cross the border. There are enough treasures on this side to keep one busy, than venturing into "uncharted waters" and perhaps landing in jail. It just isn't work the risk.

If you believe you can buck their system, give it a try. Another thing, if you think you can work out some arrangement with the local officials down there, forget it as it won't work. Remember you're in their country play their game and the rules are all stacked against you. Like they say on the 'streets': "If you can't do the time, don't do the crime."

BONUS SECTION

DONALD W. PAGE

Donald William Page, was am amateur historian and archaeologist, was born and educated in California. He worked as an engineer, city building inspector and assistant county engineer in Tucson. He did considerable research on early Tucson and Southern Arizona and wrote biographical sketches on early pioneers which appeared in the *Arizona Daily Star*. He died in California in 1958.

Additional notes: Captain Donald William Page (1884-1958) was an assistant Tucson City Engineer in the late 1920s and early 30s, and the co-author of *Tucson – The Old Pueblo* with noted historian Frank C. Lockwood. He later served on the staff of the Bancroft Research Library, University of California in Berkeley.

The following documents have been edited and compiled by Ron Quinn.

Search for El Corral Falso
      Includes: History surrounding the Corral Falso
      Page's translations of documents associated with the treasure
      1926 expedition diary

Molina Document
      Page's Translation & notes

Chapter 76

SEARCH FOR EL CORRAL FALSO

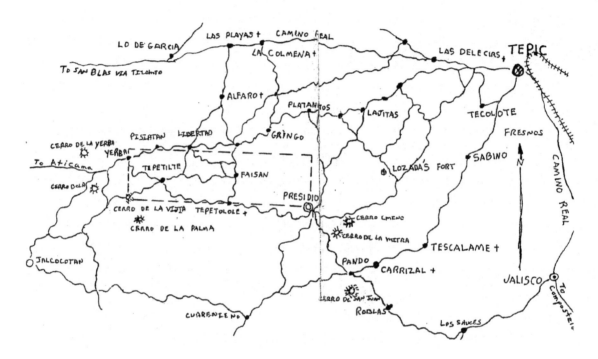

Ron Quinn's map taken from Don Page's original map.

Southern Arizona Trails, Vol. 4, No. 186-190 May 8 – June 5, 1990

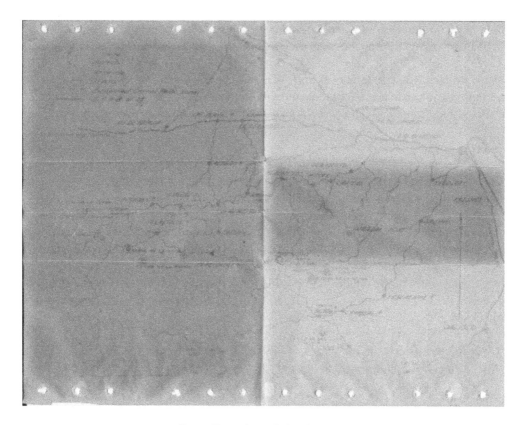

Don Page's original map.

(First of a series)

By Donald W. Page
Transcribed & edited by Ron Quinn

Tucson, Ariz. June 1, 1926

or years past and even up to the present day, the tradition of the vast treasure buried at points along the "Camino Real," is supposed to have been sealed in a cave somewhere within a bandits' mountain fortress in Mexico.

This has led many searchers to scour the mountains in search of some clue that might lead them to the hoard, and not always without success.

Mexico is a veritable storehouse of tales of buried treasure, as all must be aware who know that country intimately.

There are bandits' loot and pirates' gold, church ornaments and ecclesiastical jewels, funds abandoned by fleeing revolutionists and by overthrown governments.

And, in a more prosaic strain, money and valuables of honest folks buried during perilous times in the anticipation of its recovery at some more auspicious date.

However, there were constant disturbances and such anticipations were more often than not in the case of bandit, pirate and patriot, defeated by sudden and violent death or, as happened with so many of the Spanish priests, nobles, mine and land owners, banished by the stern laws promulgated by the first republic.

In the meantime, for one reason or another, the location of their treasure had been lost, mislaid, or passed into the hands of others who, either through loyalty to the rightful owner or ignorance of the true value of their knowledge left the cache undisturbed.

Viewed in a casual light, that statement doubtless sounds well enough for purposes of polite romance, but as the basis for a business proposition to shine a trifle too ethereally to warrant any serious consideration.

Nevertheless, a brief study of the underlying reasons for and of the known facts will quickly prove that the majority of these tales, far from being simply legends, are no more than verbal records of conditions that were the rule down to the close of the 19th century.

As late as 1880, the country was in the throes of violent political evolution. The highways and trails swarmed with patriots and bandits, with at least 80 percent of the transportation accomplished by mule back.

The telegraph was practically unknown, mail routes were few and indifferently served, and banking was only carried on in a very restricted sense by a few commercial houses in the larger towns.

In a word, it was the day of the opportunist, and these abounded in every district.

Tangible wealth, especially in the form of gold and silver, was in consequence a potential menace, to be gotten rid of as quickly as possible.

What wonder then that the malefactor, the cleric, the politician, the ordinary citizen, finding themselves temporarily embarrassed with a surplus of that treasure produced by Mexico in the days of which I write in quantities that challenge belief, and beset upon every side by the fear of retribution, forced political loans, assault or robbery, should turn to Mother Earth as the quickest and surest repository for their wealth?

Probably the majority of these hoards were eventually recovered by their more or less rightful owners, while of these remaining unclaimed many have been unearthed by others, as witnessed by the following cases selected at random from many that have come under my observations.

During the 1880s, an American named Williard, then residing in San Luis Potosí, accidentally discovered a tunnel under his house.

Upon exploring this, he came upon a considerable fortune in silver bars and old Spanish coins.

It was sufficiently large, however, for him to purchase the property that he then occupied (a large one and of considerable value) and to permit him to erect a linen mill.

In 1847 a young mail carrier, caught one night in a tropical storm on the road between Tepic and San Blas, saw two men stealthily lead a loaded mule a short distance from the road and by its burden.

Drafted immediately thereafter into the army, he was unable to return until 1889, where he devoted his time to a search for the spot.

He applied to a Mr. Alberto Gonsales for assistance. After some further search, they succeeded in locating the cache, which proved to be a small chest containing $5,000.

Capt. Villa, a Mexican sailor then in my father's employ, was one day climbing the path leading to the ruins of old San Blas when he came upon an ancient earthen pot, washed down from the bank by the rains, containing several hundred dollars in Spanish gold coins.

Pedro Borgia, mule drover of Sihuatian [Cihuatlan], Jalisco and a companion recovered a considerable portion of the million dollars in California gold that went down with the old side wheeler Golden Gate when she was burned and beached just south of Graham's Head on the west coast of Mexico on July 27, 1862.

During the construction of the Southern Pacific Railroad of Mexico, an American contractor, clearing the right of way between Mazatlan and Acaponeta, in the state of Sinaloa, came upon two loads of bullion at the foot of a tree, evidently part of some long forgotten Spanish convoy carrying the treasure down from the mines to the port of San Blas.

Another American, working from a description given to him by a Mexican woman, unearthed $750,000 in ancient coin and bullion from the ruins of an old Spanish church near Torres, Sonora, late in 1925.

Alejandro Rivera, of San Blas came upon a document telling of the location of two loads of silver buried by robbers at a point on the Camino Real between Tepic and San Blas, set down as "La Vuelta de las Calvelines."

Careful search failed to discover any such spot and Rivera was about to give up in disgust when and old drover, who had traveled the road for years, told him the place was now called "Vuelta de los Viejos." Following the instructions given in his document, Rivera located the spot and dug up silver amounting to more than $10,000 in Mexican currency.

While the following incidents are more properly negative records, I am getting them down as interesting, and at the same time furnishing still further proof that treasure actually existed and still exists in Mexico.

The foregoing is not intended as a brief at large for the existence of Mexican treasures, but as a necessary forward to the story that I now have to tell, as I realize that lacing some such preparation of local color to bare statement of the facts that I shall set forth, might well leave the reader unconvinced.

In 1912, I was for some months located in the vicinity of San Blas, territory of Tepic (now the state of Nayarit), and at this time a most interesting document came into my hands, the history of its finding alone warranting mention.

An illiterate Mexican woman, digging one day in her garden near San Blas, unearthed a small ironbound antique chest whose only contents were a few yellowed and moldy papers.
Being unable to read, the woman gave scant importance to her find and tucked the papers away in the thatch of her nipa hut, where they were quickly forgotten.

There they remained until one day a friend, an ex-schoolmistress, inquired whether she had an old newspaper from which a dress pattern could be cut. The woman remembered and gave her the old papers, without thinking to tell her how they came into her possession. They had been partly cut up before the seamstress thought to glance at the text.

Then realizing their possible importance, she preserved the pieces. These were reassembled and the complete text copied, with the exception of a few words that were illegible.

The document purported to be a record of the disposal of the loot taken by two bandit chiefs, Juan and Antonio Auriano (or Lauriano.) The writing at times was difficult to decipher but in this case the spelling probably was the latter. I shall quote the preamble and closing paragraph textually:

"This began in 1811 and ended in 1815. In the name of God and of the Virgin Mary of Guadalupe, I speak in good faith inasmuch as that which is stated in these documents is clear truth, they being enclosed in a casket of iron and wood on the 13 of May 1818.

"I charge the persons who remove them to comply with what they charge, as thus thou shalt learn of the treasure that is buried between Compostela and the Paso Blanco.

"…and further, thou shalt ascend to the Corral Falso where in the entrance thou shalt seek for a pile of mortar with which the cave was sealed. Thou shalt enter it and remove what treasure thou wilt."

As the present interest in the foregoing document centers only on the activities of the gang as referred to in the preamble, and in the spot spoken of in the last paragraph as the "Corral Falso," it may be well to dispose of the balance of the text for the time being by stating that it contained descriptions of a number of caches of plunder scattered between Compostela and the Paso Blanco.

Local investigation having proven the accuracy of the historical, topographical and geographical references made in the document, I began preparation for an expedition to verify the statements made relative to the treasure, but unfortunately just at this time Emiliano Zapata's followers invaded the territory and I was forced to postpone the trip until a safer time.

(Second of a series)

Corral Falso: Bandits' Loot

While waiting for political conditions to improve in Mexico, my business called me abroad where I remained until recently, but always with the intention of carrying out my original plan to search for the Corral Falso.

In the meantime, research in various quarters, including the Archivo de las Indias at Sevilla, the archives of the archbishopic at Guadalajara and the local records at Tepic, rounded out by interviews with the old men and women of the territory, brought to light data from which it is possible to write at least a sketch of a tale of patriotism, robbery and murder that goes back to the days of the Spanish conquest.

In 1529, barely 10 years after Hernán Cortés first landed at La Vera Cruz, Nuñez de Guzman carried the conquest over the mountains of Nayarit and down to the shores of the Pacific Ocean at the mouth of the Rio Rololacan (later called the Grande or Santiago River).

The Spaniards claimed all of the region forming the central portion of the Pacific Coast of Mexico for his Most Catholic Majesty, Ferdinand V, under the name of the Kingdom of Nueva Galicia, and founding the port of San Blas and the town of Espiritu Santo de Tepic.

The following year Espiritu Santo de Compostela, the capital of the new kingdom, was founded and this city was soon linked by a Camino Real both with the new port of San Blas and, through Guadalajara, with Mexico City—still known by its Aztec name, Tenochtitlan.

The Spaniards' insatiable lust was for gold, gold and more gold, and by the end of the 16th century many of the subsequently famous mines of Nayarit had been discovered, and those of Zacatecas were already giving promise of developing into a new El Dorado.

By 1750, Nueva Galicia boasted no fewer than 21 *reales*, or mining towns, here ore was treated, and the mines of Zacatecas alone were producing more than 5 million pesos a year.

San Blas was the seaport for the region.

Besides the Zacatecas mines, such renown properties in Sinaloa, Nayarit and Jalisco as the Sesentona (a name suggested by the fact that the ore ran sixto marcos to the carga, or $8,000 to the ton), the Condesa (whose wealth bought for its owner, a humble Spanish woman, the title of Countess of Miravalles), the Guadalupena (long lost after the Spanish exodus, but whose rediscovery elevated its new owners from the ranks of poor criollo washerwomen to the upper circles of San Francisco's old aristocracy), the Tigre, the Barrosa, the mines of Santa Maria del Oro, Las Habillas and a dozen others were sending their mule trains of gold and silver winding down to the galleons that were to carry it back to Spain, via the Isthmus of Panama, or to the Philippine Islands.

The Camino Real, or royal highway, over which all of this treasure was carried was, despite its sonorous name, in great part no better than a mule trail, climbing endlessly up over passes and twisting down through river gorges, now clinging to the sheer side of some mighty cliff, now picking its tortuous way over and among giant boulders at the bottom of a chasm, with a hundred pitfalls and natural ambuscades at almost every turn.

With such treasure abroad in a natural bandits' paradise, no wonder that not all was allowed to pass unmolested.

There was never a lack of lawless spirits and masterless men, discharged soldiers, embittered seekers after the easy wealth of the New World, rebellious Indians and fugitives from the justice of the Holy Inquisition, all of whom took such toll as they were able.

And now the first stirrings of the spirit of nationalism added still another enemy to prey upon the treasure convoys. By this time the Spaniards were extracting not less than 50 million pesos annually from the country. All of this, with the exception of possibly one fifth, was shipped to Spain, one fifth as the king's share, one fifth as the church's share and the remainder as the mine owner's portion.

This systematic despoliation of the land was one of the causes of bitterness against the Spaniards and was one of the first evils to be assailed.

A group of the earliest patriots, whose headquarters was in San Luis Potosí, foreseeing the day when Mexico's independence would be proclaimed, determined to prepare for this time by preventing the export of gold and silver by the Spaniards. They stored such booty as they were able to seize until it should be required to equip and arm a patriot army. To accomplish this end, three bands were formed, recruited from criollos (Mexico-born Spaniards) and Indians of humble origin and good character.

One of these was assigned to operate on the Camino Real between Mexico City and Vera Cruz, one on the Acapulco road and the third on the highway between Tepic and San Blas, thus covering the approaches of the only ports then authorized for export.

The instructions given these men were simple. They were to attack only such convoys as carried royal or Spanish treasure, but they were to allow no opportunity to escape by inflicting as great a loss as possible upon these.

Of the proceeds of their assault, the gold was to be held as an inviolable trust against the needs of the nation, while the balance was to be employed as might be required to further the ends of the organization.

They were bound by the strictest oaths of secrecy and, if required, they were prepared to lay down their lives for the cause. The band operating between Tepic and San Blas was composed of some 40 picked men.

All were honest artisans and mechanics, and membership was handed down from father to son, being looked upon with pride as a mark of distinction.

They lived at home, either in Tepic or the immediate vicinity, and followed their various trades except when called into the field by their local chief, acting upon information sent down from San Luis Potosí relative to the anticipated movement of some state convoy.

At such times, the band was sent to assemble at their mountain headquarters, a natural stronghold known as Corral Falso.

This spot seems to have been a small volcanic crater or similar depression in the side of a canyon, having but one narrow entrance, enclosed by precipitous cliffs so cunningly concealed by nature that it has defied searchers for more than a hundred years.

A small permanent garrison was maintained in the Corral whose duty was to guard the treasure accumulated by the band.

The gold, or national property, seems to have been deposited in one or more small caves which were walled up as filled and the silver to have been buried separately.

The favorite method of attack is said to have been for the band to divide into several small parties and to lie in wait for a convoy at some point where the road was especially narrow and difficult, and where the train would be strung out over a considerable distance.

As the convoys generally consisted of from 50 to 100 or more mules, it was easy to launch several simultaneous attacks at points some distance apart, thus the connection of the fighting enabling at least one of their parties to seize and make off with one or more loaded mules while the remainder joined to fight off pursuit.

This was not a difficult undertaking, as the robbers knew every square *vara* of ground. The country was wild and broken and the guards were generally glad enough to escape with the loss of a few mules.

After all, the treasure belonged either to the church, the king or the nobles, all of whom had unfailing sources of supply while the soldier, however brave he might be, had but one life to lose and once gone neither pope or king, to say nothing of the nobility, would return this to him.

Therefore it may be imagined that many of these attacks were concluded with a shrug, a spreading of hands, many and lurid maledictions heaped upon the heads of the "*sin verguenazas*," the fatherless sons of shame, and the convoy moved on.

Years passed, and toward the close of the century the Corral Falso band came to be looked upon as an established institution.

Their depredations were confined exclusively to property of Spaniards, these having fallen low in the favor the country folk.

What more natural than that the latter should come to look upon the patriot-bandit brotherhood as to one of the first tangible manifestations of the earnestness of their ultimate delivery from the galling oppression of the yoke of Spain, and to protect them at every turn from their natural enemies, the royal forces?

So secure indeed became their position that various improvements were undertaken in what had come to be looked upon as their undisputed domain.

At many spots the roughest portions of their most frequented trails were rudely paved, and at others the sheer sides were secured by rubble retaining walls.

The Corral itself is said to have boasted a number of quite substantially built houses and the natural difficulties at the entrance were added to by the location of stone posts drilled for the reception of gate bars, so that once enclosed their stock could, if necessary, be left to itself.

Nor was art neglected, for at three commanding points, forgotten artists in the band have left bas relief records of their leaders.

At one spot, facing down a narrow and gloomy gorge, one of their chiefs, Pedro Morúa, is sculptured armed, mounted and brandishing his machete in defiance.

At another, some forgotten *jefe* faces his enemy, Colonel Villarda, a royalist officer dressed in full regimentals of the period, both on horseback and defying each other with drawn sabers.

(Third of a series)

Corral Falso: Bandits' Loot

The fortunes of the band continued in the ascendant until 1798, by which time their organization was highly developed and their confidence so high that not a convoy could pass through their territory without suffering a loss.

Many sporadic, half-hearted attempts had been made to subjugate the robbers but to [no] end until now, when a supreme act of bold blasphemy forced the government into a determined aggression that finally resulted in their overthrow.

Smarting under constant losses, and harassed both locally and from the court by ever-growing criticism, the viceroy, Count Branciforte, a Sicilian who retired this same year with more than 5 million pesos to show for his four years tenure of office, hit upon a plan.

As the secular arm had proven powerless to stay the assaults, it was determined to invoke the powers of the church. To this end, arrangements were made whereby three friars of holy orders were to march at the head of the next convoy leaving Tepic.

The viceroy was assured that the thunders of the ecclesiastical anathema would blast his tormentors where his own had failed. The viceroy's records would be cleared, the power of the church would once more be proven and everyone would be content, excepting perhaps the bandits.

The train left Tepic, captained by its spiritual guardians. But to the horror of all concerned, far from being permitted to pass unmolested, it was fallen upon with redoubled fury.

After a fierce and bloody fight, all three priests were seized and carried captive to the Corral, where they were placed upon trial for their lives, charged with high treason in aiding and abetting the enemies of "America" (as Mexico was called at the time.)

It may be inferred that the unfortunate padres were given but scant grace, as they seem to have been convicted and executed with a speed that well might have graced a better cause. All three were buried where they fell, at the foot of a great rock that is said to rise from the center of the Corral.

This final gesture of sacrilegious defiance was the last straw, and both clergy and laity arose en masse, demanding the extermination of the band. Count Branciforte had been relieved as viceroy by General Miguel José de Asansa, a man of great energy.

Goaded into a blind fury by this prompt and dreadful defiance of his authority, the new viceroy needed no stimulation but quickly dispatched a strong column of heavy dragoons to the scene with orders to clear the country of the bandits at any cost.

Arriving in the heart of the troubled area, the royal forces established their headquarters at a spot that, strange to say, bears a striking resemblance to the descriptions of the bandits' stronghold the Corral Falso.

This is without doubt a volcanic crater, some 300 meters across.

The floor is quite level, (indeed, it is so even that at times it is planted to corn) and the entrance, which faces west, is over a ridge some 50 meters in height that forms the wall of the enclosure.

The Presidio, as the old crater is now called in memory of the days when it served as a camp for the king's troops, is located high up on a jutting corner of the San Juan Mountains. From its elevation of 1,500 meters above sea level, it dominated a considerable extent of the country.

From this vantage point the troops could swoop down upon the patriots (for such had now become their status) whenever it was learned that these were gathering for an attack.

Many and bloody were the battles that raged through the wild canyons and over the dizzy peaks that make up the country.

Even today grim mementos of that fierce struggle are occasionally met with: here a few moldering beams, there a broken and rust-eaten sword blade; further on a few blackened Spanish dollars—"pieces of eight" bearing the royal arms of Spain and the profiles of Ferdinand VI or Charles III; a horseshoe, the fragments of a blunderbuss. And finally found but a few years ago by a man named Silva, the headquarters mess kit belonging to a Spanish officer who garrisoned the Presidio more than 100 years ago, each piece of porcelain in its place, just as it was left.

Despite the most stubborn resistance, weight of numbers finally told against the patriot band and, after a year of incessant guerilla warfare, they were finally conquered.

Their end is shrouded in some doubt, and there are various version of the affair.

One is that the troops drove them in until they were forced to throw themselves into the Corral, where, after a bloody hand-to-hand encounter, they were slain to a man, no quarter being asked or given.

Another, and more probable account, is that the soldiers never found the Corral, being deliberately lured away each time they drew near the stronghold, but that in 1799 they finally succeeded in dispersing the band.

Many were killed, a few taken prisoner (and of these there is reason to believe that some were sent to Spain) and the few survivors scattered for their lives as far as California, Texas and Guatemala.

(Fourth of a series)

In Search of El Corral Falso

A gap of some five years follows and the thread of the Corral Falso story is again taken up early in the 19th century.

The viceroy, Don José de Iturrigaray, learning of the Corral Falso and the plunder said to be buried there, [he] determined to secure this and dispatched an expedition from Mexico City with instructions to locate the place and find the treasure.

The viceroy seems to have felt assured both as to the existence of the Corral and as to his being able to find it. His party arrived in Tepic fully equipped with laborers, tools and 200 pack mules to carry off the plunder. It is said that the leaders said they anticipated little difficulty in executing their task.

At the time there were doubtless still to be found a number of individual who, while probably not having been members of the band, still either knew or had a shrewd suspicion of the location of the Corral.

However, hatred of the Spanish had by this time grown to a white-hot flame and no assistance could be looked for from the natives.

The viceroy's information must have either been vague or in error, for, after spending several months in aimless wanderings about the mountains, his expedition withdrew.

Five or six more years passed, each fanning still higher the flames of the political conflagration, and in 1811 still another chapter of the history of the Corral Falso was written.

Under cover of the turbulent peon uprising following Father Miguel Hildalgo's "Grito de Dolores" on the night of the 15th of September, 1810 (Mexico's equivalent to the ringing of our Liberty Bell) and, it is believed, in the guise of partisans of the patriot priest Mercado, who had just wrested both Tepic and San Blas from the royalists, two brothers, Juan and Antonio Lauriano, gathered about them a following and set themselves up as successors of the original band of the Corral.

Despite the lack of conclusive evidence, it may be deduced that their motives were far less altruistic than those of their predecessors. If they did observe some of this tradition handed down, including that of maintaining utmost secrecy regarding the location of their headquarters, this was done, no doubt for mercenary reasons.

The Laurianos seem to have been highly successful in their chosen field of endeavor until the year 1815.

The capture and execution in the year of the soldier-priest, General Morelos, marked the end of the fortunes, as it did those of what may be termed the intermediate efforts of the war of independence.

The temporary collapse of the Mexican Revolution released the royal forces, whose efforts were now directed to hunting down any unfortunate who might in any way be identified with the political uprising that had just been crushed.

The Laurianos fell into that class and the viceroy, General Felix Galleja [Calleja], lost no time. He fell upon them like a thunderbolt and the gang was ruthlessly hunted down until it is believed that none escaped.

Forty-one years elapsed before the Corral was heard of again, and during that time much history was written.

The last viceroy, O'Dontroujou, signed the recognition of Mexico's independence, but Ferdinand VII refused the crown of the new nation.

General Iturbide was crowned Agustin I, Emperor of Mexico, and was executed.

The war of 1847 was fought with the United States and that stolid, upright Indian statesman, Benito Juarez, as president of the Republic, was trying to establish order out of chaos and at the same time present a firm front to Napoleon III, whose threats of intervention now loomed on the political horizon.

In Tepic, the English house of Barron, Forbes & Co. had risen to baronial grandeur by means of supplanting the king in his royal monopoly of the sale of quicksilver to the mines.

Numbered among their staunchest supporters, and the recipient of many marked confidences was Don Ignacio Pintado, judge of the first instance and member of one of the first families of the county, who now adds a dramatic chapter to the story of the Corral.

I will let his daughter, Doña Guadalupe P. viuda de Casillas, tell the tale in her own words.

Self explanatory as Sra. Casillas' recital of her father's experience will be found, still, in view of the data at my disposal a few words of comment in the form of footnotes to the following translation have been thought proper.

It may be added that this is the first time that the full story of Sr. Pintado's trip has been made public, and for reasons that will readily be appreciated, certain points have been omitted or slightly altered, as is also the case with the recital of my own experiences and deductions.

(Pages 16 to 20 are missing.)

The next page starts with: was crowned Maximilian I, Emperor of Mexico, to fall before the firing squad on the Cerro de las Campañas at Queretaro. General Porfirio Díaz ruled with an iron hand for 30 years.

Francisco Madero awakened the country with his slogan of political equality — only to die beneath the bayonets of his guards, and President Venustiano Carranza rose to power as his avenger.

In 1918 a lady arrived in Mexico City from Spain bearing certain documents relative to the Corral and secured a personal interview with President Carranza.

Carranza examined her data and evidently impressed, dispatched two inspectors of schools to Tepic with instructions to secure all the information possible at first hand.

These gentlemen had barely begun their work when they were forced to flee by the outbreak of General Obregon's revolution in 1919.

Their chief was killed shortly thereafter and the matter was dropped. This was the last serious effort that was made to rediscover the Corral until January of 1926.

Ever since the documents described in this story came into my hands, a friends of many years standing, Mr. M. D. Strong of the real estate firm of Strong & Bashine of New York, has been equally interest in them.

While in England in December of last year, another old friend, F. W. DeValda, managing director of Visual Education, Ltd., of London, also became interested in the matter.

As the time seemed ripe, it was agreed that these gentlemen should finance an expedition to examine the various locations described and incidentally to endeavor to verify the rumors and tales centering about the Corral Falso.

In explanation of the secondary importance in which the Corral Falso was held at the time, it may be well to state that I had then collected but little of the data upon the subject that subsequently came into my possession.

We were not unnaturally more interested in certain locations that were carefully described than in one spot that was simply referred to, and of the existence of which, we were at the time in considerable doubt.

Capt. DeValda and I departed from New York on Feb. 10, arriving at Tepic on the 24th, when we immediately set to work to locate the various caches.

There were 22 in number, including the Corral Falso, and it was found that 14 of these lay to the south, between Tepic and Compostela, and the balance, including the Corral, to the west between Tepic and Jalcocotan

The direct distances involved are short, it being barely 29 kilometers in an air line between Tepic and Compostela and 24 to Jalcocotan, but the terrain is so wild and broken that it's often as far again or farther by trail.

There are no roads that merit the name in this section of the country, and once off the main trails, the tracks are of the most elementary nature. Many of these can be negotiated only by a good mule.

With the exception of a very few days, we are constantly in the field from the date of our arrival until our departure on May 4, exploring more than 250 square kilometers of territory and localizing all the spots described in the documents, including the Corral Falso.

Nine of these we were able to definitely identify, but lack of time prevented the completion of the work.

It may be of interest to state that at each of the nine spots we were able to identify, we found that we had been anticipated.

There was of course, no method of telling whether the treasure had been unearthed or not, although at one point we heard a rumor to the effect that considerable money had been unearthed in the vicinity.

(Fifth of a series- -conclusion)

Search for El Corral Falso Booty

During our investigation of the western locations, we ascertained that popular belief located the Corral Falso somewhere within a parallelogram roughly 2 ½ kilometers North and seven by seven kilometers East and West.

The southeastern corner of it was formed by the Presidio and the northwestern by the hacienda La Yerba, the first point lying about 10 and the second about 16 kilometers in a south- southwesterly direction from Tepic.

The principal reasons assigned for this location were that the area is bounded on the east by the Presidio (from where, it may be remembered, the Spanish troops were to wage warfare upon the robbers,) on the west by an isolated peak known as the Cerro de la Vijia (Watch Mountain), popularly believed to have been the bandits' lookout, on the south by a trackless wilderness and on the north by an old Spanish road connecting Tepic with San Blas, via Lajitas, Libertad, Yerba and Aticama.

This trail, running up along the northern flank of the Cerro de San Juan, was the one supposed to have been taken by the convoys, and consequently the one along which the attacks were made.

But in reality, it was no more than a vague track in those days, used principally by smugglers in [word missing] their goods up from the coast, the true Camino Real of the date being the road described in Note 2 on page 18 (missing).

By the time we had sufficient data in hand to prove to our satisfaction that the story of the Corral Falso warranted serious consideration, we undertook the search with much more conviction than that with which we had looked upon this phase of the matter at the start.

278

A systematic survey of the scene just described failed to discover the Corral but did prove that from the time of Sr. Pintado's efforts, each succeeding generation of searchers had devoted their energies to this particular region, to the exclusion of all others.

As the area under consideration was not large, about 17 ½ square kilometers, we were at a loss to understand why, if the Corral was located in this section of country, it had not been discovered time and again.

Nor were we able to wholly reconcile the few available scraps or description of the surrounds and approaches of the place, later found to be distorted fragments of the story that Sra. Casillas was to tell us.

At this point, were we not entirely surprised to find that the deductions made from a chance discovery strongly indicated a different section of the country as the probable location.

Careful inquiries proved that the scenes that we now had in mind had never been considered as a possible location for the Corral, and that consequently it had never been explored.

But as we were satisfied of the soundness of our deductions (and I may state that these were amply supported by Sra. Casillas' description of the route taken by her father), we proceeded with a survey of this new area.

We had completed about five square kilometers when a hurried trip into the state of Jalisco became imperative and it was decided to postpone the completion of the work until our return.

The trip took longer and was much more expensive than we had anticipated, so that upon our return to Tepic we were forced to make immediate preparations for our departure to the United States. Continuation of the search for the Corral Falso would be held in abeyance until our return.

Upon the eve of our departure, we met Sra. Casillas and for the first time heard the story of her father's experience at first hand and while we both felt that this would prove to be the key to the puzzle, it was absolutely impossible for us to delay our departure to conclude the investigation in the light of the new data.

The point where Sr. Casillas turned off from the Tepic to San Blas road, the direction that he took and the description of the ridges that he traversed all point to the confirmation of our last deductions about the probable location of the Corral.

Furthermore, they point to its being within the five square kilometers that we were unable to survey, so that we feel confident that in taking up the work again we will only have to explore that area.

There are two outstanding questions that seem to be involved by this story of the Corral Falso and by Sr. Casillas' experience.

The first is, how is it possible that a bandit stronghold of such importance could be maintained in such close proximity to a city of the importance of Tepic?

Second, why was it that Sr. Casillas was wholly unable to rediscover the Corral himself or to direct his associates so that they could find the place, barely four years having elapsed since he was taken to the spot?

In reply to the first query, it must be remembered that in those days the region of which I write was a veritable no-man's land, uninhabited and given over to criminals, Indians and wild beasts.

An old lady who rode over the Camino Real in 1841 states that at that time the entire country was covered with heavy brush and timber and that the trail was so narrow that, despite the fact that soldiers of the escort marched behind each mule, the party might have been successfully attacked at almost any point.

It will also be of interest to note that no longer ago than 1862 that arch bandit, Manuel Lozada, maintained one of his strongholds in this same region but less than seven kilometers distance from the Plaza de Armas of Tepic.

The second question is somewhat harder to explain. To fully realize the reason for the apparently casual manner in which the problem has been attacked from the first, it is necessary to know the easy-going way of the *hidalgos* of the old school.

They were not to be hurried and any matter that could not with all convenience be concluded today was a matter of course postponed until tomorrow, or the following week or month. It really made but little difference.

Also they took much for granted and bothered themselves not at all over details that were part of the responsibility of subordinates.

I can visualize Sr. Pintado riding behind his guides and paying little or no attention to the trail or to the landmarks.

Also, neither Sr. Casillas nor his companions were country bred. The region abounds in hills and peaks, all more or less the same in appearance, and their trips were always made in fear of attack.

Such seemingly improbable things do happen, however, as witnessed by the story told by Pedro Vizarraga of San Blas about the bandit dictator of Tepic, Manuel Lazada. Having reason to suspect the good faith of his banker, the House of Aguirre, and in anticipation of his eventual overthrow, Lazada began to ship part of his vast accumulation of wealth to Spain in about 1886.

One of the treasure convoys was in the charge of Commandant Antonio Rodriguez, one of Lazada's officers. He was camped for a week at La Palma, a hacienda lying a short distance inland from Aticama that at that time belonged to Rodriguez.

Vizarraga was one of the guards and it occurred to him that it would be a good plan to lay by a load or so of silver against the time of retribution that would undoubtedly arrive with Lazada's fall.

He felt confident that he could do this with impunity, as the amount would never be missed in the hurry and excitement of embarkation.

Accordingly, the same night he buried two *cargas* of dollars at the fork of a little arroyo, just east of the hacienda.

As it was so close to the building, he paid little attention to landmarks. When he returned a few year later for his plunder, he found that he could by no means identify the place, and despite his many endeavors, lost something like $10,000.

Under the terms of our original agreement, Mrs. Strong and DeValda were to finance the search up to a certain figure and I was o furnish the data.

In return for these considerations, all three were to share alike in any profits that might accrue. As originally planned, we were all to go on the expedition, but at the last moment Mr. Strong was unavoidably detained.

The information furnished by Sra. Casillas made a new agreement necessary. To this end a contract was executed with the lady and her son, whereby they agreed to deliver to us all of the information relative to the Corral now in their possession or that may in the future come to their knowledge.

They were to assist us in the search in every way (such as furnishing headquarters in Tepic, supplying reliable memos, the use of their influence, etc.) and to enter into no negotiations in any way upon the Corral Falso with others.

In return for this, they have accepted a 12.5 percent interest in the returns of our explorations, under the following arrangements:

A private stock company was to be formed for the purpose of continuing the search for the Corral Falso and 20 shares (or fractions thereof) valued at $1,000 each (U.S.) were to be issued as follows. Paid up and non-assessable promoters stock: Sra. Guadalupe P. viuda de Casillas and Sr. Ignacio Casillas, 2.5 shares; Mr. M. D. Strong, 2.5 shares; Capt. F. W. DeValda, 2.5 shares; Capt. D. W. Page, 2.5 shares; Treasury Stock, 10.0 shares. Total 20 shares.

Upon concluding the arrangement, we planned to return to the United States, re-equip and reorganize and in about a month's time return to Tepic to conclude the search. The financing of the second expedition was to be handled, as was the first, by Strong and DeValda.

Unfortunately in the meantime, both these gentlemen suffered serious financial reverses, and for the time being it was impossible for either of them to furnish the necessary funds.

Capt. DeValda had been forced to return to England and it was doubtful if he would be available to help carry out the work.

Under these altered conditions, and in view of this fact that we all three feel the utmost confidence in our ultimate success and are, therefore, to carry on the search at the earliest moment, it has been agreed that he Treasure stock originally intended to be assumed by Strong and DeValda, be placed upon the market to cover the expenses of the final expedition which, based upon my going along and the trip lasting three months, are estimated at about $3,500.

It may be remarked that all of the costs are based upon our experience during the trip, just completed, and are accurate as is possible to make them:

Equipment, $300; R.R. transportation, $150; 4 mules at $50 each, $200; 2 mesos [mestizos] at $30 each per month, $180; 1 cook at $15 per month, $45; house rent at $30 per month, $90: 720 rations corn at $0.15, $108; 1,080 rations food at $0.50 $450; personal expense, $1,500; incidental, $387.00. Total, $3,500.

While under the above plan I am the only member of the company assigned to the final expedition, one, or even two others would be welcomed, provided that they possess a fair knowledge of Spanish and were prepared to pay their expenses.

Finally, the question of prospective remuneration is to be considered. I have as yet been unable to secure reliable data on the number and value of the robberies committed on the Camino Real between Tepic and San Blas from 1750 to 1815 and cannot hazard a fixed estimate of the value of the plunder that may be looked for from the Corral Falso.

But from the fact that the viceroy's expedition of 1805 arrived with 200 pack mules to carry off the treasure, and assuming the value thereof on a silver basis, a minimum estimate at any rate can be arrived at.

The standard mule load of minted silver of the old coinage was 5,000 pesos. Therefore, under the foregoing assumption, the value of the treasure of the Corral Falso cannot be less than 1 million pesos, or $500,000 gold.

[The manuscript ends at the point.]

DONALD W. PAGE'S 1926 EXPEDITION IN SEARCH OF THE CORRAL FALSO

Copied from Page's notes by Roy Purdie

In February of 1926 D. W. Page arrived in Tepic to begin the search for the Corral Falso treasure. The following diary entries are taken from his personal notebook.

2/25: Tepic – Compostela via Jalisco N°. 8, Doc. N°. 1. Determined that route via Jalisco N°. 11, Doc. N°. 1 is correct one.

Road crosses Rio de las Pasos ??? 22 times and car was stuck each time. Left Tepic 8 a.m., arrived Compostela 3:30 p.m. Left 5:30 p.m. arrived Tepic 1 a.m. Out of gas at Jalisco and walked in. Terrain very rough and broken and will present great difficulty to identification of points. Believe that we determined the general location of N°. 1, Doc. N°. 1 between Miravalles & Puente.

2/26: Walked 5 kilometers and reconnoitered N°. 13, Doc N°. 1. Dep. 9 a.m., returned 1:30 p.m.

2/27: Drove 6 km & walked 8 km to further reconnoiter N°. 13, Doc. N°.1 but failed to find point as described. At <u>A</u> found excavation with flat rock overturned and at <u>B</u> rock with very faint marks (thus IIII). This may have been a natural mark and shallow very old excavation 8 meters in direction of 4 marks. Excavation "A" quite recent great number of rocks both isolated & in groups on west slope of N°. 13, Doc. N°. 1, but examined all. Heavy brush ½ way up slope 45°, balance pine 60°. Water at "C" & said to be a valuable mine up Arroyo de Resudo Paisano at Rancho N°. 13, Doc. N°. 1 reported a mine near head of Arroyo de Raisuda, owned, located and known of by an oak gall collector.

2/28: Arranged to hire horses and saddles & mozo [lad], Manuel Rodriquez from Nicho Valley of the Meson de la Luz next to hotel at 2 pesos per day per head.

3/1: Departed for reconnaissance trip to N°. 13, Doc. N°. 1. A spring located S.E. of south peak N°. 13, Doc. N°. 1, peak as possible location of N°. 13. Found terrain very rough and broken and no possibility of reconstructing direction for location. Found the spring (the trees had disappeared) and endeavored to trace back to mountain, but found impossible as many deep barrancas [slopes] and high ridges intervened. Progressed on Tepic – Jalisco, Los Sauces Trail almost to latter point, returning from there to Los Aguacates & Tepic. Departed 8 a.m., returned 5 p.m. Inclined to believe that location examined on 2/27 is correct one.

3/2: Ascertained from Deluis that peak referred to in location N°. 2 is on Quarenteño [probably Cuarentenño] ranch now property of Mr. A. C. James, an American coffee planter. Secured trailing [tracing] of Deluis Land map of sector S.W. of Tepic.

3/3: Depart 8 a.m. for Quarenteño by Salino [probably Sabino], El Pando Trail, very steep and rough, steady climb to El Pando (El. 6175') from where steady descent. Reached El Pando 1 p.m., lunched, no water but said to be a spring on south peak of S. Juan. Arrived Quarenteño 3 p.m. and put up by Mr. James. Told that ridge running S.W. N°.2, Doc. N°. 2, was referred to under N°.4, Doc. N°. 2, arranged for guide. Photographed peak from Pando Trail.

3/4: Accompanied James to his ranch at Cuarento, an hour's ride south of Quarenteño and met a Mr. Carr who seems to be looking for coffee land & calculated roughly elevations for James' proposed flume. At 1 p.m. climbed ridge supposed to be N°. 2, Doc. N°. 2 and went to so called water hole on N.W. side which was really a small brook at point where Pisoneño and Quarenteño crossed. Inclined to believe that we are at fault. Returned to Quarenteño at 6 p.m.

3/5: Dep. 8 a.m. for N°. 2, Doc. N°. 2 arr. 10^{30} a.m. Found mountain to be sharp conical peak (El. 4100') attached to southern peak of N°. 13, Doc. N°. 1 (El. 7250') by sharp steep ridge and 1/3 way along which on E. is small valley "Lo de Alonzo." Deep barrancas E., S.E., N.W. while to S. & S.W. long ridges lead to lower coast country, heavily pine timbered. Trail leads up to N.E. at the highest point and low stone wall or breastwork has been thrown across ridge, trail winding to east thereof. Formation very soft limestone, weathered and partly leached, on stone at center of peak two oblong depressions cut, another south and another west thereof, while at south is a cut in the hillside. S.E. a level spot all as below.

Shallow excavations were effected at points marked X [X] within a circle] as lying roughly between the 2 pines as indicated altho these cannot be more than 20/30 years old. Subsequently it was ascertained from Nasbar ??? Pintado of Jalisco, a friend of Manuel Rodriquez, that this peak was a strong point of Mexican patriots during the war of independence and that by digging at the flat spot a prospect would be found. As indicated, a shallow pit was dug but in common with other test pits the ground or rock was found to be in place so was abandoned. Upon return to Quarenteño advised that the places referred to in N°. 3, N°. 4, & N°. 6, Doc. N°. 2 are near to Jalcocatan and that the ridge and consequently the water hole is not that name in N°. 4, Doc. N°. 2.

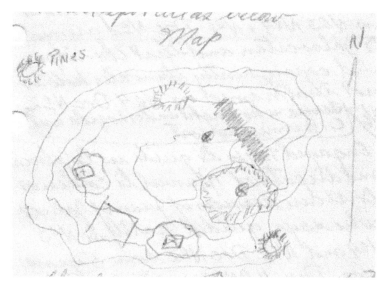

3/6: Terma who fought under Lozada [Manuel Lozada] used C. Bermejo as fort. [The last sentence is particially circled in the diary.] Engaged mozo to guide us to Jalcocotan and dispatched Manuel to endeavor to secure services of Juan of Jalisco who says guided party to N°· 3, N°· 4 and N°· 6, Doc. N°· 2 some 5 years ago. Dep. 11 a.m., arr. 5³⁰ p.m. Put up at Estanislaus Alemans, village baker. Jalcocotan a little village of some 100 houses. Elev. 1415'. No authority, squalid. Road or trail, Tepic, La Yerba – Aticama – and San Blas was used during war of independence in preference to Camino Real as it offered quicker touch with the coast. That operations of N°· 12, Doc. N°· 1 are common record and that many efforts have been made to locate N°· 3, N°· 4, N°· 6, Doc. N°· 2, but as far as he knows without success. States that a woman came some years ago and was referred to one Franco Valdez, a hunter, as knowing terrain. Stopped at his hut and read over to him several times description of prospect on El Voladero. "See map Page 28." Valdez stole paper that nite and spent years searching. Finally located tree as described against cliff but could find no ring driven in same. Some stone steps and wooden door closing cave burned door and cut bark until discovering ring. Removed to talegas [sacks] from cave and nails from door. On way home taken ill and hid talegas at foot of higuerras. Dying [he] told his wife but was overheard by Margareto Rodriguez, who benefited by Valdez discovery. Became very well to do and at death much money in jars was found on his coffee plantation. Two years ago Aleman purchased from Merced Villa (ancida [possibly anciana elderly woman] of Rodriguez) a Spanish dollar, having thereon Carlos III 1807.

Commandante Silvestre Montanez of Jalcocotan was want to warn all inhabitants to stay in their homes whenever a treasure train passed. Money was Lozada's and was in sacks of beans which were later distributed.

Pedro Vizarraga tells of guarding a treasure train for a week for Commandante Antonio Rodriguez at La Palma. He buried a carga of silver at small fork of arroyo just east of La Palma but later was unable to find spot. This money was part of Lozada's loot that he was shipping to Spain after breaking with house of Aguirre. Anastacio Rodriquez, an old man living at La Yerba was want to come to Jalcocolan for a spree. His money would be exhausted and he would take a boy or two ascend N°· 4, Doc. N°· 2 to an ancient stone wall known as La Cruz de N°· 4, Doc. N°· 2. Leaving the boys there, he would alight from his horse and go down the mountain side probably to N°· 5, Doc. N°· 2 and return shortly with a talego of silver which he gave the boys to carry.

Alejandro Rivera came to Tepic with a document in search of 2 cargas of silver said to be buried at La Vuelte de Los Clavlinas on the Tepic, Aticama road. Finally determined that original name had been altered to Vuelte de Los Viejos. Found silver, see page 99 for further data.

3/7: Walked to Cerro de la Bola (nee Cerro Colorado, nee Doc. N°· 2, N°· 2.

3/8: Rode with guide to N°· 4, Doc. N°· 2 to La Cruz, 5 km and walked to N.E. and went down to water hole and found all indications to check with N°· 4, Doc. N°· 2.

A = Top of Cerro Bola, land monument & excavations.

B = Remains of Indian village idol, various excavations.
C = Stone wall = La Cruz
D = Water hole = Ojo de Agua
E = Cliffs among which Valdez said to have found cave.
F = Cerro de la Vigía. Lookout for man mentioned in Nº· 12, Doc. Nº· 1.
G = Cerro de la Marjonera/Maijonera – land monument.
H = Cuchillo de los Muchachos
I = El Voladero

3/9: Went with Juan around Cerro de Bola (up arroyo de Tepechilche) to Potrero de Tepechilche and back by way of La Yerba. Found remains of Indian village at "B" rude stone foundations, mounds, etc. No indications of Nº· 2, Doc. Nº·2. No pines. Returned 6 p.m.

3/10: Aleman states that his son Arturo went to see Juan Martinez at El Malinal re a span of oxen. They went up the cerro to the S. of El Malinal looking for the oxen and Martinez asked Arturo if he could see anything that looked like the Corral Falso that was said to be in the vicinity of Jalcocotan. Martinez then lead him to a spot and looking down he saw a small circular valley with but one entrance and precipitous sides. This is on land belonging to Perez Hernandez.

3/11: Manuel states that a pal of his, Carlos Navarro, knows of a mine at the head of the Arroya Resudo (Raisudo) on the W. flank of Nº· 1, Doc. Nº· 1. Navarro has brought several rocks to Ventura who has paid as high as 2^{50} for a piece the size of 3 fists from which he extracted about an oz. of oro [gold]. He has urged Navarro to take him to the mine but without success as Navarro seems content to make a living from it. He says that the opening is small about 2 ft. by 3 ft. and that a paved road leads up to it. It is supposed to be an Antigua.

3/12: Told Navarro that I would go to his mine tomorrow. Met mining agent who says no denuncios [reports] on Cerro San Juan. Says that several parties have asked about rich Antigua gold mine on San Juan and that two men said they tried to explore a cave in a relis. [?] to which an old paved road ascended but had failed due to draft and bats.

3/13: Navarro proved to be in last stages of TB and stated that he had lived at Rancho "A" in 1911 and was burned out by Maderistas and forced to move to Tepic. A friend of his showed him the mine on way up passed 3 small circ plateaus with many excavations made by searchers for Lozadas Treasure. Arrived at "B" after extremely steep difficult climb and Navarro pointed out a small stone corral called the Chiqueros de los Buarros [Burros] of Lozada, whose stronghold was on a ridge somewhat higher and running S. where there was still stone breastwork (see C). Navarro stated that in 1911 a spirit told him that close to his house at "A," Lozada had buried 8 loads of silver from a train of 60 mule loads captured on the Camino Real in the plain below, and that at "La Joya" – "G" – he had buried another 18 loads of silver and 11 loads of gold, killing and burying 4 arrieros [muleteers] at the same spot, which Navarro claimed to have located from the ghostly description given him but was afraid to touch. Standing before the stone corral he pointed to a stone that once formed the base of the "E" gate post and calmly stated that under this stone Lozada had buried 16 loads of silver. A large excavation had been made a few meters "W" of the corral X [X in a circle] = spot pointed out by Navarro

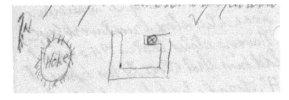

Arriving at "D," left, [word "plateau" underlined is written under "D"], Navarro who almost collapsed with fatigue and following his directions, proceeded some 500 meters "E" to the upper reaches of the Cañada de la Raisuda (?) Trail continued down, much travelled by

woodcutters and charcoal burners and to north of same and on W. side of Cañada found a series of broken cliffs 10-15 meters high extending north for 100-300 meters. At base of these found series of shallow caves, partly erosion, partly excavation in a reddish brittle formation. No indication of opening of tunnel nor of the ore which he stated was black and very heavy with brite spots. Rode down cañada and Navarro seemed uncertain as to cliffs. He subsequently met a woodcutter he knew who told him the mine is still there but in another cañada. About 1000 meters up from mouth of cañada found large brown rock "F" W. of trail with what seemed to be marks as per N°. 13, Doc. N°. 2. Did not investigate as Manuel and Navarro were present. Rode in by trail around N. Base of S. Juan and found many excavations apart from "A & B" of 2/27 as per XXX

Navarro stated he believed a carga was about 5000 pesos.
1 Carga = 12 arrobas
1 Arraba = 11.5 Kg
Navarro also stated that N°. 6, Doc. N°. 2 was close to El Malinal (S. of El Gringo) and that the trail led by way of the Cuchilla [ridge] de Tequitosa. Has not been there himself, but says he understands the Laurianos banked there.

3/14: Dep. 8 a.m., arr. "El Gringo" 10 a.m., arr. La Yerba 12^N, arr. Jalcocotan 1^{30} p.m. Raphael Najara still away from El Gringo. Manuel stated that coming down the Cuehilla de los Muchachos, (properly called Los Siete Cuchillas de Muchaschos) the first one branches to the left or S. Halfway between this and the next one the Laurianos had their Almacén [store or warehouse].

Called on Padre of church of Santa Cruz de Tepic in p.m. He states that about 1600, an arriero [mule driver] noticed this cross, which is of course grass about 20 cm high above a bare, hard earth foundation 50 cm thick x 2.5 m wide and 3.5 m high, enclosed by a high wall and with a grilled door opening into the N. nave of the church. The cross is supposed to be of divine origin and said never to wither. Padre stated the N°. 6, Doc. N°. 2 was well known by the country folk as bank of the Laurianos, bandits who flourished during the war of independence 1810-1824.

Aleman states that a bandit band had their O.H.Q. in a house in a small level clearing in the Cañada Majer by some Zapotes with a lookout on a small peak close by. House was surrounded by troops and bandits buried loot, covered by their aparrejos in so shallow a trench that the leather of the aparrejos showed. Fired house at 4 corners and escaped. Location has been sought in vain.

De Valdo states that he was at Cuchilla 4 days & explored all points in vicinity of water hole. See page N°. 28 "D."

3/15: Explored various small draws leading down from Cuchilla to N. as well as ridge to N. of Cuchilla. Page 51 (corrected map superseding that on page N°. 28.) Found old diggings at "I."

3/16: Jalcocotan to Tepic 12^{30} p.m. – 6^{30} p.m.

3/17: Juan Sanchez claims that he and several partners were at the Cuchilla de los Muchachos in 1925 and found a fairly deep cave "open" and another closed with a masonry arch at Point "E."

3/18: Dep. 8^{30} a.m. to investigate rock "F" (Page 42 & 43) arr. 10 a.m. Found 5 marks to be about 5 cm long and 5 mm deep, evenly spaced at 7 cm & all pointing N.E.-S.W. on the flat upper surface of the rock.

Could find several smaller rocks in the direction that marks S.W. but could find no marks on them on hillside. 25 m S.W. found low rubble wall built in between 2 rocks and backed with rock and loose earth. About 40 m S.E. found very old excavation on small mesa and against hillside small cave recently dug under two boulders. (See X [within a circle] for cave on map, page 43.)

Juan Sanchez did not wish to show caves or masonry arch to anyone. (Caves on the Cerro de la Vijia, Pages 55 to 76 offered nothing, so were not copied.)

Juan Fousea stated that he had seen an antigua mine with masonry arch and dumps in a high cliff face in an arroyo beyond Platanitos and somewhat off the trail which at this point was long a hillside. (Tepic, Aticama road.)

3/21: Dep. Tepic 7^{30} a.m., arr El Malinal via Las Lajitas at 11^{30} a.m. Manuel and De Valdo inspected El Presidio, evidently crater of extinct volcano 400 M diameter at top, 250 m at bottom & 150 m in depth with entrance to W. Martinez states that years ago chest of porcelain was found among rocks and learned also that Spanish Column pursuing Laurianos made the presidio their HQ 1798-99.

3/22: Camped at base of "Cerro de la Palma" (or Tigra.)

3/23: De Valdo investigated arroyo "A" large rocks and cliffs but running water and walked to Cerro de la Vijia as per "B" (map page 82) to see if any signs of a cave closed with mortar and a brick arch were to be seen. Neither of us successful.

3/24 & 3/25: In Tepic —

3/26: De Valdo left on train for Puente, where Manuel is to meet him to examine N$^{os.}$ 1-9, Doc. N$^{o.}$ 1. HQ to be at Las Majados.

3/27: In Tepic —

3/28: De Valdo returned, reports all locations dug up by others but don't think anything found.

3/31: Dep. 7 a.m., arrived at Mesa de Tepetolele via La Libertad & El Faisan at 5 p.m. En route investigated Cañada de los Perricos as per route "A." Met Raphael Cruz again at El Faisan & learned of sculptures on Rock at "C" (page 82) with words Pedro Morua carved underneath rock overturned by treasure hunters. Assumed that Cañada de Faisan might have been central canyon that Gonzales Sr. claimed to have gone up. Also assuming that La Libertad was the long ranch on a flat that he referred to as his point of departure from Tepic, La Yerba road — seems too far away however and there is no possibility of "Perricos" having been arroyo as there is no trail, road, or mountain at its head, and the Pando drops sheer away to S.W. No descent being possible.

Full details of Gonzales trip as follows.

Left Tepic 5-6 a.m. by old road running S.W. to Garrita near Rancho Tecolote and thence N. and N.W. around N. end of Cerro de San Juan. I now believe this road to have been the original Spanish road to San Blas which leaves the new road built in 1842 at Lo de Alameda and runs thru La Colemana [Colmena], the vanished Rancho de la Playa, Lo de Garcia (just N. or the road), Tizonita, La Libertad where it again joins the main road to San Blas.

The road travelled was good and no deep barrancas were crossed. Just before arriving at Al Long ranch on a llano (a description that fits La Playas as it was in 1842) they turned off to the left and followed the right hand bank, looking up, of the central one of three wooded green barrancas that were seen to run down the mountain side from S. to N. Every now and then Gonzales noted small stone calzado or revetments at the turns of the arroyo. Down towards the bed shortly before the trail reached the end of the barranca they turned ½ right and continued until reaching the top of the mountain ridge or plateau they were ascending where they crossed a wide well travelled trail running from S to N. "?" A short distance further on they went down a long ridge or cuchilla running W. covered with malinal or guinea grass and having scattered ancenos or live oaks. Gonzales picked several of the pods from an oak. They next turned down a small steep cuchilla running N. (or S?) which curved to the East (or W.) the trail running along the edge of a cliff that formed one side of the "Corral Falso."

Arriving at the bottom the cliff was only 1.5 m high and on the right hand side looking in were 3 holes 5m in depth for bars to bar the narrow entrance to stop stock from escaping. Going in the cliff rose gradually to 15 m in height at the back of the corral where it merged into a number of perpendicular cuchillas which in turn gave way to rock piled slope that formed the left hand entrance. The first half of the corral was level, covered with short grass, while the rear half was rough and stoney. The area was that of a city block, while well inside the entrance and just to left of the center was a rock, as large as a jackal, the top being flat, sloping gently and a young oak grew by its side, the only tree in the corral. There was no water in the corral but a small arroyo starting from the entrance was thought to have water lower down. At the entrance was a flat that extended down the cañada, the head of which the corral formed (?) The entrance faced W. and from it two small round, bare hills could be seen, apparently but a short distance away and bearing W. When the party were seated resting Gonzales looked at his watch. It was just 11 a.m. Josefa showed them a flat rock just outside the entrance and under it they found a large hole filled with coin. She showed them a small cave in the cliff (or hole at its foot) sealed with masonry and said that the bulk of the treasure was there. They did not open this but Gonzales chipped of a piece of cement. Stress was laid on the fact that the distance from Tepic was short and that after leaving the road they only crossed one mountain or ridge before arriving at the corral. The route followed I believe to be as follows

4/1: Investigated all cañadas S.W. slope of Mancuceras to no effect. Cows raided camp which was at "D." (Page 82)

4/2: Moved camp to "E" (Page 82) and finished examination of terrain.

4/3: Examined both sides of Espinoza del Diablo ("Page 84") from Tepetilte to Tepetolele as per red track (Page 84) and camped at "B."

4/4: Went with Seferina Cruz to examine cañada between Cuchilla de los Muchachos & Cerro de la Tigra. Failed to find Pedro Moreno stone, bricked up cave or stone pavement.

4/7: Dep. 7 a.m. for spot above El Gringo said by Martinez to resemble corral. Arrived at 12^N — No good – Examined all of terrain between La Libertad, El Faisan & El Gringo.

4/8: Dr. Gonzales states that at the time of the revolution in 1810 there were many rich mines about San Pablo near Mascota in Jalisco and that the church was ornamented with solid silver candlesticks, lamps and a solid gold Christ 24" high, a silver cross and 40 to 60,000 pesos in cash. When the order came expelling all Spanish from Mexico the Padre buried these in the nave of the church, a short distance from the principal door and on the left hand side facing the alter. The Sacristan left to guard the secret passed the secret down to his sons who near death finally told a Padre about it. The Padre told Gonzales of it and asked him to search for the treasure but Gonzales had not done so yet.

4/9: Nothing offered.

4/10: Dep. 7 a.m., arrived Las Delecias 8 a.m., arrived La Playa 10 a.m., arrived Rancho Alfaro 12^N. Followed the original Tepic – San Blas Spanish road from Las Delicias to Los Playos [Las Playas], passing thru La Colmena both places having totally disappeared. From a point just "E" of La Colmena the cañada can be seen leading down from lower ridges of San Juan and emptying into Arroyo La Colmena at Los Playos the same thing occurs. Followed up middle arroyo to Rancho Alfaro. Scouted up ridge forming "E" bank of Arroyo Libertad. Rode to Mesa del Guayabito] — and down to point where Bartelo was killed X [X within a circle] (Page 112) and thus East to Lo de Lamedo. No signs of corral — (Map 112)

4/11 thru 4/19: Nothing offered.

4/21: Having gone to church at San Pablo where we hired men to dig in the old church but found nothing but the sword hilt mentioned.

5/4: To Tucson

Chapter 77

MOLINA DOCUMENT

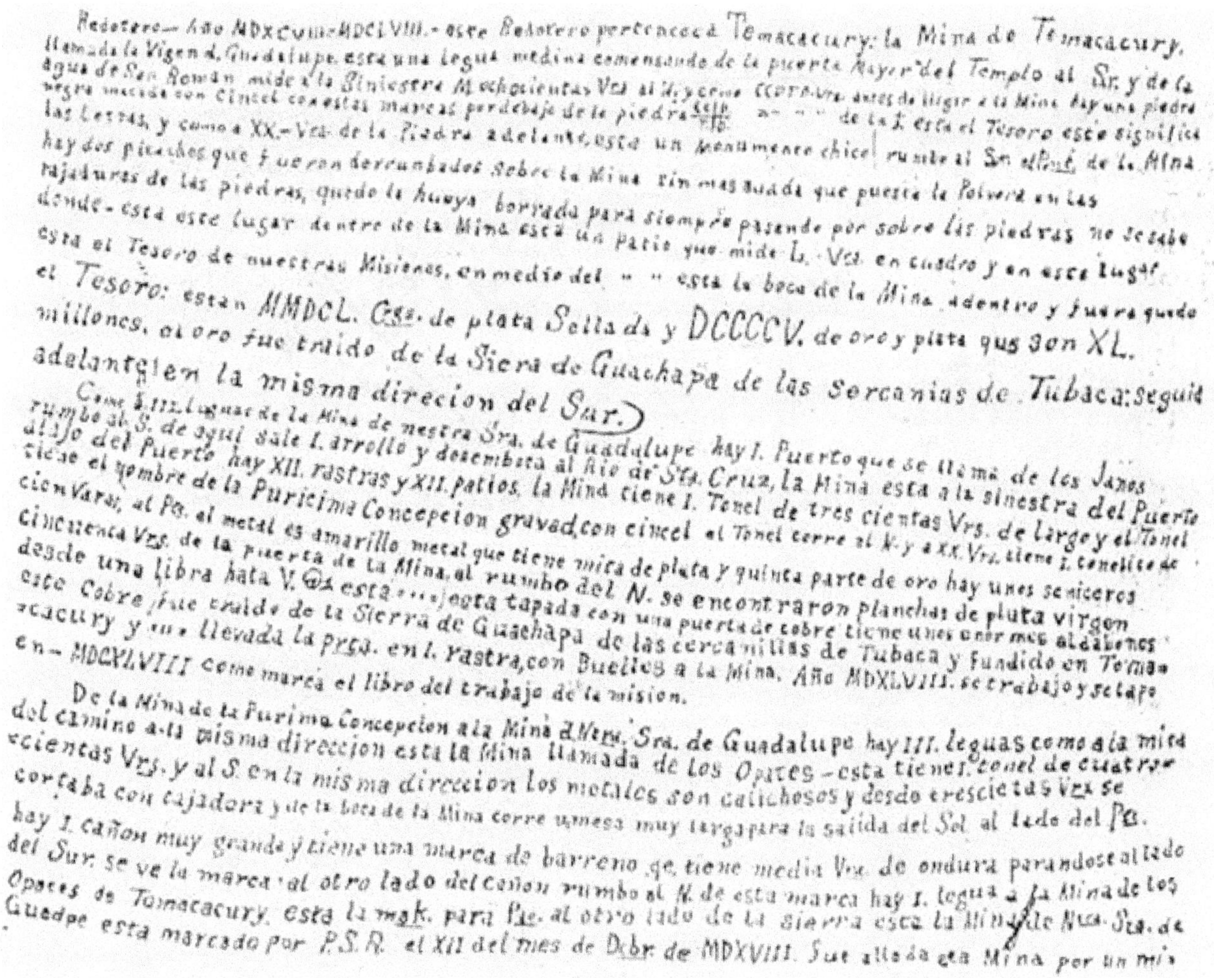
Derrotero — Año MDXCVIII — MDCLVIII. — este Derrotero pertenece a Temacacury: la Mina de Temacacury,
llamada la Virgen d. Guadalupe. esta una legua medina comensando de la puerta Mayor del Templo al Sr. y de la
agua de San Roman mide a la Siniestra Mochocientas Vrs al Mayor como CCCVI Vrs. antes de llegar a la Mina hay una piedra
negra marcada con Cincel conestas marcas por debajo de la piedra ... de la I. esta el Tesoro esto significa
las Letras, y como a XX. Vrs de la Piedra adelante, esta un monumento chico rumbo al Sr. ... de la Mina
hay dos picachos que fueron derrumbados sobre la Mina sin mas nada que puesta la Polvora en las
rajaduras de las piedras, quedo la huya borrada para siempre pasando por sobre las piedras no se sabe
donde esta este lugar dentro de la Mina esta un Patio que mide L. Vrs. en cuadro y en este lugar
esta el Tesoro de nuestras Misiones, en medio del " " esta la boca de la Mina adentro y fuera quedo
el Tesoro: estan MMDCL. Cgs. de plata Sellada y DCCCCV. de oro y plata que son XL.
millones. el oro fue traido de la Siera de Guachapa de las sercanias de Tubaca: seguir
adelante en la misma direcion del Sur.)
Como a III. leguas de la Mina de nuestra Sra. de Guadalupe hay I. Puerto que se llama de los Janos
rumbo al S. de aqui sale I. arrollo y desemboca al Rio de Sta. Cruz, la Mina esta a la sinestra del Puerto
abajo del Puerto hay XII. rastras y XII. patios, la Mina tiene I. Tunel de tres cientas Vrs. de largo y el Tunel
tiene el nombre de la Purisima Concepcion gravad con cincel el Tunel corre al N. y a XX. Vrs. tiene I. tunelito de
cien Varas, al Po. el metal es amarillo metal que tiene mita de plata y quinta parte de oro hay unos seniceros
cincuenta Vrs. de la puerta de la Mina, al rumbo del N. se encontraron planchas de plata virgen
desde una libra hata V. @s esta ... esta tapada con una puerta de cobre tiene unos enormes aldabones
este Cobre fue traido de la Sierra de Guachapa de las cercanillas de Tubaca y fundido en Temacacury y fue llevada la prsa. en I. rastra, con Bueyes a la Mina. Año MDXLVIII. se trabajo y se tapo
en — MDCXLVIII como marca el libro del trabajo de la mision.
De la Mina de la Purima Concepcion a la Mina d. Ntra. Sra. de Guadalupe hay III. leguas como a la mita
del camino a la misma direccion esta la Mina llamada de los Opates — esta tiene I. tunel de cuatro
... cientas Vrs. y al S. en la misma direccion los metales son calichosos y desde trescientas Vrs. se
cortaba con tajadora y de la boca de la Mina corre una mesa muy larga para la salida del Sol al lado del Po.
hay I. cañon muy grande y tiene una marca de barreno qe. tiene media Vr. de ondura parandose al lado
del Sur. se ve la marca al otro lado del Cañon rumbo al N. de esta marca hay I. legua a la Mina de los
Opates de Temacacury. esta la mak. para Pte. al otro lado de la Sierra esta la Mina de Ntra. Sra. de
Guadpe esta marcado por P.S.R. el XII del mes de Dbr. de MDXVIII. Fue allada esta Mina por un mis

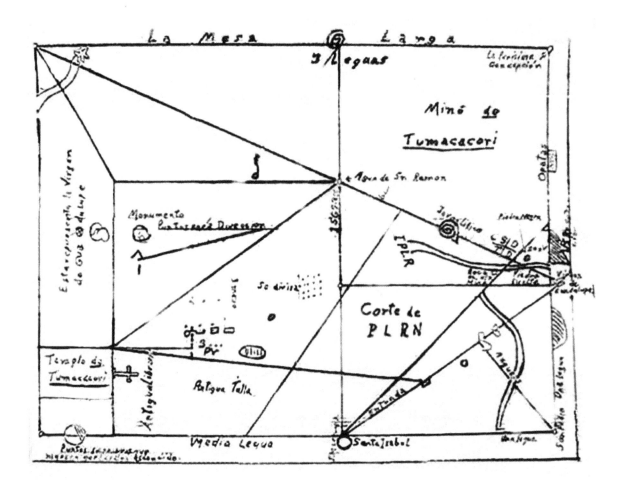

Translations and Notes by Donald W. Page

T he following are Donald W. Page's translations of the famous Molina Documents. Many believe the documents are authentic while others disagree. Also included are Page's reports on his trip(s) to southern Arizona in regard to the Spanish mines and treasures. This report was written by Don during the 1930s and would be quite valuable to those interested in this highly controversial subject.

Modern Measurement Conversions:
Arroba = 25.357 USI pounds often rounded off to 25 pounds.
Legua/League = 2.597 USI miles often rounded off to 3 statute miles.
Vara = 32.9 USI inches often rounded of to 33 inches.
[Conversion calculator *varas castellana*: http://www.unitconversion.org/unit_converter/length-ex.html]

INTRODUCTION

In the following English version of the *Derroteros* [14] (it being apparent that two separate documents are involved), no attempt has been made to interpret the Spanish sense of the wording and phraseology, except in the case of certain archaic words and terms. Rather a literal translation has been made, this permitting the reader to draw his own conclusions as to the correct meaning of several passages that are patently open to dual interpretation. In the following analysis and deductions, however, the process has been reversed, and an effort has been made to arrive at the true meaning of the *Derroteros* text, without regard to literalism or continuity.

MOLINA DOCUMENTS

Derrotero I

Descriptive guide of the year 1648.
This description refers to Tumacácori.

The Tumacácori Mine, called the *Virgen de Guadalupe*, is located at a measured league, starting from the main door of the temple toward the south. From the *Ojos de San Román*, measure 1800 *varas* to the left, 200 *varas* before arriving at the north there is a black rock marked on the underside with chisel:
CI
C C I B
TD
200 *varas* from the cross is the treasure. This is the meaning of the letters. And about 20 *varas* toward the south there is a small monument to the south toward the west from the mine there are two peaks that were thrown down enormous rocks by means of powder onto the mine obliterating the latter. In the middle of

---

[14] *Derroteros* = course or direction.]

this scene is the mouth of the mine. Native silver, minted gold and silver. The gold was brought from the Guachapa Mountains from the Tubac Range. Minted 2,650 loads of native silver 905 of gold.

Continue forward about three leagues beyond the mine of *Nuestra Señora de Guadalupe* there is a pass called the pass of the Hornos [Janos]. To the south from this pass an arroyo emerges and empties into the Santa Cruz River. The mine is on the left of the pass. Below the pass there are 12 ore dressing floors and 12 mills. The mine has a tunnel 300 *varas* in length. The tunnel bears the name *Purísima Concepción* cut out with chisel. The tunnel runs toward the north and at about 20 *varas* it has a tunnel of 100 *varas* toward the west. The metal is yellow and runs half silver and the fifth part gold. At some ash heaps 50 *varas* toward the north from the mouth of the mine will be found plates of silver of from one pound to five *arrobas*. This mine is closed with a copper door. This has large handles. The copper was brought from the Guachapa Mountains, from the Tubac Range. The door was made at Tumacácori and carried on ox drawn sleds in the year 1648.

About half way between the Nuestra Señora de Guadalupe and the Purísima Concepción Mines, on a line about northeast, is the mine called the *Opatas*. This mine has a tunnel 400 *varas* in length that runs toward the north. The metals of this mine are second grade silver (or are mixed with calcium carbonate). From the mouth of the mine a very long plateau runs toward the rising sun. On the western side there is a very large canyon that has a landmark a large plane of sloping rock (or landslide) and this has a drill hole one *vara* deep, standing to the south the mark of the drill hole can be seen. To the other side of the canyon toward the north from this mark it is approximately a league from the *Opatas de Tumacácori* to the west.

The mine of Nuestra Señora de Guadalupe graven by (or is described by) P.S.R. the 12th day of December of 1508 this mine was found by some prospectors. The affairs of these mines (or the documents relating to the affairs) were left entrusted in (or to) the Tumacácori Mine. There is a copper box that has the key in one corner it is a screw and then there is an iron bar. This bar is pulled and the box opens. All of the maps are there. Enormous treasures. And if by chance anyone now living comes to find them they are obliged to give tithes to the holy mother church. Ten percent for the good of their soul. Buried in 1648.

***

This writing is acquired by the grandfather of my husband Santiago Molina. My husband named Juan de Dios Molina, my son who was present David Molina. My name is Micaele Vallorica de Molina.

***

Derrotero II

Year 1548 descriptive guide of the year 1648, referring to Tumacácori.

The San Pedro Mine. This will be about three leagues from the Santa Ysabel Mine. There is a river half a league north of the Santa Ysabel Mine. The mine is close to a small black mountain. At the point of the mountain of this mine starts the road to the San Pedro Mine along the crest of the mountain. A road that was opened in parts by the work of bars.

The San Pedro Mine is one and a half leagues from the temple toward the west and when the sun is rising it strikes first on the door of the mine. From this mine Arivaca can be seen and from the mine of Nuestra Señora it is about a league to the San Pedro Mine.

Between the mines (or in the center of the mines) there is an immortal sign, a drill hole half a *vara* in depth. The rocks rolled from the trail down to the mine of N. Sra. de Guadalupe. And continue by the canyon toward the south half a league there is the Ojos de San Román Mine. The eyes are graven in the rock.

There are enormous plates of silver in the San Pedro Mine. There are two buried caches of virgin silver. The mine has a wooden door. On the west side there is a drill hole in a sloping wall of rock. On the east there is another drill hole. There are three deposits in mortar. In these great treasures, the person who comes to find these is obliged to give ten percent for the good of their soul to the Holy Mother Church.

Children do not forget this temple. Repair it and God will help you. Help the poor and God will help you. This is a condition formed in heaven and the earth.

With respect to the authenticity of the documents, at the moment [1930s] nothing is known of the originals or of their discovery beyond the statement appearing in the introductions hereto. It is only fair to say, however, that certain investigations are now being made that it is hoped will prove this point conclusively, but as these involve personal interests nothing further can be said for the present, and the text must be dealt with at its face value.

Referring to the Spanish text, there are several points that might lead to the immediate conclusion that the documents are either not what they purport to be, or that they were written at a considerably later date than that claimed, and these will be dealt with first.

CONS

The first of these points is that it appears that at least the *Virgen de Guadalupe* was discovered as early as 1548 (it being safe to assume that the statement made in the last paragraph of the first document, to the effect that the mine was found in 1508, is a mistake in copying), and that by 1648 all of the mines referred to were being worked, only to be abandoned for some unstated reason probably in that same year. It is highly improbable that these or any other mines located in what is now Arizona were actively worked as early as 1648, and here again I am of the impression that an error was made either in copying the Roman numerals (in which both dates and quantities appear to have been set down in the original manuscript) or in translating these into Arabic notation, as in at least two cases it is perfectly evident that this occurred.

The region was perhaps visited by the first Spaniards as early as 1538 when the Franciscan padres, Juan de la Asunción and Pedro Nadal, are believed to have penetrated as far north as the Colorado River, having been commissioned by the viceroy of New Spain to explore the country north of the then known limits of the kingdom in search of the fabled Chicomoztoc, the mysterious land of origin of the Aztecs.

In 1539 Fray Marcos de Niza made a reconnaissance of the country looking for the glittering seven cities of Cibola, as reported by Alvar Nuñez Cabeza de Vaca in 1536, at the end of his eight years of wandering westward from the coast of Florida. And in 1540 Francisco Vasquez de Coronado made his famous military expedition into the region, when plentiful reports of rich gold and silver deposits were brought back.

The early Spanish miners [were] a hardy crew, and whilst there is no historical evidence to support the theory, it is not at all impossible that some of these did indeed penetrate the hitherto *Tierra Incógnita* [Unknown Land] of the north as early as 1548 and locate a few rich prospects. As a matter of fact, at least three writers stoutly maintain that Spanish settlements were established in the valley of the Santa Cruz

River between 1555 and 1560, namely, the authors of "Treasure Land," [by John George Hilzinger] "With The Invader: [Glimpses of the Southwest]" [by Edwards Roberts] and "Arizona As It Was, [1877]" [by Hiram C. Hodge].

Still another possible explanation lies in the fact that it was an early Spanish custom to omit the first two figures in dates, and if this was the case in the original documents it is easy to understand how, in attempting to complete the years, the error occurred. However this may be, it is known that by the year ~~1748~~ [1698 [15]] the original church had been built at San Cayetano ~~(later rechristened San José)~~ de Tumacácori, and that the Jesuit padres were hard at work upon a number of very rich mines that had been discovered in the vicinity of the mission. Also, at just about that time a fierce Indian uprising [1751*] forced them to flee for their lives, all of their establishments being plundered and burned by the savages.

Finally, in 1767 the Jesuits were expelled from New Spain, and it is perfectly safe to say that they left nothing of any value uncovered for their successors, the Franciscan, to make capital out of. Indeed, it is a well known fact that after March 28, 1741, when Felipe V of Spain declared the fabulously rich *Planchas de Plata* discovery of native silver to be a part of his royal patrimony, the Jesuits carefully refrained from making public any of their mining operations. Stating openly (to quote Fray José Ortega, in his "Apostólicos Afanes de la Compañía de Jesús") "that dependence upon royal commissions is an illusion."

The second question point is the use of the name "Rio de Santa Cruz," whereas this stream was originally called the "Rio de Santa María." This however, appears to be in favor of the *Derroteros* authenticity and my belief in the error is copying the dates, as by ~~1748~~ 1766 the river bore the former name.

The third point is the use of the name "Arivaca," as the Pima *ranchería* was first known as "Aribac," the Spanish rancho as "Arivac" and the village finally as "Arivaca." But as the date of the final transition is questionable, this is perhaps not of great importance.

The fourth and final point in question is the rambling, incoherent and disjointed construction of the *Derroteros*, as this is not at all in accord with the usual careful and meticulous manner in which the Jesuits were wont to set down matters of such importance. The only explanation that can be offered in this case is that either the writer greatly hurried or that he was someone other than one of the padres. A Spanish miner, perhaps, who, in view of what must have appeared to be the impending downfall of civilization in the region, sought by these means to leave a record of the mines for posterity. In view of the reference to maps and other documents said to have been left in the *Virgen de Guadalupe* enclosed in a copper box, this would seem to be a not entirely unreasonable suggestion.

PROS

On the other hand, there are an equal number of points about the *Derroteros* that might as easily lead to the conclusion that the documents are perfectly authentic.

The first of these is the use of obsolete Spanish letters and words. Such as the "o" in place of "s", *"siniestra"* instead of *"izquierda"* (left); *"oriente"* and *"poniente"* for *"este"* and *"oeste"* (east and west); *"tonel"* in lieu of *"tunnel"* (tunnel); *"tentores"* in place of *"gambusinos"* (prospectors). The word *"tentor,"* by the way, is quite archaic and *"intereses"* for *"documentos"* (documents).

---

[15] According the National Park Service: http://www.nps.gov/history/history/online_books/explorers/sitea3.htm

The second favorable point are the references to the *"Sierra de Guachapa"* (the Santa Rita Mountains), as this name has been obsolete for at least a hundred years.

The third are the references to *"Planchas de Plata."* The famous *Planchas de Plata* discovery already referred to was made in 1736, but twelve years before the assumed date of the *Derroteros,* and naturally made a deep and lasting impression on the minds of all of the Spaniards of those times and especially of that vicinity, and it would have been but natural for them to describe any other great amount of silver in the same terms.

Finally, it is an historical fact that a number of very rich mines were worked at various times by both the padres of the Tumacácori mission and later by lay miners of the vicinity. Of these, the "Salero," "Ojero" "Cerro Colorado" and perhaps the "Santa Ysabel," are known, having been worked with profit down to comparatively recent times. And it is equally certain that there were several other old mines that have never been rediscovered.

DEDUCTIONS

In approaching the problem of the location of these old mines, it would appear at first glance that the *Virgen de Guadalupe* was the logical starting point, as this mine is said to be located at a "measured league, starting from the main door of the temple toward the south." There are, however, several reasons why this is not the case.

In the first place, *"comencando de la puerta mayor del templo al sur"* may mean either that the league is to be measured from the main door of the temple toward the south or that it is to be measured from the main door of the temple, which faces south.

In the second place, the ruins that are to be seen at Tumacácori today are not those of the original church but of an edifice built ~~in 1802~~ [between 1800-1821], and whilst it is understood that the first church stood somewhere in the immediate vicinity. The exact site thereof is not known.

In the third place, whilst the *Derrotero* says "toward the south" (assuming that the bearing of the mine from the church is meant) this does not necessarily mean due south, as any point of the compass between southwest may have been meant.

Finally, one league south from Tumacácori, measured either to the astronomical south or to the magnetic south of 1748, ends in a series of rolling ridges formed by erosion from the Tumacácori Mountains, where there is not the slightest indication of mineralization.

From a careful study of the *Derroteros,* supplemented by a thorough general knowledge of this country involved, it appears to me that the logical starting point is the San Pedro [Mine]. According to the second *Derrotero,* it is said to be one and a half leagues westward from the temple to this mine, which on the map sites the latter somewhere about half a league west of the crest of the Tumacácori Range. Of necessity, this league and a half was measured along the trail taken from the mission, and assuming that this more or less roundabout way to have been a league longer than the direct distance, the mine might be looked for somewhere along the crest of the range and bearing between northwest and southwest from the temple. Plotted on the map, this would appear to narrow down the search to include not above five miles of the mountain crest, but as will be seen presently, the limits within [which] the mine is probably located are much narrower than this. The *Derrotero's* next two statements seem to prove this deduction correct, as, from a glance at the map, it is obvious that there is only one point from which Arivaca can be seen and that will receive the first rays of the rising sun. Namely, the crest of the Tumacácori Range.

Turning back for a moment to the Santa Ysabel Mine, we find that this is said to be located about three leagues from the San Pedro, close to a small black mountain and half a league south of a river, and that from the point of the mountain where the mine is located a road that was in parts cut out of the rock leads to the San Pedro along the crest of the mountain.

Again, it is obvious that the mountain referred to is the Tumacácori range, and at the northern end of this, close to a small black peak and a little more than half a league south of Soporí Creek is the Saucita Mine. According to local tradition, this is one of the old mines that formerly belonged to the mission, and assuming this to be the case a further account of the property will be given later together with descriptions of the Salero, and Cerro Colorado Mines. Referring to the road or trail that is said to lead from the Santa Ysabel to the San Pedro, whilst I have never been through the northern end of the Tumacácori Range, I have seen an ancient trail that descends from the southern end of the crest and that I believe to be the extension of the one just mentioned, and will describe this in its proper place.

Returning to the San Pedro Mine, this is said to be three leagues from the Santa Ysabel, and three leagues measured from the Saucita Mine southward along the crest of the Tumacácori Mountains [and] ends at the highest point of the range, the bearing being due magnetic west (as of 1748) from the mission. This fixes the location of the mine from four different angles, namely, its distance from the temple, the fact that the first rays of the rising sun strike on the door of the mine, that Arivaca can be seen from the site and its distance from the Santa Ysabel or Saucita Mine, and, as I stated a moment ago, the presumed location is narrowed down to a radius of but a few hundred yards. Whilst at the moment I know of no data on this mine other than that given in the *Derrotero*, the statement that it contains masses of virgin silver may not be an exaggeration, as this was not at all an uncommon occurrence in other mines in the vicinity.

The Virgin (or Nuestra Señora) de Guadalupe mine is said to be about a league from the San Pedro [Mine], and if the first is a measured league southwest instead of south from the church at Tumacácori the location, as determined on the map by the intersection of these two distances, would be on the eastern slopes of the Tumacácori mountains and somewhere in the vicinity of an ancient stone enclosure known as the "*corral de piedra*" [rock corral] I have not visited this spot and know nothing about it other than that for some reason it is held by the old Mexican miners of the vicinity to have something to do with the location of the Guadalupe Mine, which, if I am right in my deductions, would be perfectly natural.

The *corral de piedra* is located on the southeastern side of a short, steep canyon that runs roughly southwest from the mission and an ancient trail leads to it from the latter up through this gorge. The northwestern wall of the canyon runs up to the crest of the range, and if the mine is located in this canyon and the trail from the Santa Ysabel to the San Pedro runs along this crest, it would be perfectly feasible for rocks to roll down from the trail onto the mine, even as is said to have happened.

The *Derrotero* now says that one is to continue by the canyon toward the south for half a league, where the Ojos de San Román Mine will be found, the eyes being graven in the rock. As I interpret this, one is to go half a league down a canyon that lies to the south of, and not half a league down a canyon from the San Pedro Mine, and for reasons that will be given presently there is only one canyon that can be meant.

About four and a half miles south of the mission the Palaco Canyon [16] (formerly known as the Cañada de los Fresnos) runs down to the Santa Cruz River from the west, and about four and a quarter miles up this

---

[16] GNIS identifies Palaco as Peck Canyon.

from the Tucson-Nogales Highway a tributary canyon runs up to the northwest, the latter bearing no name on the modern maps of the region but formerly having been known as the "Cañada de San Román."

In 1928 I was making a topographical survey of the eastern end of the Palaco Canyon. And on a low cliff in the northwest angle formed by the two canyons an old Mexican miner showed me a pair of eyes out in the rock and told me these were the "Ojos de San Roman." I knew nothing about the old mines of Tumacácori at the time, and naturally even less about the *Derroteros*. So was not particularly interested and did no more than to examine the eyes carefully. The line of sight bore about northeast, and I noted that as the so-called "desert varnish" had begun to cover the cuttings these must have been well over a hundred years old.

About half a league up to the Cañada de San Román, and about the same distance from its head, I found that at some time in the past a considerable amount of excavating had been done, and learned later than this was in search of the great treasure said to be buried at the San Román Mine, but that nothing had been found.

Along the southwestern wall of the canyon I found numerous traces of an ancient and well-traveled trail that appeared to lead down from the head of the canyon and that in spots had been cut out from the living rock. The same Mexican told me that he had traced this up to and along the crest of the range to the north, and that a branch of the trail led down the canyon in which the *corral de piedra* is located, and these are the circumstances that led me to mention this connection with the trail said to connect the Santa Ysabel and the San Pedro Mines. I may add that my informant made no reference to the *Derroteros* nor did he appear to place any importance on the trail other than that it might perhaps have had something to do with the padres mining activities.

The *Derrotero* gives no description of the Ojos de San Román Mine apart from the description of the treasure said to be buried there, but in writing of Don Dionisio Robles' search for the *Planchas de Plata* in 1817, Jose Francisco Velasco [17] makes an interesting reference to what appears to have been the same mine on page 192 of his "Noticias Estadísticas del Estado de Sonora," published in 1850, the following being a translation of the Spanish text:

"...Don Teodoro Salazar, a truthful and practical man who has had great experience in mining in Sonora,...speaking of this (the mineral richness of the region under discussion), referred to a mine that he saw a short distance beyond (to the north of) the Arizona (the *Planchas de Plata*) when he was in those parts (with Robles), that had been worked superficially by the ancients by the open method of mining, as was their custom. He examined the metals as best he could in view of the surprise and fear caused by the fact that the Apaches had seen him and his few companions, and from whom they barely escaped. Notwithstanding, he brought out samples from the mine, which they called the 'Ojito de San Román,' and according to the assays that he made the mine is very rich."

Returning to the second paragraph of the first *Derrotero*, at first glance this appears to be highly involved and in parts contradictory, but I believe that most of it can be correctly interpreted.

To begin with, it is stated that 1,800 *varas* are to be measured from the "Ojos de San Román" to the left, and that 200 *varas* before arriving at the "north" (or the end of the 1,800 *varas*) a certain rock will be found. This would seem to indicate that the bearing along which the measurement is to be made is north,

---

[17] Source: José Francisco Velasco, Noticias Estadísticas del Estado de Sonora (1850) (Hermosillo, Gobierno del Estado de Sonora, 1985) p. 81-111.

and furthermore, if one stands with their back to the cliff on which the sign of the eyes is graven, prepared to begin measuring, the Cañada de San Román will be found on the left hand and bearing about north-northwest.

It will be remembered that the second *Derrotero* states that half a league down a canyon toward the south from the San Pedro the Ojos de San Román Mine will be found, and the only canyon that lies to the south of the San Pedro and that also runs toward the south is the Cañada de San Román. It seems certain, therefore, that the 1,800 *varas* are to be measured up the later. At 1,600 *varas* it is said that a black rock will be found having certain characters chiseled in the form of a cross on it's under or lower side. The meaning of the letters forming the cross being that the treasure (and presumably the mine) is to be found 200 *varas* farther on.

The only sense that I can make out of these letters is that perhaps the CI stands for *"Capitulum I,"* the CC for "200," the IB for *"ibidem"* and the TD for *"tu dibige."* Or freely rendered, "As per section (or chapter) one (of the *Derrotero*) two hundred (*varas*) in the same place (direction) I direct thee."

Admittedly, this is a somewhat fanciful interpretation, and its correctness depends upon the orientation of the cross, it is further stated that about 20 *varas* toward the south (presumably from the end of the 1,800 *varas* there is a small monument (which probably means a pile of stones), and that to the west of the mine there are two small peaks (or crags) from which great masses of rock were blown down to cover the mine. Whilst these directions are not particularly explicit, I believe that they are clear enough to locate the mine and the alleged treasure in a general way, and color is lent to my deductions by the fact that considerable excavating has been done in the neighborhood, as has been said.

With respect to the treasure said to be buried at this spot, the statement that the gold was brought from the Guachapa (or Santa Rita) Mountains is quite in order, as there are (or were) rich gold mines in that range.

If the statement that there are 2,650 *cargas* (mule loads of 300 pounds each) of mined silver is to be taken at its face value, then with silver at $0.45 per ounce (then) and the fineness of the coins assumed at 900, the value of the cache is $3,863,700.00. (A great deal more at today's price of silver.)

The meaning of the reference to "905" is not all clear, but if this should mean that the 905 *cargas* of silver (the 2,650 referring to something else), the value of the treasure is $1,319,490.00. Personally, I believe that it is much more likely that what is meant is that there are 2,650 *pesos* and 905 *cargas* of native silver, which, with the average weight of the peso at 415 grains and its fineness at 900, and the purity of the native silver at 800, would make the value of the treasure stand at $1,173,807.85, without allowing any gold content in the silver.

The *Derrotero* now states that one is to continue for about three leagues beyond the Nuestra Señora (or Virgin) de Guadalupe Mine to a mountain pass called the *"hornos"* (ovens), to the south of which an arroyo empties into the Santa Cruz [River], and that the Purísima Concepción Mine is on the left of the pass. Assuming the Virgin de Guadalupe to be located somewhere in the vicinity of the *corral de piedra,* three leagues to the south (this bearing being indicated by the continuity of the descriptions) ends at a steep and difficult pass in the Atascoso Mountains (also known as the southern extension of the Tumacácori Range). I do not know the name of this pass. But there is an ancient trail leading up to it that makes me believe that it may have been used in the early days in traveling between the mission and the Real de Arizona, Sáric, and points south, as this route would have been much shorter than by way of Nogales [which did not exist at the time] and the Santa Cruz River.

About a mile southeast of this pass the Peña Blanca Canyon (or arroyo) flows down into the Atascoso Canyon and thus to the Santa Cruz, and about a mile and a half to the northeast and some seven hundred feet below the pass there is said to be a group of ruins of ancient buildings, and these may have been connected with the patios and *arrastras* referred to by the *Derrotero*. If the statement that the ore of the Purísima Concepción runs one half silver and one fifth gold be accepted, then with silver at $0.45 per ounce and gold at $35.00 this would be worth $173,400.00 per ton of 2,000 pounds, which might do well enough for "jewelry" or specimen ore but never for the run of the mine.

The next statement to the effect that at some ash heaps 50 *varas* toward the north from the mouth of the mine, plates or sheets of silver weighing anywhere from one to five arrobas (25.4 to 126.80 pounds, U.S. Standard) are to be found, may not be so far from the truth. The location is a scant twelve miles due north of the famous *Planchas de Plata* discovery, where masses of native silver weighing as high as 2,000 pounds were found in a volcanic ash deposit. If this mine really existed, and was even a hundredth part as rich as it is said to have been, it is not surprising that the padres closed the portal with a copper door, and the statement that the copper was brought from the Guachapa (or Santa Rita) Mountains is perfectly natural, as the closest copper deposits are located in that range.

About half way between the Guadalupe and the Purísima Concepción Mines, the *Derrotero* continues, and on a line about northeast, is the Opatas (or the Opatas de Tumacácori) Mine. From about the mouth of the mine a long plateau is said to run toward the rising sun, the bench or table-land being bounded on the west by a very large canyon. A little over a league to the northeast of the deduced location of the Purísima Concepción, the topographical maps show such a plateau, a mile and a quarter in length and about half a mile in width, running due east and bounded on the west by a canyon that is from three to four hundred feet in depth, and it may be that this is the location described. In the absence of anymore definite landmarks, I believe that this mine will be the most difficult of all to locate, but as it also appears to be the least important of the group no more time need be spent on the matter at this point.

The last paragraph of the first *Derrotero* states that the Guadalupe Mine was "Grabada por El P.S.R." [Recorded by El P.S.R.] this statement probably means either that the name of the mine was chiseled somewhere in rock (presumably over the portal) or that the mine was described by a certain Padres S... R... The natural assumption is that "Padre San Román" is meant, but I have been unable to find any record of such a name in the annals of the Pimería Alta, nor was it usual for a priest to add the "San" (saint) to whatever saint's name he may have assumed upon taking holy orders.

At this point I wish to confess that when I first read the Spanish text of the *Derroteros* I was so satisfied that it was nothing but nonsense that for five years I did not even look at them again. Now, however, after checking back into the history of the mining operations of the padres of Tumacácori, comparing the several distances and bearings given with the map topography of the region and my own knowledge of the terrain, and making the foregoing painstaking analysis and deductions of the information contained in the documents I have completely changed my mind as to their authenticity. I am certain that the mine described as the Santa Ysabel is today the Saucita, and am persuaded that the remaining five mines will be found at the approximate locations that I have deducted from the *Derroteros'* descriptions. The only point that remains to be settled to prove the authenticity of the documents beyond the shadow of a doubt is the matter of their discovery, and as I have stated, this is being investigated at this time.

(More From Don Page's Notes)

AN IMPORTANT DOCUMENT

T*he original of this document is in the Paris museum in Paris, France. A document dating 1508 to 1538 reads as follows:*

The mine known as the Virgin of Guadalupe near the Temple of the Opatas of Tumacácori, located one league from the main door of the Temple, on the west side, to the south from the waters of San Román, and to your left looking north 1800 *varas* from this mine. To the north, after reaching this mine, 200 *varas* there is a black rock marked with a chisel, a hole one/half a vara deep and will last forever. Near this mine is another rock, marked on the underside like a cross

CC | B
_____

T | D

Two hundred bars of treasure are buried near this rock. That's what these letters signify, and 20 *varas* toward the southwest is a monument carved in a large stone (Montezuma guarding the treasure) and towards the west are two peaks that were blasted down to cover the mine and treasure and rock fell in large masses over the mine. Powder was placed in the crevices and the place was blotted out forever. People could pass over without seeing it.

In this cliff there is a cross. There is a virgin carved in said place. There is a square of 50 *varas* outside of the mine. It is a square within a square and the treasure is in the center of the square. At the mouth of this mine there are gold and silver bars. The gold was brought from the Tubaca Range in the Guachapa Mountains 250 ox cart loads of gold and silver, and 905 ox cart loads of pure silver, making a total of Forty-five Million Dollars ($45,000,000) in gold and silver.

Continuing in the same direction towards the south, on this road of the pass, rims a canyon that empties into the Santa Cruz River. It is three leagues [9 miles] from the Virgin of Guadalupe mine to this pass called Agua Honda (deep water.) This mine, La Purísima de la Concepción (pure conception) is to the left of the pass. Below this pass are twelve arrastras and twelve patios (stone mills), and stone walls (corrals). This mine has a tunnel 30 *varas* long. A little further there is another tunnel 300 *varas* long running north and at 30 *varas* it has a tunnel 100 *varas* long running west. The ore is yellow and contains one-half silver and one-fifty gold.

50 *varas* from this [La Purísima de la Concepción] mine there is found silver virgin in a northerly direction, the minimum being of one pound and maximum five *arrobas* (125 lbs.). This mine is covered with a copper door, with enormous iron hinges that will as forever. The copper was mined in the Huachapa mountains, smelted at Tumacácori and transported by oxen to the mine between the years 1508 and 1538. This mine is the Purisima de la Conception. It is three leagues from the Virgin of Guadalupe and half way between the two mines in the same direction is the mine of Las Opatas. It has a tunnel 400 *varas* long and it runs in a southerly direction. The ore in this mine is in contact with lime (*calichoso*) and about 300 *varas* from the mouth of this mine they commenced to cut pure silver with hammer and chisel.

A long mesa runs in the direction from [where] the rim rises. From the mouth of this tunnel and to where the sun sets is a large canyon. On a rocky incline there is a mark made with a chisel. A drill-hole nearly one-half vara deep and will remain forever. It is on the south side of the canyon and points toward the north. You will notice the mark of gold in a northerly direction. From this mark it is one league distant from the mine of the Opatas to the mine of Tubuca. There the mark or drill-hole is on the west side and on the other side of this mountain you arrive again at Nuestra Señora de Guadalupe mine towards the north. The letters P.S.R. December 5, 1506 are carved over the mine.

It was found by an Indian Chief of the Opata tribe known as Ostentota. All the interests of all these mines are in charge of Nuestra Señora de Guadalupe mine, which has a copper chest that contains the documents and maps of the enormous treasure. The key is to be found in a corner. You will find a sort of bolt; that you take out, and you will find a rod that opens the box. But if anyone is fortunate enough to find these mines they will be under obligation for the good of their souls to give ten percent to the Holy Mother Church as tithes, and rebuild it.

In the year 1538 the mine is known as the San Pedro belonging to Tumacácori. This mine is about three leagues [9 miles] from the mine called the Santa Isabelle; a small river is to the north about one league distant that runs west. This mine is near some black rocks where the ox cart road ends from the San Pedro mine. The San Pedro is on the highest point of this mountain range, and it is one and one-half leagues from the Temple of the Opatas of Tumacácori, and when the sun first rises it strikes into the entrance of this mine or tunnel, which is on the east side of this mountain. From the top of this mountain you can see Arivaca and from the Nuestra Señora de Guadalupe mine it is one league north.

There is also a tunnel on the west side of the San Pedro. It is covered with a large wooden door. There is a large rock slide and dump. Large slabs of silver are buried in this slide. Between these two mines there is an incline of one and one-half *varas* to descend down the canyon, and it is about half way between the 2 mines. There is also a sure sign, a [vein ?] of [rich ?] rock about 5 *varas* wide around this [corner ?] of this canyon. This bar was blasted out in a triangle of about three *varas*. This triangle is near the mine of the Eyes [Ojos] of the San Román. One path descends from the San Pedro mine. It goes from the [que/cue ?] of the mountain to Nuestra Señora de Guadalupe mine. The other goes down the canyon in a southerly direction, passing the Eyes of San Román, which is near the waters of the San Román [spring] and continues down the canyon in a southerly direction to the mine of Santa Isabella; from the San Pedro mine you could also see Arivaca.

In the mine of San Pedro will be found enormous slabs of silver; two hidden treasures of virgin silver. Near the tunnel on the west side are some piles of rock. Some silver slabs will be found there. There are others on the east side. There will be found in this district three deposits mixed with clay. South and east are these clay deposits. In these mines are millions in placer gold, also bars of silver, also gold bullion buried, and when these mines are uncovered they will yield millions more.

Montezuma was the chief of many tribes and ordered them to put all the gold and silver of the seven northern tribes under those two peaks that were known as the Virgin of Guadalupe mine. This was a natural crater and was worked also as a mine, and was also the principal mine of the Seven Cities of Cibola.

Cibola means buffalo. The carts used to haul this bullion were pulled by buffalo, as there were no other oxen in this country until they were brought over by Spaniards. The location of these mines was 200 leagues (600 miles) north of Culiacan, Sinaloa, Mexico. The principal city stood on the Mesa del Lobo, in the center of the Huachapa Mountains, and one and one-half leagues south of Montezuma Peak.

Guaquiverti por la puerta Lobo esta el Gran Quivira Lobo, to where the sun rises in the Golden Kingdon through La Puerta Lobo, to where the [sun] sets, the Gateway to Liberty (La Puerta a La Liberatad).

CPSIA information can be obtained
at www.ICGtesting.com
Printed in the USA
LVHW062357080922
727939LV00014B/696